pg 143-153

Cesare Pavese

Twayne's World Authors Series

Italian Literature

Anthony Oldcorn, Editor

Brown University

TWAS 785

CESARE PAVESE
1908–1950
Photograph courtesy of Giulio Einaudi Editore

Cesare Pavese

by Áine O'Healy

University of Southern California

Twayne Publishers
A Division of G. K. Hall & Co. • Boston

Cesare Pavese
Áine O'Healy

Published by Twayne Publishers
A Division of G. K. Hall & Co.
70 Lincoln Street
Boston, Massachusetts 02111

Copyediting supervised by Barbara Sutton
Book production by Gabrielle B. McDonald
Book design by Barbara Anderson

Typeset in 11 pt. Garamond
by Compset, Inc., Beverly, Massachusetts

Printed on permanent/durable acid-free paper
and bound in the United States of America

Library of Congress Cataloging-in-Publication Data

O'Healy, Áine.
Cesare Pavese / by Áine O'Healy.
p. cm.—(Twayne's world author series ; TWAS 785. Italian literature)
Bibliography: p.
Includes index.
ISBN 0-8057-8242-7
1. Pavese, Cesare—Criticism and interpretation. I. Title.
II. Series: Twayne's world authors series ; TWAS 785. III. Series:
Twayne's world author series. Italian literature.
PQ4835.A846Z76645 1988
853'.912—dc19 88-14682
CIP

Contents

About the Author

Áine O'Healy was born in Ireland and educated in Ireland, Italy, and the United States. In 1976 she received her Ph.D. from the University of Wisconsin. Since then she has taught at the University of Notre Dame, the University of Georgia, and the University of Southern California, specializing in modern Italian literature and cinema. She has published articles on Natalia Ginzburg, Alberto Moravia, and other Italian writers of the twentieth century.

Preface

Cesare Pavese was one of the foremost writers to emerge in Italy during the first half of the twentieth century. He was not only an acclaimed novelist and accomplished poet, but also exerted influence in his work as an editor, translator and critic. He is generally regarded, along with Elio Vittorini, as one of the key figures in the cultural resistance to fascism. During the 1930s he became a prominent scholar and promoter of American literature, introducing the Italian public to important English and American works in translation and to discussions of the problems raised by modern American fiction and poetry, at a time when the Fascist regime was attempting to enforce an increasingly isolationist cultural policy. Yet, unlike Vittorini, Pavese was not motivated during this phase of his career by a conscious ideological agenda. Throughout his life, he remained largely uncomprehending and intolerant of politics, even during his highly publicized postwar affiliation with the Italian Communist party.

The secondary literature on Pavese is vast and continues to proliferate. I have found some of these studies useful and challenging. Many of Pavese's critics and biographers, however, have helped over the years to prepetuate myths and misunderstandings about him, including the image of Pavese as a consciously engaged anti-Fascist intellectual, as a representative of the Piedmontese peasant class, or as a doomed, decadent figure. These distorted perceptions have sometimes obscured and even replaced a serious examination of his very real gifts as a writer. In this study, which provides a biographical sketch and a chronological reading of Pavese's literary works, I have attempted as much as possible to avoid the pitfall of repeating the popular myths that have fossilized around him.

Almost all of Pavese's works have been translated into English. Nevertheless, his unique use of language presents particular problems for the translator that have rarely been satisfactorily resolved. All translations in the text are my own.

With the exception of Pavese's verse, all quotations are from *Opere,* 14 vols. (Turin: Einaudi, 1968). The following abbreviations are used in this volume to refer to the primary sources.

BE	*La bella estate* (three novels: *La bella estate, Il diavolo sulle colline,* and *Tra donne sole*) (*Opere,* vol. 8)
C	*Il compagno* (*Opere,* vol. 4)
DL	*Dialoghi con Leucò* (*Opere,* vol. 6)
FA	*Feria d'agosto* (*Opere,* vol. 5)
L	*Lettere, 1926–1950* (*Opere,* vol. 14)
LF	*La luna e i falò* (*Opere,* vol. 9)
MV	*Il mestiere di vivere* (*Opere,* vol. 10)
P	*Poesie edite e inedite* (Turin: Einaudi, 1962)
PG	*Prima che il gallo canti* (Two novels: *Il carcere* and *La casa in collina*) (*Opere,* vol. 7)
PT	*Paesi tuoi* (*Opere,* vol. 2)
R	*Racconti* (*Opere,* vol. 13)
S	*La spiaggia* (*Opere,* vol. 3)
SL	*Saggi letterari* (*Opere,* vol. 12)

I would like to express my appreciation to Giulio Einaudi Editore for the use of its archives during my several visits to Turin over the past eight years, and for permission to print the frontispiece photograph of Pavese. I also wish to thank Marziano Guglielminetti and Giuseppe Zaccaria of the University of Turin, and the staff of the Centro Studi Cesare Pavese at Santo Stefano Belbo. I am indebted to Natalia Ginzburg, Bianca Garufi, Pinolo Scaglione, and Cesarina Sini for their willingness to answer my questions about Pavese. I wish to express my deep gratitude to Tibor Wlassics for his thoughtful and challenging comments on my manuscript. I extend my thanks to Professor Anthony Oldcorn, the editor of this series, who provided invaluable editorial help and suggestions. I also wish to express my appreciation for the personal support and assistance of Barbara Borini Criscuoli, Judith Skeldon, R. J. Zeldin, and Maria Javier Garcia. Finally, my heartfelt thanks to Edward McGlynn Gaffney for his patient and generous support throughout every stage of the process.

Áine O'Healy

University of Southern California

Chronology

1908 9 September, Cesare Pavese born at his family's summer home in the village of Santo Stefano Belbo in Piedmont in northwest Italy. Shortly thereafter the family moves back to Turin.

1914 Father dies of brain tumor.

1923 Enters Liceo Massimo d'Azeglio to complete high school education. Augusto Monti becomes his teacher and exerts a strong influence.

1926 Enrolls in the Faculty of Letters at the University of Turin. Retains ties with Monti and former school friends, Leone Ginzburg and Massimo Mila.

1929 Pursues study of American authors.

1930 Begins relationship with Tina Pizzardo. Graduates from university with a thesis on Walt Whitman. Writes the first poems of the *Lavorare stanca* cycle. Begins to contribute essays on American authors to *La Cultura*.

1931 First translation, *Our Mr. Wrenn* by Sinclair Lewis. Writes experimental stories, *Ciau Masino*.

1932 Translations of Melville's *Moby-Dick* and Anderson's *Dark Laughter*. Joins the Fascist party to become eligible for teaching career in state schools.

1934 Takes over editorship of *La Cultura*, recently merged with the new Einaudi Publishing House.

1935 Arrested and sentenced to political detention in Calabria, for possession of the letters of an imprisoned Communist dissident. Begins diary, *Il mestiere di vivere*.

1936 *Lavorare stanca*. Released from exile in Calabria, he returns to Turin, and is rejected by Pizzardo. Begins writing short stories.

1937–1939 Begins full-time position with Einaudi. Continues translations. Writes *Il carcere*, his first short novel.

1939 Writes second novel, *Paesi tuoi*.

1940 Writes third novel, *La bella estate.* Becomes involved with Fernanda Pivano. Begins writing *La spiaggia.*

1941 Begins to associate with members of clandestine Communist party. Meets Giaime Pintor.

1943 Sent to Rome to set up a branch of Einaudi. Returns to Turin. After escalation of Nazi control in Turin, takes refuge in Serralunga in the hills of Monferrato. Continues writing the stories of the *Feria d'agosto* collection.

1944 Accepted as a teacher in a monastery school. Meditates on myth. Begins to study Scripture and theology and makes an attempt to embrace religious faith.

1945 Returns to Turin at the end of the war. Joins Communist party. Meets Bianca Garufi. Writes the poems of *La terra e la morte* and begins *Dialoghi con Leucò.*

1946 Writes *Il compagno* and collaborates with Garufi on *Fuoco grande.*

1947 Writes *La casa in collina.* Begins to organize a series of ethnological publications for Einaudi.

1948 Writes *Il diavolo sulle colline.*

1949 Writes *Tra donne sole* and *La luna e i falò.* Begins collaboration with *Cultura e realtà.* Relations with his Communist associates deteriorate.

1950 Ultimately unhappy affair with Constance Dowling. Writes his last love poems, *Verrà la morte e avrà i tuoi occhi.* Awarded Strega prize for the trilogy, *La bella estate,* which includes *La bella estate, Il diavolo sulle colline* and *Tra donne sole.* Suicide in Turin on 27 August.

Chapter One
The Life of Cesare Pavese: Myth and Reality

Pavese's writings are a rich, if problematic, source of information on his life and literary output. He kept a diary intermittently for fourteen years, wrote hundreds of letters, and meticulously preserved his manuscripts and drafts. A major difficulty in constructing a biography of Pavese is that the subject was himself intensely involved in a literary effort not only to provide the sources for future biographers, but also to set the limits of their inquiry and even to provoke and puzzle them.

The testimony provided in Pavese's diary, *Il mestiere di vivere* (*The Business of Living*), is sketchy and often confusing. This diary, which he wrote with an eye to eventual publication, rarely makes direct allusion to the external circumstances of his life, and never offers a description of his friends, lovers, or family. It is preoccupied to a large extent with literary and philosophical reflections. Yet it also contains a compelling record of intense feeling and suffering, of love, disappointment, a tragic sense of predestination, and frequent reference to the possibility of suicide. Most of the entries that document Pavese's emotional disillusionments are at once both intimate and deliberately oblique, and conceal at least as much as they reveal.

Even in the act of writing his diary and personal letters, Pavese was extremely self-conscious and always vigilant of the image he was attempting to project. He regarded his life as a necessary performance, as an artifact to be constructed, rather than as a process to be accepted. Because of his tendency to posture and pose, to create a persona in one situation that he might reverse in the next, the difficulty of achieving an accurate interpretation of this complex figure has been considerable.

Another major difficulty for the biographer of Pavese is that almost all accounts of the writer's life published since the early 1960s have been influenced by the "definitive" biography of Pavese by Davide Lajolo, *Il vizio assurdo* (*The Absurd Vice*).[1] Lajolo maintained that Pavese had personally chosen him to write this work. *Il vizio assurdo*, however, contains numerous errors and distortions that have been absorbed into most of the secondary literature on Pavese. The publication of Tibor Wlassics's challenging monograph in 1985, however, has reversed that trend.[2] Apart from indicating several of Lajolo's omissions and embellishments,[3] Wlassics demonstrates that several of the letters that first appeared in *Il vizio assurdo* and were reprinted without further verification in the definitive edition of Pavese's collected letters were almost certainly altered or forged by Lajolo himself.[4]

Born in the village of Santo Stefano Belbo in the Langhe hills of Piedmont, Pavese regarded his rural beginning as a vital part of his identity. His poetry and fiction are replete with images of the rough, impoverished landscape of his birthplace, and he managed single-handedly to put this virtually unknown corner of the provinces on the Italian literary map. Yet his birth in the countryside was something of an accident. Pavese's father, Eugenio, was himself a native of Santo Stefano and had inherited a farmhouse on the outskirts of the village. He had lived, however, for many years in Turin, where he had married Consolina Mesturini, the daughter of a relatively well-to-do merchant family from a nearby industrial town. Employed as a clerk at the Turinese law court, Eugenio Pavese returned to Santo Stefano with his wife and young daughter, Maria, only in the summer months, when the weather in the city became stifling and oppressive. It was at the end of one of these long summer vacations, as the family was already preparing to return to the city, that Cesare Pavese was born on 9 September 1908.

Although the myth of Pavese's peasant origins has become a widespread cliché, his contact with the Langhe countryside, even during his early years, was not very extensive. Because of his mother's fragile health, he was sent, shortly after his birth, to be cared for by a wetnurse, a peasant woman who lived in Moncucco, not far from the Pavese farmhouse. Later, when his family returned to Turin, a young girl from Santo Stefano, Vittoria Scaglione, came to work in the Pavese household, where she helped to look after the infant Cesare and his six-year-old sister, Maria. Although she married and moved away when Pavese was still a young boy, he always retained contact with the Scaglione family in the village, particularly with Vittoria's younger brother, Pinolo—six years older than Pavese—who became a lifelong friend.

Even as a very young child, Pavese took great delight in the summer visits to the Langhe countryside. His earliest memories were forever dominated by the discovery of nature during these magical vacations.

Just as he was about to begin elementary school in Turin, his sister Maria became ill with an infectious disease, causing the family to move temporarily to their house in the country. Pavese thus received his first year of schooling in Santo Stefano—the longest period he ever spent in the countryside. The people of the Langhe are renowned for their diffident reserve. Yet Pavese felt at ease among them as he did nowhere else throughout his life, and he learned to speak the Langarolo dialect fluently and with pride.

When Pavese was six years old his father died of a brain tumor, a condition that had been diagnosed several years earlier. The children may not have been aware of Eugenio Pavese's impending death, but they cannot have failed to observe the tensions in the family atmosphere. Their parents, each very different from the other in background as well as temperament, did not enjoy a harmonious relationship.[5] There is no allusion to these domestic difficulties in Pavese's work, however, and he always displayed considerable reticence about the facts of his family life, including his personal reaction to the early loss of his father.

Consolina Pavese chose to remain in Turin with her children after her husband's death. Strongly marked by the social aspirations of her own family background, she wanted a middle-class upbringing for her children, and insisted on the virtues of frugality and self-discipline.[6] She eventually decided to sell the farmhouse in Santo Stefano Belbo, and with the proceeds of the sale was able to move from her apartment near the city center to a more desirable residential neighborhood off the elegant Corso Re Umberto. She also purchased a smaller summer home in Reaglie, a village in the hills near Turin. From this time onward Pavese returned to Santo Stefano only for brief vacations, usually as the guest of his relatives. In this way he was able to keep up the friendship with the Scaglione family, and Pinolo eventually came to live for a time with the Paveses in Turin. Under Scaglione's tutelage he learned to observe the secrets of the Langhe countryside and gained an intimate knowledge of the values and customs of the local people.

Pavese's mother was painstaking in her effort to provide her son with the best education available in Turin. He was duly enrolled in several private institutions, including a Jesuit school, where he associated with the sons of the city's elite. Pavese was almost certainly unable to appreciate his mother's disciplined sense of ambition. Yet he was never openly rebellious, despite the strict discipline at home. Throughout his life Pavese remained loyal to the memory of his upbringing, providing in his journal only one explicit reference to any childhood unhappiness:

> Certain trivial or unimportant actions that would rid me of psychological uneasiness (making the bed in the morning when I stay at home; spending a lot to make a fuss of someone who expects it; washing myself with an abundance of soap, etc.) require me to make a huge effort. This is the mark of a harsh upbringing, inflicted on a shy and sensitive nature. It is the result of the terrors of so much of my childhood. Yet my family was neither mean nor excessive. . . . How did those who were really abused end up? (*MV,* 185)

The years of Pavese's childhood and adolescence corresponded with a turbulent period in Italy's history, from the experience of World War I to the great political and economic upheavals that followed. The postwar years saw the inception of fascism and the beginnings of the spirit of resistance in Turin, a city of traditionally socialist sympathies and home for several years to Antonio Gramsci, founder of the Italian Communist Party (PCI). Turin was also the birthplace of Piero Gobetti, leader of *Giustizia e Libertà* (Justice and Liberty), a group that became an important part of the anti-Fascist Resistance. Since Pavese's family was not politically involved, the historical upheavals did not catch his attention until 1922, when a violent incident left a profound mark on his sensibilities. On 18 December of that year the Fascist squads of Turin conducted a punitive raid on representatives of the Left, in the course of which several innocent men were slaughtered on the street. Pavese's memory of this episode appears to have provided the inspiration for "Una generazione" (A generation), a poem written twelve years later, which describes the interruption of a children's game with the sound of gunfire, followed by the vision of blood-stained streets and the silent helplessness of the onlookers.[7] The childlike perspective through which the historical material is filtered is of great interest, reflecting Pavese's view of political events as something extraneous and bewildering, in the face of which a sense of powerlessness is his dominant response.

In 1923 Pavese enrolled at the Liceo Massimo D'Azeglio, one of the finest high schools in the nation. He was fortunate in having as a teacher of Latin and Italian the powerful and exacting figure of Augusto Monti. Monti's own intellectual training was strongly influenced by the idealist philosophy of Benedetto Croce. He was also an admirer of Antonio Gramsci and gradually became convinced of the necessity of political activism. His political ideas found expression in articles written for Gobetti's *Rivoluzione Liberale* (Liberal revolution). Because this journal advocated a program of social reform based on cooperation between the forces of bourgeois liberalism and the proletariat, it was suppressed by Fascist censorship in 1924. Pavese was captivated by the magnetism of his teacher's moral conviction and by the example of a strong personality so very different from his own. Monti attempted to convey to his students a keen sense of civic and historical awareness. Without specific mention of the contemporary political scene, he succeeded in inspiring a spirit of resistance toward totalitarianism through his skillful readings of ancient and modern texts. Monti was admired, respected, and loved by his brightest pupils, many of whom chose to remain in contact with their teacher upon graduation from the *liceo.*

Pavese had been singled out by Monti at an early stage in their acquaintance, and the teacher had attempted both to encourage the boy's intellectual gifts and to correct what he accurately perceived as morbid psychological tendencies. It was during this period that one of Pavese's companions, Elio Baraldi, committed suicide, which led Pavese to contemplate taking his own life. Monti greatly disapproved of this morbid fantasy on ethical grounds. He connected Pavese's attraction to the idea of self-destruction with his taste for aestheticism, nurtured by abundant exposure to late-romantic and decadent writers. Urging his pupil to abandon his fascination with Giacomo Leopardi, Gabriele D'Annunzio, and the Crepuscular poets, Monti guided him toward the more morally edifying and civic-minded works of Vittorio Alfieri. As Pavese's admiration and affection for Monti increased, he made a genuine effort to change in the direction suggested by his teacher. Nevertheless, Pavese's introspective and melancholic personality, his tendency to focus on events of his intimate experience rather than on the realities of the social and historical scene, made it difficult for him to accept the necessity of placing ethical considerations above aesthetic and emotional issues.

Pavese's letters to his friend Mario Sturani during the same period reflect his tendency toward aestheticism, as well as a preference for those literary texts that echoed his own feelings of melancholy and despair. In one of these letters he cites a stanza from a poem by Rabindranath Tagore and adds: "No joy surpasses the joy of suffering."[8] Yet Pavese's struggle to create something positive from his despair through the constructive process of writing is also documented here. This theme was repeated throughout Pavese's subsequent life: "My sickness is no longer the usual depression I used to feel in the past: it is a battle I have to fight every day, every hour, against laziness, uneasiness, and fear; it is a struggle, a conflict that sharpens and refines my spirit as metal is smelted and hardened in the fire. This struggle, this suffering, which is so painful and yet so sweet, keeps me alert and ready, and is in fact what draws my works from my soul."[9] These letters also contain Pavese's earliest efforts at writing poetry—juvenile verses, reminiscent of late-romantic and decadent models, chiefly preoccupied with the time-worn themes of love and death.

It was undoubtedly during the years of Monti's greatest influence that the two distinct poles of Pavese's self-image came into focus. He strove, on the one hand, to present himself as highly disciplined and self-willed, driven by moral concerns and particularly by a commitment to social justice. Yet there also emerged a contrasting image of a man in the grip of what he later described in his diary as *voluttuosità,* an attitude of weakness and self-indulgence, characterized by daydreaming, corrosive insecurity, and fantasies of impending doom. The depressive, antisocial side of Pavese's personality led to a highly ambivalent attitude toward his own isolation, which he sometimes cherished and sometimes struggled to transcend.

Augusto Monti's influence did not end with the classroom. In the summer of 1926 Pavese wrote his teacher to report on the rigorous reading program that he had assigned himself and to announce that he was in the process of teaching himself classical Greek. The letter is an explicit plea for continued friendship, revealing both the desire for intellectual approval and a longing for affection and support. In addition to a report on scholastic matters, Pavese informs Monti that he has recently been initiated into the mysteries of sex at a local brothel. The style of his disclosure already betrays an uneasy ambivalence toward sexual issues: "I managed to visit those places recommended by Cato. . . . The struggle was difficult, but I won, and an entirely new part of the world was revealed to me."[10]

In 1927 Cesare Pavese enrolled in the Faculty of Letters at the University of Turin. Although he had little interest in politics, the tensions generated by the totalitarian regime were becoming increasingly difficult to ignore in the university setting. Some critics have viewed Pavese's decision to specialize in American literature, an area generally ignored in the contemporary academic scene in Italy, as a defiant political choice. Nevertheless, to attribute a conscious sense of antifascism to Pavese at this point is certainly mistaken. Pavese had come to

American literature by way of the cinema. Since adolescence, he had been an avid fan of American films, and his taste for the English language had developed out of his interest in the cinema and his fascination with jazz and blues. He was now drawn to American writers for their vitality and independence from stifling traditions. In the guarded atmosphere of contemporary academic life, American literature presented itself as an irresistible intellectual adventure.

Pavese was mainly attracted to what he perceived as a marked sense of place in American writers. He was fascinated by the fact that the Americans were able to evoke the specific qualities of their native regions while endowing them with universal significance. He was also impressed by their use of slang as a literary device and began to wonder if Italian dialects might be used for similar effect. He put this idea to the test almost immediately, drafting some experimental prose fragments in Piedmontese dialect.

Pavese's comprehension of American colloquial language was enhanced by his friendship with Antonio Chiuminatto, an Italo-American conservatory student from Chicago, then living temporarily in Turin. With the self-confidence that grew from his contact with his American friend, Pavese began to translate Sinclair Lewis's *Our Mr. Wrenn.* When Chiuminatto returned to the United States, Pavese initiated an eager and amusing correspondence with him, with the purpose both of receiving American books then unavailable in Italy, and of keeping up with new colloquialisms as he encountered them in his readings. His favorite authors were Walt Whitman, Herman Melville, and Sherwood Anderson, followed by Sinclair Lewis, Edgar Lee Masters, and Ernest Hemingway. During the same period he began to draft his university thesis on Whitman, whose poetry appealed to him particularly for its optimistic vitality, and its freshness of rhythm and language.

The gatherings of Monti's fraternity of former students were a crucial part of Pavese's social life during his university years. The group usually convened at cafés and restaurants in Turin, occasionally making excursions to Monti's home in the countryside. In spite of the lighthearted mood of these gatherings, there was a serious undercurrent at work, for the spirit of antifascism engendered in Monti's pupils during their schooldays was now taking a more focused and articulate form. Several of the participants in these outings, including Leone Ginzburg, Massimo Mila, and Monti himself, later took an active part in the militant Resistance. Pavese, however, remained detached from the passionate interest in politics shared by the others in the group. In his correspondence with Monti during this period, contemporary political issues are conspicuously absent. Instead, his letters deal almost exclusively with aesthetics and literature with some allusions to his personal, existential problems. A letter dated 18 May 1928 reveals Pavese's awareness of the tensions between the ideals of his chosen model, Monti, and his own contrasting insights:

> You say that in order to create great art one has only to live as profoundly and as intensely as possible one's real life, whatever that happens to be, since if our spirit has within it the ingredients of a masterpiece, it will emerge almost on its own, healthily and naturally, as happens with all living things. . . . I believe instead that art requires a long gestation and mortification of the spirit, and such a relentless, painful, usually futile repetition of effort that it ought to be classed among the most unnatural activities of mankind. (*L,* 45)[11]

In this letter we see the genesis of an attitude toward literary creation that became more marked with the passage of time, and that Susan Sontag describes as "the artist as exemplary sufferer."[12] The letter also reveals that in spite of the outgoing, lighthearted mood manifest elsewhere in Pavese's writing during this period, a more complex and tormented sensibility was also developing in his consciousness. Later the same summer Pavese wrote again to Monti in a tone of troubled self-disclosure: "Literature has already worn me out too much. . . . I cannot throw myself into the act of living. I cannot. To live one has to have strength and understanding, one has to know how to choose. I have never known how to do this. I neither understand anything about politics nor about any of the other entanglements of life. I scribble, I spew out poems, in order to have a territory, a place where I can stop and say: 'This is me'" (*L,* 51).

Despite this declared ineptitude for living, his university years were productive. In addition to translating *Our Mr. Wrenn,* he had brought out translations of Anderson's *Dark Laughter* and Melville's *Moby-Dick* by the time he graduated. Though often the object of generic praise, his translations are rather unorthodox. Pavese's command of English was more enthusiastic than profound. Nevertheless, the importance of his making these works widely available to the Italian reading public—increasingly affected by the xenophobic cultural policies of the regime—is undeniable. In addition, Pavese began to contribute essays on American writers for the progressive periodical *La Cultura.* Years later he commented on the historical importance of the trend he had helped to establish during those crucial years:

> It could be frankly said that the new mania [for America] was a considerable help in perpetuating and nourishing the political opposition, however vague and futile, of the Italian reading public. For many, the encounter with Steinbeck, Caldwell, Saroyan, or even Lewis before these . . . aroused the first suspicion that not everything in the world's culture ended with the Fasces. . . . It dawned on us that America was not *another* country, a *new* beginning in history, but only the gigantic theater where the drama of everyone was being acted out with greater freedom than elsewhere. (*SL*, 173–74)

The death of Pavese's mother in 1930 was difficult for him since he had never resolved the tensions in his relationship with her. There is no allusion to this bereavement in any of his writings apart from a cursory mention in a letter to Antonio Chiuminatto. After his mother's death Pavese decided to continue living with his sister and her husband in the family home on Via Lamarmora, which was to be his residence for the remainder of his life.

In 1930 Pavese presented his thesis to the examining board of the university, where it was rejected, apparently because of the influence of Crocean aesthetics, obviously in disfavor during fascism. Nevertheless, thanks to the intervention of Leone Ginzburg, whose talents were highly esteemed at the university despite his dissident politics, Pavese's thesis was eventually accepted and he was granted his degree with highest honors. For some weeks after graduation he considered the possibility of going to America, and he initiated a correspondence with Columbia University to inquire about the prospect of studying and teaching there. He eventually lost interest in the project, however, suspecting perhaps that the America that so fascinated him was to be found in the pages of literature rather than in the concrete reality of a geographical location. Tenaciously attached to his own part of the world, Pavese did not enjoy dislocation. He resisted travel whenever possible and never ventured beyond the borders of Italy.

Now ready to begin a career in teaching, Pavese found that there were no openings available to him, and he was obliged to take a number of poorly paid part-time jobs to support himself. Though he had already published several translations and continued to work on others, his income from this activity was small. Finally, in order to improve his prospects of employment, he took out membership in the Fascist party, a prerequisite for eligibility in the state teaching system. He was fundamentally alien to all political activity and later admitted that this expedient was against his nature.

Thanks to his ongoing association with Monti's intellectual circle,

Pavese observed at close quarters the growth of an increasingly organized anti-Fascist spirit among Turinese intellectuals. In November 1933, Giulio Einaudi, the son of the liberal economist, Luigi Einaudi, founded a publishing house in Turin, with the goal of exposing Italian culture to foreign contact and ideas. Einaudi's earliest interests—reflected in the first books chosen by his editors—were in the area of political, financial, and economic questions. But the range of the Einaudi publications soon displayed a growing interest in literature and the humanities. An important step in this direction was the takeover of the periodical *La Cultura,* then edited by a board comprised of several outspoken intellectuals including Arrigo Cajumi, Sergio Solmi, and Bruno Migliorini. Their contributions expressed an explicit anti-Fascist stand as well as opposition to certain aspects of Croce's ideology. Pavese's pioneering essays on Lewis, Anderson, Masters, Melville, Dos Passos, Dreiser, Whitman, and Faulkner, along with Leone Ginzburg's articles on Russian writers, were among the early articles published on foreign literature in *La Cultura.*

Leone Ginzburg was editor of *La Cultura* for a short time, until he was arrested in 1934 for his association with *Giustizia e Libertà.* Later, Pavese was appointed to the position of general editor, because of a new law requiring all editors to be members of the Fascist party. He held this post for about a year, after which he resigned, weary of the fact that his editorship was merely a titular position and that Arrigo Cajumi had retained effective control of the journal.

In spite of many difficulties, the years between 1930 and 1935 were among the most serene of Pavese's life. Though erratic and underpaid, his jobs as a substitute or part-time teacher in Turin and in provincial towns gave him the taste of a career that he found engaging and rewarding. In the meantime, his work as a translator and critic was already receiving modest recognition. More important than this, the outcome of his efforts to create a radically new form of poetry convinced him that his was the strongest poetic talent in Italy at the time. Publication of his first collection of verse, *Lavorare stanca,* was not, however, an easy achievement. He eventually sent the manuscript to Solaria, a small, progressive publishing house in Florence, whose periodical, also entitled *Solaria,* had begun to foster promising new writers. Here *Lavorare stanca* came to the attention of Elio Vittorini,[13] who was impressed by Pavese's talent and took a personal interest in trying to overcome the difficulties that stood in the way of its publication.

Around 1930 Pavese met the woman who was to exert a profound influence on his emotional life. For many years after his death, this woman's name was withheld from the public, and she became widely known as "the woman with the hoarse voice," echoing a reference to her in one of the early poems of *Lavorare stanca.* Not much is known about this friendship, since the woman herself, Battistina Pizzardo (known to her friends as "Tina"), subsequently refused to release Pavese's letters to her for publication. Nevertheless, the impression of obligatory anonymity perpetuated in Lajolo's biography was shattered in 1980 when Pizzardo published two short articles in *Il Messagero* describing her relationship with Pavese.[14] A committed activist in the clandestine Communist movement, Pizzardo was a forceful and pragmatic personality, and she seemed to embody many of the qualities that Pavese lacked. His biographers have not failed to point out that he seemed drawn to her for her domineering demeanor and attitudes, traits also attributed to his mother.

Pavese's association with Pizzardo led eventually to political consequences he could scarcely have foreseen. In March 1934 many of his friends in the Justice and Liberty movement organized the distribution of anti-Fascist propaganda. Subsequently several of the conspirators were arrested, including Leone Ginzburg and Augusto Monti. The group was disbanded but soon reorganized under new leadership. In May 1935 the activities of Justice and Liberty again came to the attention of the police, who immediately conducted a search of all those known to be connected with the group, or with *La Cultura,* the periodical for which many of these dissidents wrote. Recognized by the Fascists as an important contributor to and until recently the editor of *La Cultura,* Pavese was duly investigated and his house was thoroughly searched. It is possible that he might have been arrested for subversive activity simply by virtue of his professional association with well-known dissidents, but other more incriminating evidence was revealed during the search of his room. Finding among his private papers the letters of an imprisoned Communist dissident, the police arrested and imprisoned Pavese on 13 May 1935. The compromising letters were not, in fact, destined for Pavese himself, but had been received at his address at the request of Pizzardo, for whom they were intended. Thus, on the same date that Pavese had planned to go to Rome to take the qualifying exam for the state teaching system, he found himself in a Roman prison. From there, in August 1934, he was sentenced to three years of internal exile in the village of Brancaleone Calabro on the Ionian coast.

During this period many of Pavese's friends and associates suffered the same fate of the *confino.* According to this system of political detention enforced by the Fascist government, dissidents were deported to remote rural areas. Here they were supervised by local police and subjected to curfew, but were otherwise free to live among the local people and to move about within the community. The advantage of this system for the regime was that it isolated dissident intellectuals from contact with each other and from access to publicity. The unintended result of the *confino,* however, was that it brought these same intellectuals into direct contact with Italy's oldest and most intractable problem, the poverty of its southern provinces. This problem constituted a major obstacle to the glorious self-image that imperial fascism wished to project. At the end of the war, many of the *confinati* were instrumental in drawing the nation's attention to the abject circumstances of the South in articles of political journalism, as well as in works of fiction and autobiography. Among these writings, Carlo Levi's *Cristo si è fermato a Eboli* (Christ stopped at Eboli)—based on his own *confino*—emerged as a classic.

Pavese's own reaction to the southern environment was entirely solipsistic. This was his first exposure to an environment radically different from his native region. He felt neither curiosity nor sympathy for the plight of the southern peasants with whom he now lived in close contact. Outraged that he had been exiled to Calabria because of a miscarriage of justice, he repeatedly sent letters to the Fascist authorities, insisting that he was innocent of subversive activity and indifferent to politics in general. His sister Maria also wrote to Mussolini on his behalf pleading for clemency.[15] This correspondence led eventually to Pavese's release after less than eight months of exile.

Pavese's inability to come to terms with the strangeness of Calabria and his tendency to withdraw into the private contemplation of aesthetics and literature are the most striking elements that emerge from the abundant correspondence of this period. His main defense against loneliness and despair was the world of books, and most of his letters to Turin contain requests for volumes to be forwarded to him. His reading lists in this period are prodigious and reveal such diverse interests as the Bible, Greek and Roman classics, Shakespeare, the authors of the French Enlightenment, Hawthorne, Nietzsche, and Kafka.

In Pavese's letters to his sister and friends he unburdened his unhappiness in a long litany of complaint, mixed with a burning nostalgia for his beloved Piedmont. His generally petulant, self-pitying tone was often mitigated by a bitter, sarcastic humor. An excerpt from a letter to Adolfo Ruata is the most frequently quoted record of his southern experience: "I have the most sordid pastimes. I catch flies, translate from Greek, abstain from looking at the sea, wander through the fields, smoke, take notes, reread letters from my native land, and observe a useless chastity" (*L,* 299).

On the positive side, however, it was during his political detention that Pavese began to keep a journal—published posthumously as *Il mestiere di vivere*—that became the complex document of the unfolding of a spiritual, emotional, and intellectual journey. The early entries, all written in Brancaleone, are concerned almost exclusively with the problem of constructing a personal poetics and of renewing poetic inspiration, which Pavese feared he was losing.

It was also during his detention in Brancaleone that Pavese began to acknowledge the importance of place in his own poetry. His diary tells of how, during a moonlit walk, he was tempted to write a poem about a god incarnate in the red cliffs nearby, and how he immediately rejected the idea, deciding that these cliffs were not his, that he could not experience their presence in a persuasive way. He thus realized that only his native Piedmontese landscape had the power to generate poetic inspiration, concluding that "the fundamental basis of poetry may be the subconscious awareness of the importance of those bonds of sympathy, those biological vagaries, that are already alive, in embryo, in the poet's imagination before he starts to create a poem" (*MV,* 12).

In March 1936 Pavese was released and left immediately for Turin. He was anxious to hear of the fate of his recently published collection of verse, *Lavorare stanca,* and even more preoccupied with the desire to be reunited with Tina Pizzardo, whose silence during his long absence had tested him beyond endurance. On both counts he experienced bitter defeat. His poetry, despite its novelty, had failed to provoke a critical response, and few copies had been sold. In addition, Pizzardo proved indifferent to his attachment. Their relationship was now, more than ever, a painfully one-sided affair. Pavese's disappointment was intense. For some time, however, he was unable to relinquish the hope of reclaiming Pizzardo's affection, and the unresolved nature of his attachment can only have increased his emotional suffering.[16] In an attempt to regain his composure and self-esteem, he isolated himself from his friends. Overwhelmed with a sense of loss, both personal and artistic, he began a new phase of self-questioning in his journal. The misogynistic note, already present in his poetry, became from this time onward a stridently obsessive theme.

Pavese was now without secure, full-time employment. His police record permanently excluded him from the possibility of teaching, and he returned to his translations and literary essays in an attempt to earn a meager living. The Einaudi publishing house offered him part-time employment for which he received only a modest salary, despite his ever-increasing responsibilities. These were among the bleakest years of his life. Although his long-established tendency toward melancholy gradually assumed pathological proportions, he never sought professional help for his psychological problems. Allusions to suicide recur in his diary, which is dominated during this period by a tone of unrelenting depression. It is clear that the absence of economic security also contributed to his despondency. On 26 March 1938 he wrote: "My inner strength is gone: Look at my experience in the *confino.* The illusion of my genius is gone: look at my stupid book and my translator's mentality. I lack even the strength of the ordinary man in the street. At thirty I still have no trade" (*MV,* 89).

In January 1938 Pavese confessed in a letter to his friend, Enzo Monferini, that he had made "a half-hearted attempt" to gas himself. The letter reveals clearly that his intense immersion in his work at this point was an attempt to escape from the insoluble anguish generated by the end of his hopes for reconciliation with Pizzardo. He also confessed to his friend that he was sexually impotent and that he believed himself incapable of satisfying a woman. The fear of sexual inadequacy was to torment him for the rest of his life.

Gradually, almost in spite of himself, Pavese recovered his creative inspiration, and in a short time wrote his first novel, *Il carcere* (literally "The prison," but later translated under the misleading title *The Political Prisoner*), which remained unpublished until 1948. The novel describes the detention of an urban intellectual in a remote village in southern Italy, and has an obvious autobiographical basis. Its fundamental theme is the "prison" of existential solitude, understood both as a self-willed isolation and externally imposed alienation. The novel reflects very clearly Pavese's own conflicting feelings about human relationships and his inability to escape the restrictive confines of the self. This theme was repeated in almost all his subsequent works, most explicitly in *La casa in collina* (*The House on the Hill*).

Although Pavese did not become a permanent member of the Einaudi staff for several years, he threw himself into the commitments offered to him with the most scrupulous dedication, and his contribution to the publishing house was substantial and lasting. Even before obtaining his full-time contract, he helped to launch a new interdisciplinary series for the publishing house. This series, entitled *I Saggi,* introduced important foreign works as yet relatively unknown in Italy. One of its earliest numbers was Huizinga's *Crisis of Civilization,* to be followed eventually by the same author's study of Erasmus. Later, Pavese launched another series entitled Biblioteca dello Struzzo (Ostrich library), committed to the publication of new Italian novelists. His own novel, *Paesi tuoi* (*The Harvesters*), published in 1941, was the first to appear in this series,[17] and was followed by the works of important emerging writers such as Natalia Ginzburg, Quarantotti Gambini, and Elsa Morante. In addition, within the short space of three years (1938–41), Pavese translated seven books for Einaudi, including novels by Dickens, Defoe, Melville, and Stein.

In 1940 Pavese began to develop a romantic interest in Fernanda Pivano, a former pupil who was several years his junior. This relationship grew under the guise of intellectual tutelage. Pivano was a promising student with a genuine interest in American literature, prompted and sustained by Pavese's example and advice. Her attachment to him was no doubt enhanced by her admiration for him as a scholar and teacher and also perhaps by the modest prestige he was beginning to enjoy. A large collection of letters documents their association. Although Pavese revealed a great deal of himself in this correspondence, his relationship with Pivano was extremely repressed. Pavese's letters have a paternal, sometimes condescending tone, and even when he is attempting an attitude of intimate self-disclosure, as in the striking self-portrait that he attaches to a letter of 5 November 1940, he still exhibits a manipulative restraint and control. The distance between Pavese and his former pupil is reflected in their continued use of the formal manner of address. Never, in the many years of their association, did they cross the threshold to the familiar "*tu.*" Yet Pavese does not hesitate to reveal to Pivano his dissatisfaction with the unfulfilled erotic potential of the relationship. In one extraordinary letter (20 October 1940) he offers a lengthy Freudian analysis of her alleged "frigidity." This letter, referring to Pivano in the third person, inadvertently reveals far more about the writer than about his correspondent. Despite these obvious difficulties with the relationship, Pavese made many petulant proposals of marriage to her over a period of several years, which she consistently refused. It was not until his return to Turin in 1945 at the end of the war that he accepted the inevitable demise of this attachment. His encouragement of the young woman's intellectual talents, however, bore lasting fruit; Pivano went on to become one of the leading *Americanisti* of her generation in Italy.

In 1940 Elio Vittorini requested Pavese's collaboration in his preparation of the 1,000-page anthology, *Americana.* This immense volume was intended to introduce Italian readers to a selection of American works in translation, and was the product of the combined effort of all the prominent *Americanisti* of the day. Pavese contributed the Melanctha section of Gertrude Stein's *Three Lives,* which had already been published by Einaudi. *Americana* appeared in 1941 but was suppressed by Fascist censorship almost at once, due to the pro-American essay with which Vittorini prefaced the volume. Pavese, who had received one of the early volumes, wrote immediately on 27 May 1942 to Vittorini to compliment him on his work. In another letter addressed to Oliviero Bianchi on 15 May 1943, he spoke of Vittorini as "the strongest moral conscience and the most straightforward of our generation." The admiration of these two writers was reciprocal. Vittorini had written to Pavese on 16 June 1941, claiming that his *Paesi tuoi* was vastly superior to the works of Steinbeck (*L,* 397).

As Italy became involved in the war, Pavese began to attend meetings of the clandestine Communist party with his former school companion, Geymonat, and one of his pupils, a southern Leftist, Capriolo. In this setting, he met Giaime Pintor, a young Sardinian lieutenant, who was at first considered with some suspicion by the Communists because he was the nephew of General Pintor, and because he had devoted himself to the study of German literature, on which he had already written several articles. Yet Giaime Pintor was one of the most dedicated anti-Fascists of the group, and deeply convinced of the necessity of armed resistance. Pintor, also an intellectual and an academic, made a profound impression on Pavese, who saw in his decisive, humane, and courageous personality the qualities he admired but could not imitate. Pintor rejected the decadent, late-romantic literary and ethnological tradition that captivated Pavese's imagination, and he saw in post-romantic aesthetics the seed of the moral downfall of Europe. At Pavese's suggestion, Pintor began to read American literature and discovered in it an invigorating new vision, free from insidious academic traditions. This friendship, though important, was short-lived. Pintor eventually joined the armed resistance and was killed by a German mine. His essays, published posthumously as *Il sangue d'Europa* (The blood of Europe), were a source of inspiration to the postwar generation.

In 1943 Pavese was sent to Rome to set up a new branch of the Einaudi publishing house. He was summoned almost immediately to report to the army for active service, but was released after a medical examination revealed the severity of his chronic asthma. While great political upheavals were transforming the world, Pavese's journal remained preoccupied with personal and emotional concerns, as well as with questions of aesthetics and literature. This was a period of intense intellectual discovery. In conjunction with his readings in classical literature, he began to develop a more systematic interest in ethnology, psychology, and psychoanalysis.

Pavese's indifference to the events of the war was shattered when, on 19 July, Rome was bombed. Panic-stricken, he wrote to Giulio Einaudi, asking to be allowed back to Turin. When he returned there a week later, the day after the fall of Mussolini, he found the city in chaos. The Einaudi headquarters had been bombed, and even his sister's home had not escaped damage. Discovering that Maria and her family had fled to the home of relatives in Serralunga, a village in the province of Monferrato, he followed them there in September as Nazi control escalated in Turin. In the meantime, some of his friends had left for the mountains to join the Partisan struggle.

Pavese remained in Monferrato until the end of the war. This was an important parenthesis in his life, marked by an attempt to withdraw from the reality of historical struggle into the realm of timeless myth. During his twenty months of retreat his diary never mentions the terrible events that were taking place in his country, nor does it allude to the presence of Nazis and Repubblichini[18] in the nearby countryside and the reign of terror they evoked. His concerns remained focused on aesthetics and ethnology, although he also exhibited a growing interest in religion, stimulated by his encounter with a congregation of priests at a monastery not far from his brother-in-law's home. At this monastery Pavese taught for a time and formed a close friendship with one of the priests, Father Baravalle, at whose suggestion he began to read church history and theology. Pavese had been an agnostic for several years, but the serene atmosphere of the monastery seemed to provide an answer to a deep need in his anguished mind. He turned to prayer and meditation, and even began to participate in the Catholic liturgy. This episode is fictionalized in *La casa in collina,* where Baravalle provides the model for Father Felice. There are also allusions to Pavese's religious experience in his diary, notably an entry on 1 February 1944: "We feel this same glow of divinity when suffering has brought us to our knees, so much so that the first pang can give us a sense of joy, gratitude, anticipation. . . . We reach the point of wanting pain. This rich symbolic reality, heralding another even more true and sublime, what is it but Christianity? To accept it means, quite literally, entering into the world of supernatural" (*MV,* 248–49).

This religious experience has been underplayed by most of Pavese's biographers, most of whom have difficulty in accepting its sincerity. Yet Pavese appears as sincere in this quest as he was in his pursuit of absolute love, and even more so than in his subsequent attempt to embrace political commitment. These were all motivated by the desire to relinquish his profound sense of solitude and alienation.

In addition to reading the works of theology lent to him by Baravalle, he was simultaneously rereading Giambattista Vico, whose writings exerted considerable influence on the development of Pavese's theory of myth. He also reread the classics and tried to reevaluate their formulation of myth in the light of his increasing familiarity with ethnological theory. Of all contemporary writers, Thomas Mann now became the figure whom Pavese regarded with the greatest fascination, since Mann's novels offered a modern reworking of the age-old myths at the heart of Western civilization. The hilly landscape of Serralunga provided the ideal setting for Pavese's readings and reflections, reminding him of his childhood summers in the Langhe. The superimposition of the two regions in his imagination led him to focus on the importance of childhood perception in the creation of universal myths. The ideas formulated during this period are expressed in the essays of the final section of *Feria d'agosto.*

When Pavese returned to Turin after the liberation he found to his horror that some of his friends had been killed during the war. The news of Ginzburg's death had already reached him in Serralunga and prompted the only entry in his diary during that period, which acknowledges, however obliquely, the violent realities of the war: "Do others exist for us? I wish it were not true so as not to feel the loss. I'm living in a kind of fog, aware of it vaguely but constantly. You end up getting used to this state, putting off real pain till tomorrow" (*MV,* 251). Also dead were Giaime Pintor, Capriolo, and the eighteen-year-old Gaspare Pajetta, whom Pavese had tutored.

In an attempt to deal with his feelings of loss and inadequacy, Pavese joined the Communist party, registering in the cell that bore Pajetta's name. Though fundamentally incapable of a genuine involvement in political issues, Pavese tried for a time to adapt himself to this new commitment by attending cell meetings regularly. In this environment he established a friendship with Italo Calvino, who was at the time a virtually unknown young writer and to whom Pavese offered encouragement and support. Pavese also began to contribute essays to the Communist daily newspaper, *L'Unità,* and occasional articles to the Communist review, *Rinascita.* In 1946 he attempted to write an ideologically "correct" novel, *Il compagno* (*The Comrade*), which was unappreciated by the majority of readers, regardless of political affiliation.

Pavese's political commitment was not solidly based. It was prompted by an emotional need for an outlet that would save him from a sense of futility and despair. After a time it became obvious to him that Party membership did not bring automatic salvation and his participation cooled. He also began to grow disillusioned with some of the inner workings of everyday political life. The divisions within the Party itself—particularly between intellectuals who had been drawn to Marxism through their participation in the Resistance and hard-line Party bureaucrats—gradually alienated him further. His relationship with his Marxist friends grew increasingly strained after 1947 when the PCI officially adopted the position urged by Stalin's cultural watchdog, Andrei Zhdanov, that art should reflect the Party position on socialist realism. In 1948 the tension between Pavese and his Communist colleagues reached a crisis after the publication of *La casa in collina,* which was severely attacked by critics on the Left for its failure to glorify the Resistance. In 1950, *Rinascita* published a strong critique of *Cultura e realtà,* a journal of the Catholic Left with which Pavese had begun to collaborate. The article was written by Palmiro Togliatti, the leader of the PCI, under a pseudonym. Feeling under personal attack, Pavese observed in his diary with a note of sarcasm: "'P. is not a good comrade' . . . tales of intrigue everywhere. Shady dealings that are the talk of those you care about the most" (*MV,* 353).

There is a marked disparity between Pavese's public pronouncements on political issues and the reflections on the same topics noted simultaneously in his diary. Much as he tried to keep up the appearance of the "good comrade"—especially at the beginning of his association with the Party—his private observations indicated that his deepest interests lay in a very different direction. Questions of aesthetics, spirituality, and myth continued to predominate in his diary, along with the simultaneous expression of a skeptical attitude toward the very positions he was taking on the public level.

Between 1946 and 1947 Pavese wrote *Dialoghi con Leucò* (*Dialogues with Leucò*), a book of existential meditations cast as dialogues between mythological characters. It was begun during his brief affair with Bianca Garufi, a colleague at the Einaudi office in Rome where he was sent for a few months after the war, and it contains many disguised allusions to their association. Though saddened by the book's failure to capture an audience, Pavese remained fiercely attached to it and insisted that it was his true masterpiece. Simultaneously with its composition, he wrote a small group of love poems, also inspired by Garufi. Published in 1947 under the title *La terra e la morte* (Earth and death), these poems resemble to some extent the contemporary Hermetic vogue that Pavese had once so much despised.

The last years of Pavese's life were a time of great creative energy. In a short span of four years he blossomed as a novelist, producing *Il compagno*, *La casa in collina*, *Il diavolo sulle colline* (*The Devil in the Hills*), *Tra donne sole* (*Among Women Only*), *La luna e i falò* (*The Moon and the Bonfires*), and the unfinished *Fuoco grande* (Great fire), coauthored with Bianca Garufi. His talent won him widespread public recognition and he received a number of literary accolades. These included the coveted Strega prize, which he was awarded for *La bella estate,* a trilogy that contained *La bella estate, Il diavolo sulle colline,* and *Tra donne sole.* Nevertheless, his novels came under fire repeatedly from colleagues on the Left for their lack of adherence to acceptable ideological positions.

In January 1950, Pavese made another desperate attempt at romantic involvement. During the New Year celebrations he was introduced to Constance Dowling, a struggling American actress who had already appeared in a number of undistinguished Hollywood films and had recently come to Rome in search of work. She embodied for him the lure of America (toward which his attitude was now more complex and critical than his enthusiasm of the early 1930s) as well as the promise of a mutual commitment. To his new love he dedicated *La luna e i falò,* the novel he had finished just before their first encounter. For a few weeks he was happy, but by the time Dowling returned to America in the spring it was already clear that the relationship presented difficulties. Pavese's letters to her have a desperate urgency, betraying the fear that his dreams had once more eluded him. Yet he persisted in clinging to the possibility that she would come back, and began to draft screenplays with roles designed for both Constance Dowling and her sister,

Doris. Gradually he realized that the affair was over. For a short time he sought consolation in the company of Doris Dowling, who had remained in Italy after her sister's departure and who accompanied Pavese to the Strega prize-giving ceremony in late June. Even the acquisition of the Strega itself was not enough to ward off a profound, familiar sense of depression and defeat. Just before his death, Pavese pursued briefly another romantic relationship, about which almost nothing is known apart from its ultimate failure.

Pavese's emotional difficulties were compounded by the alienation he felt from several of his acquaintances on the Left because of his inconsistent political behavior. His involvement with the journal *Cultura e realtà* had unwittingly drawn him into the center of a heated political controversy. On 27 May 1950, reacting to the personal attacks in the communist press, he expressed in his diary a bitter regret at having lost the sense of detachment he had achieved during the two previous years. Here again the consideration of taking his own life emerges explicitly.[19]

During the summer many of his intimate friends found him moody and difficult to deal with, and some who tried to offer help were rudely rejected. Toward the end of August he organized his personal papers and left his sister's house to check in as a guest at the Hotel Roma, near the Turin railway station. He arranged his death with meticulous care, clearly wishing to salvage the sense of accomplishing a positive, necessary act. Yet the last, brief messages to his friends are abrupt and desolate.

Just as he was in the process of planning his suicide, Pavese made an entry in his diary that serves as a modest epitaph: "I have done my public share—as much as I could do. I have worked. I have given people poetry. I have shared the sufferings of many" (*MV,* 361). On the night of Saturday, 26 August, he wrote on the title page of his favorite work, *Dialoghi con Leucò,* echoing the suicide message of the Russian poet, Vladimir Mayakovsky: "I forgive everyone, and ask forgiveness from all. Not too much gossip, please!" He then took a lethal dose of sleeping medication, and was found dead by the hotel staff on the evening of 27 August.

Chapter Two
The Craft of Poetry

Lavorare stanca (Work is wearying),[1] the collection of verse written between 1930 and 1940, is one of Pavese's most challenging and ambitious works, and it contains the nucleus of all the thematic preoccupations of his subsequent writing. The first edition, containing forty-five poems, was published by Solaria, a small literary publishing house, in 1936, after some difficulties with Fascist censorship. Despite Pavese's expectation of immediate recognition and acclaim, the volume was greeted with almost total indifference. Nevertheless, still convinced of the unique importance of his poetics, he continued writing verse, and by the end of the decade had expanded the collection to seventy poems.

In the 1943 edition of *Lavorare stanca* published by Einaudi, Pavese presented this work in its final form. Though he had previously dismissed the validity of an organized anthology, in the second edition he divided the collection into six sections, organized according to theme. He also appended to this edition two essays of self-criticism that he considered vital to an understanding of his work.

For Pavese, poetry was not an innate or spontaneous gift, but the product of effort, ambition, and conviction. From the start, he approached the shaping of his own poetic craft with the analytical aloofness of a critic and polemicist. With the earliest poems of the *Lavorare stanca* collection he sought—with an almost missionary sense of purpose—to create a radically new form of poetry. He was aware that the literature produced in contemporary Italy manifested a growing tendency to reject realistic forms of expression. Inspired by his early training under the tutelage of Augusto Monti and by his exposure to American literature (especially to the poetry of Walt Whitman and Edgar Lee Masters), Pavese set out to oppose this flight from realism. Rejecting both the sensual aestheticism of D'Annunzio and his imitators—so popular in Fascist circles—and the contrasting trend toward the private allusiveness of Hermeticism witnessed in the work of some young emerging poets (Ungaretti and Montale in particular), Pavese was determined to create a new narrative poetry that would be "virile," "sober," and objective. Pavese's view of himself as a narrative poet at the outset of his career was of great importance to him both aesthetically and morally.

"Il mestiere di poeta" (The poet's craft), the earlier of the two critical essays included in the Einaudi edition of *Lavorare stanca,* describes his initial quest for the "essential expression of essential facts" and his rejection of "the usual abstract introspection expressed in that bookish and allusive language, which, all too often, poses as essential" (*P,* 194). He now presented himself as antilyrical, anti-decadent, and anti-hermetic, abandoning the sentimental effusiveness of many of his own early experiments in verse.[2] The essay links this transition from a "lyricism of explosive personal feeling" to the quest for narrative clarity with two creative experiments of his own: some short stories containing dialogues written in dialect, and his playful "pornoteca," a collection of parodic verse written in ottava rima. The short stories helped him discover and develop an interest in regional characters, settings, and speech. This process was reinforced by his admiration for the realistic way in which American writers portrayed their native regions in a fresh colloquial language. On the other hand, the "pornoteca" taught him the discipline of technical craftsmanship and eventually served to persuade him that traditional meters were obsolete for all purposes other than parody.

Early in the process of formulating his new poetics, Pavese invented the concept of the *poesia-racconto* (poem-story). Insisting on an absolute austerity of style and rejecting all conventional imagery and rhetorical devices, he decided that every poem should tell a story. Convinced that traditional Italian meters would be of no use to him in creating his new poetry, he nevertheless hesitated to adopt the model of Whitman's free verse, which he felt was unsuited to his temperament and at odds with the residual influences of a classical education. The problem of choosing a meter thus remained for a time the only obstacle to realizing his expressive goals. Finally and almost by accident—or so he would have us believe—this problem was resolved. In "Il mestiere di poeta" he describes how one day he was muttering to himself a "rigmarole of words" when he stumbled across a phrase that provided the inspiration for his unique poetic meter: "Ha veduto fuggire balene tra schiume di sangue" ("He saw whales fleeing in a froth of blood"). Around this anapaestic line of fifteen syllables Pavese constructed his first poem-story, "I mari del Sud" (South Seas).[3]

In both editions of *Lavorare stanca* Pavese placed "I mari del Sud" in the foremost position, acknowledging its importance in his quest for a distinctive poetic voice.[4] The poem has a hundred and four lines, divided into stanzas of irregular length, and is the longest that Pavese ever wrote. Even today, more than half a century after its composition, the originality of its rhythm and cadence is immediately apparent. Pavese's metrical line can be identified under scrutiny as an inventive variation on a traditional meter, the decasyllable. Each line in "I mari del Sud" begins with a decasyllable composed of three anapaestic feet. Then, instead of moving on to the next line, Pavese adds several more syllables in a less pronounced cadence. Realizing that he could vary the number of syllables that would round out each line, he created a casual, discursive meter of his own.

"I mari del Sud" merits special attention as an introduction to the enterprise of the *Lavorare stanca* cycle, since it contains many of the major themes and expressive tensions that recur in the evolution of Pavese's poetry in the early 1930s. Its opening stanza seems to set the stage *in medias res* for the telling of a tale of almost epic dimensions:

> Camminiamo una sera sul fianco di un colle,
> in silenzio. Nell'ombra del tardo crepuscolo
> mio cugino è un gigante vestito di bianco,
> che si muove pacato, abbronzato nel volto,
> taciturno. Tacere è la nostra virtù.
> Qualche nostro antenato dev'essere stato ben solo
> —un grand'uomo tra idioti o un povero folle—
> per insegnare ai suoi tanto silenzio.
>
> (*P,* 11)

> We walk along the flank of a hill one evening
> in silence. In the shadows of late dusk,
> my cousin is a giant dressed in white,
> moving calmly along, his face tanned by the sun,
> not speaking. Silence is our strong point.
> Some ancestor of ours must have been a lonely type,
> —a great man surrounded by half-wits, or a poor old fool—
> to teach the rest of us such silence.

Against this backdrop of the Langhe hillside (identified later in the poem through allusions to Santo Stefano Belbo and Canelli) the narrator—a young peasant transplanted to the city—continues on his walk with an older cousin, who has returned home after years of traveling around the world. In a language that sometimes echoes the cadences of dialect, fragments of the wanderer's past are evoked, including the experience of whale-hunting and his eventual return to the Langhe where he failed to put to use the entrepreneurial ideas learned abroad. These episodes are interwoven with the narrator's reflections on his own less eventful past, as the young man laments the end of childhood and his painful initiation into the terrors and loneliness of urban life.

The epic quality observed in the opening stanza of "I mari del Sud" tends to diminish as the poem progresses. Though the giant figure of the seafaring cousin dominates the poem at various moments, he is not in fact its protagonist. The true protagonist turns out to be the young narrator, whose memories, illusions, and aspirations carry forward the thread of the narrative from sequence to sequence. A careful reading of "I mari del Sud" reveals a subjective stream of consciousness at work, rather than the narrative objectivity that Pavese painstakingly sought and claimed to achieve. In some passages, a tone of derivative lyricism, reminiscent of the author's rejected models—Pascoli and Gozzano in particular—emerges. The scene of a whale hunt near the poem's conclusion provides a rare episode of vivid narrative action. Yet even this scene is filtered through the narrator's idealized fantasies of his cousin's exotic adventures:

> E ha veduto volare i ramponi pesanti nel sole,
> ha veduto fuggire balene tra schiume di sangue
> e inseguirle e innalzarsi le code e lottare alla lancia.
> Me ne accenna talvolta.
>
> (*P,* 13)

> And he saw the heavy harpoons flying in the sunlight,
> he saw whales fleeing in a froth of blood,
> and then the chase, with the huge flukes rising up and thrashing out
> against attack.
> He talks about it sometimes.

In the next stanza, which brings the poem to an abrupt, almost prosaic conclusion, Pavese appears to expose and reject the romantic excesses of the narrator's perceptions. Here it is the laconic cousin who is given the last word in an exchange that juxtaposes the reality of the need to earn a living with the temptation of aestheticism and escapist illusions:

Ma quando gli dico
ch'egli è tra i fortunati che han visto l'aurora
sulle isole piú belle della terra,
al ricordo sorride e risponde che il sole
si levava che il giorno era vecchio per loro.

(*P,* 14)

But when I tell
him how lucky he is to be one of the few who've ever seen
the dawn breaking over the loveliest islands in the world,
he smiles at the memory, and says that by the time the sun came up,
their day was already half over.

The demystifying note upon which the poem concludes casts into question the initially heroic stature attributed to the "giant" cousin, and raises the issue of the narrator's reliability. Though at odds with Pavese's expressed goal of objective clarity, this ambiguity is symptomatic of the tensions at the basis of his creative inspiration.

The most enduring discovery that "I mari del Sud" brought to Pavese's art was its development of a marked sense of place. The Langhe hill against which the poem unfolds is at once both the specific territory of Pavese's earliest memories and the universal hillside of his mythical configurations. At the opposite pole the urban setting is also introduced. The image of the city that emerges here is highly ambivalent. It is presented both as a place of pleasure and independent endeavor, and as a source of solitude and terror.

With the juxtaposition of the two contrasting landscapes, rural and urban, Pavese articulated a series of interrelated themes in antithetical pairs: youth and maturity, innocence and disillusionment, escapism and work, wandering and return, the familiar and the foreign. As Pavese's work developed, the terms of these thematic polarities took on an increasing ambivalence. The motif of escapism or leisure, for example, linked in "I mari del Sud" with the notion of self-sufficient solitude and a disdain for women, evokes in later poems a more desolate sense of alienation and loneliness.

The free-spirited cousin who encapsulates the theme of proud independence in "I mari del Sud" is the first in a series of solitary, antisocial types who appear in many of the poems of the *Lavorare stanca* cycle. Pavese's cast of characters grew to include whores, thieves, drunks, runaway boys, tramps, and even a hermit. These protagonists are usually presented in an apparently objective, unsensational manner. Yet

Pavese's themes and characters have less to do with his declared objective of formulating a new narrative poetry, than with the working out of his most pressing existential preoccupation: the problem of identity and solitude, and the relationship of the self with the external world. The tensions and ambiguities of his major themes are symptomatic of a sense of internal conflict and division, and the alienation that characterizes many of his protagonists living outside the strictures of a social code reflects his own deeply felt isolation. Pavese's predilection for socially alienated provincial types is not, therefore, the manifestation of a precocious neo-realism, but rather the projection of a personal existential quest.

Unlike the author, the narrator created by Pavese in "I mari del Sud" and in several of the early poems of this cycle is an unlettered lower-class youth. In order to sustain the fictional mask of this persona, Pavese fashions a loose, paratactical syntax, often echoing the ungrammatical or repetitive structures of uneducated speech.[5] The elliptical vernacular narrator who serves as a disguise for the cultivated poet is not, however, a consistently plausible presence. In "I mari del Sud" and in a few other poems of this early period, the artifice is unevenly applied.

"Antenati" (Ancestors), written a year after "I mari del Sud," reflects Pavese's continued effort to refine the technique of the *poesia-racconto.* The scope of this poem is more compact than the previous one and lyrical lapses are completely avoided. Central to "Antenati" is again the narrator's proud affirmation of his peasant ancestry. The opening lines reiterate the qualities of self-confidence and laconic self-sufficiency:

> Ho scoperto che prima di nascere, sono vissuto
> sempre in uomini saldi, signori di sé,
> e nessuno sapeva rispondere e tutti eran calmi.
>
> (*P,* 23)

> I found out I had lived, before my birth,
> in strong, independent men, masters of themselves.
> None of them knew what to say, so they all kept quiet.

Although there are fewer unresolved tensions apparent in the texture of this poem than in the previous one, Pavese's attempt to achieve greater narrative objectivity is only partially successful. "Antenati" is both anecdotal and sententious. The opening stanzas present some vivid character sketches, but later the brisk narrative rhythm gives way to a more static and insistent tone. In the final two stanzas the theme of evasion from work is interwoven with the expression of a heavy-handed misogyny:

> E le donne non contano nella famiglia.
> Voglio dire, le donne da noi stanno in casa
> e ci mettono al mondo e non dicono nulla
> e non contano nulla e non le ricordiamo.
>
> (*P,* 24)

> In our family, women don't matter.
> What I mean is, our women stay home
> and bring into the world children like me, and keep their mouths shut.
> They don't matter and we don't remember them.

In his quest for an unembellished discursive style, Pavese occasionally lapsed into a language barely distinguishable from prose.

With "Fumatori di carta" (Men smoking paper cigarettes), written shortly after "Antenati," Pavese attempts another poem-story. In its description of a young peasant forced by economic necessity to become part of the urban proletariat, the poem presents a challenging departure from the unwillingness of almost all contemporary poets to deal with social or political themes.[6] Yet, although the setting is a workers' political meeting, a decidedly personal, emotional tone dominates, where the influence of Piero Jahier—a contemporary writer with a strong subjective tendency—has been detected.[7] The concluding stanza, even at a cursory reading, reveals the desire for sentimental impact over ideological intent:

> D'un tratto gridò
> che non era il destino se il mondo soffriva,
> se la luce del sole strappava bestemmie:
> era l'uomo, colpevole. Almeno potercene andare,
> far la libera fame, rispondere no
> a una vita che adopera amore e pietà,
> la famiglia, il pezzetto di terra, a legarci le mani.
>
> (*P,* 31)

> Suddenly he shouted
> that it wasn't fate that made the world suffer,

> that made men curse the light of day.
> It was man's fault. If at least we could pull out,
> and starve to death in freedom, and say no
> to a life that makes use of love and family and pity
> and a little plot of land to bind us together, and shackle our hands.

Here, as in several passages of "I mari del Sud," it is evident that Pavese, while making a claim for a rational, objective aesthetics bound to the interests of the real world, is at the same time struggling to control the effusive emotionality of his spontaneous inspiration, which he had previously found echoed in literary models he was now attempting to ignore.

"Pensieri di Deola" (Deola's thoughts) is the poem that most scrupulously obeys Pavese's self-imposed standards of the *poesia-racconto,* since it avoids both the severity of "Antenati" and the excessive sentimentality of "Fumatori di Carta." Its central character is Deola, a Turinese prostitute, glimpsed in the serenity of the early morning as she faces a new day, without illusion or self-pity. In Pavese's cast of characters the prostitute is among the most empathetically drawn. Here, with a few deft narrative details, Pavese evokes a sense of ineluctable isolation which can become self-conscious and courageous.

There are moments during the same period when Pavese abandons his conscious ambitions of creating colorful narrative characters in a clearly defined social setting and allows a new and distinctive lyricism to emerge. This is most evident in "Incontro" (Encounter):

> L'ho incontrata, una sera; una macchia piú chiara
> sotto le stelle ambigue, nella foschia d'estate.
> Era intorno il sentore di queste colline
> piú profondo dell'ombra, e d'un tratto suonò
> come uscisse da queste colline, una voce piú netta
> e aspra insieme, una voce di tempi perduti.
>
> (*P,* 29)

> I encountered her one evening; a brighter spot
> under the dim stars in the summer haze.
> The smell of these hills was all around me,
> a smell deeper than shadow, and suddenly I heard a sound,
> as though it came from these hills, a voice at once clearer
> and harsher, the voice of things past.

The female figure is presented as an emanation or an echo rather than as a physical being; visual clues are avoided. The woman's voice, the landscape, and the narrator's memory are fused together to form a single experience. This poem already points forward to a time when Pavese, no longer feeling compelled to present himself as a rational, realistic poet, began to subordinate character to landscape, and psychology to mythical illumination.

Through his growing appreciation of Elizabethan writers, Pavese became more open to the use of conventional poetic imagery, and soon he began to acknowledge the limitations of his quest for "muscular objectivity." Eventually an image appeared (spontaneously, he tells us in "Il mestiere di poeta") during the composition of a poem about a hermit which was to be entitled "Paesaggio I" (Landscape I). The image, a simple analogy and not a symbolic metaphor, describes the hermit as being the same color as the burnt bracken on the hillside ("è del colore delle felci bruciate"). Pavese was elated by the discovery that this image was not merely an arbitrary decoration superimposed on his narrative but that it was, in some mysterious way, the story itself. Perceiving an "imaginative link" between the hermit and the landscape, he decided that this relationship was the motivating force of the tale he wished to tell. The focus of his poetic endeavor thus shifted away from the concept of the *poesia-racconto* to a technique based on the narration of interrelated images, later described as the *poesia immagine* (poem image).

The unstated advantage of Pavese's acceptance of imagery, even on its most elementary application, was that it allowed him to develop his preoccupation with existential themes without the subjective intrusion of a dominant narrative persona. Thus the social isolation of the hermit in "Paesaggio I," unlike that of the prostitute in "Pensieri di Deola," is evoked without psychological penetration or pathos. Pavese's hermit becomes, in the images that link him to the hillside, a natural phenomenon. He gets his clothing from the mountain goat, and in return he impregnates the landscape with his own odors.

In "Il dio-caprone" (The goat-god) Pavese develops the poetic fusion of human and landscape elements one stage further, foreshadowing the mythical preoccupations of his later work. The composition of this poem was inspired by his recent, enthusiastic discovery of Sir James Frazer's ethnological classic, *The Golden Bough.* "Il dio-caprone" describes a city boy's discovery of the sensual mysteries of the countryside through the observation of human as well as animal behavior. Using the device of interweaving clusters of associated images, Pavese transforms this material into a complex, expressionistic, vision of the rural landscape. The boy's perceptions, filtered through a third-person narrative voice, combine crudely erotic description with imaginative intuitions about the mysterious bond that connects humans, animals, and the living landscape. From the vividly detailed observation of human and animal sexuality in the first stanza, there is an abrupt shift in the second to a nocturnal scene that evokes the lingering presence of archaic and numinous realities. Here the boy's sinister fantasy of a moonlit orgy is dominated by the Dionysian figure of the wild goat, and the rapidly paced description of sexual frenzy culminates in bloodshed reminiscent of Bacchic rites.

E la cagne, che abbaiano sotto la luna,
è perché hanno sentito il caprone che salta
sulle cime dei colli e annusato l'odore del sangue.
E le bestie si scuotono dentro le stalle.
Solamente i cagnacci piú forti dàn morsi all corda
e qualcuno si libera e corre a seguire il caprone,
che li spruzza e ubriaca di un sangue piú rosso del fuoco,
e poi ballano tutti, tenendosi ritti e ululando alla luna.

(*P*, 50)

And the bitches howl in the moonlight
because they've caught the smell of the wild goat leaping
on the hilltops. They've sniffed the smell of blood.
And the animals begin to stir in the stables.
Only the hounds, the biggest ones, are gnawing at the leash,
and a few of them break loose and chase the goat,
and the goat sprays them with blood redder than fire, making them drunk,
until they all dance upright, wailing at the moon.

As Pavese discarded the quest for logical or naturalistic narration in favor of an imaginative stream-of-consciousness technique, his poetry began to deal in a more focused way with the themes that were awkwardly expressed in the earlier period. Thus in "Mania di solitudine" (Passion for solitude) we find an entire poem explicitly dedicated to the theme of solitude. From the opening presentation of the solitary narrator eating supper at a window facing the evening sky, Pavese develops a series of images that suggest both the subject's connectedness on the biological level with all living things, and his aloofness from human companionship. The poem evokes a typically Pavesian moment of waiting and potentiality, where the subject is temporarily suspended from the tormented struggle between the self and the external world.

Not all the poems of this period show an appreciable advance toward the discovery of Pavese's true poetic voice. There are times when the *poesia immagine* technique yields to a showy display of superficial imagery. A striking example of the extremes of such virtuosity is seen in "Grappa a settembre" (Grappa in September). The poem weaves together a series of autumnal images, all evoking a sense of ripeness that unites landscape, buildings, and even women. Though visually compelling, it ultimately offers nothing more than an accumulation of clever images, illustrating though not developing a single idea. Pavese's use of imagery at this stage is still restricted to the level of simple analogies. His grasp of metaphor and the more complex reaches of symbolic language came much later in his stylistic development.

After Pavese's arrest and subsequent detention in the remote village of Brancaleone Calabro, his poetry underwent a striking transformation. Even the few poems written at the beginning of this period and submitted in time for inclusion in the first edition of *Lavorare stanca* already reveal this change. The verse Pavese wrote from now onward has a more lyrical, introspective quality than his earlier work. The protagonist of many of the lyrics of the *confino* period is an exile, a man who for different reasons feels alienated from the world of his fellows ("the solitary man," "the old man," and "the Negro"). Pavese's treatment of solitude gradually began to take on a cosmic or mythical dimension.

"Paternità" (Fatherhood) and "Lo steddazzu" (Morning star)—written in 1935 and 1936, respectively—are among the most compelling in Pavese's repertoire. With the desolate seaside landscape of the South as their setting, both poems transform Pavese's personal preoccupation with loneliness and futility into universal existential themes.

> Uomo solo dinanzi all'inutile mare,
> attendendo la sera, attendendo il mattino.
> I bambini vi giocano, ma quest'uomo vorrebbe
> lui averlo un bambino e guardarlo giocare.
> Grandi nuvole fanno un palazzo sull'acqua
> che ogni giorno rovina e risorge, e colora
> i bambini nel viso. Ci sarà sempre il mare.
>
> (*P,* 130)

A man alone facing the useless sea,
waiting for evening to come, waiting for morning.
There are children out playing, but this man would like
to have a son of his own, to watch him playing games.
Over the water huge clouds build a castle,
every day it falls down and rises up again, coloring
the children's faces. The sea will always be there.

The irony of the title "Paternità" becomes apparent in the third and fourth lines, in the poignant use of the conditional tense. The ocean, potentially a symbol of sexual union, becomes instead an image of sterility and separation. In the second stanza a woman and later a man are visualized in their nakedness and ineluctable separation. Again the conditional tense conveys the impossibility of fulfillment:

Il mattino ferisce. Su questo umida spiaggia
striscia il sole, aggrappato alle reti e alle pietre.
Esce l'uomo nel torbido sole e cammina
lungo il mare. Non guarda le madide schiume
che trascorrono a riva e non hanno piú pace.
A quest'ora i bambini sonnecchiano ancora
nel tepore del letto. A quest'ora sonnecchia
dentro il letto una donna, che farebbe l'amore
se non fosse lei sola. Lento, l'uomo si spoglia
nudo come la donna lontana, e discende nel mare.
(*P,* 130)

The morning strikes. Over this damp beach the sun
creeps, sticking to nets and stones.
The man steps out in the murky light and walks
along the sea. He doesn't look at the gurgling froth
which runs endlessly along the shore, never at peace.
This is the hour when children are still dozing
in warm beds. This is the hour when a woman lies
dozing in her bed—she'd make love
if she weren't all alone. Slowly, the man strips
naked as the woman in her bed, and walks into the sea.

"Lo steddazzu," which is placed in the final position of the definite edition of *Lavorare stanca,* reinforces and amplifies the themes of "Paternità." Once again, the solitary protagonist is depicted on a bleak sea shore at the dawn of a day "when nothing will happen." This recurrent motif of a solitary man in a state of waiting, imagined against a backdrop of the stars and the infinite sky, first appeared in "Mania di solitudine" where it was interpreted in a serenely meditative key. In "Lo steddazzu," however, the image is used to express an unequivocal pessimism. The final stanza states simply and powerfully the futility of the human condition:

> Val la pena che il sole si levi dal mare
> e la lunga giornata cominci? Domani
> tornerà l'alba tiepida con la diafana luce
> e sarà come ieri e mai nulla accadrà.
> L'uomo solo vorrebbe soltanto dormire.
> Quando l'ultima stella si spegne nel cielo,
> l'uomo adagio prepara la pipa e l'accende.
>
> (*P,* 134)

> Why should the sun bother to rise from the sea
> or the long day begin? Tomorrow
> the warm dawn with its transparent light will be back,
> and everything will be like yesterday, and nothing will happen at all.
> The man alone would like nothing more than to sleep.
> When the last star in the sky is quenched and gone,
> the man quietly taps tobacco into his pipe and lights up.

Pavese demonstrates more technical control in "Paternità" and "Lo steddazzu" than in any of his earlier poems. His repetition of key words and phrases, especially in "Lo steddazzu," conveys with relentless insistence the impression of existential tedium. The strategic effectiveness of his sentence structures and lexical choices reveals a conscious stylistic economy. Now the characteristically long, uneven lines in his earlier poetry are replaced to a large extent by lines of thirteen syllables. Echoes of dialect no longer occur. These changes are necessitated by Pavese's need to give more incisive expression to the increasingly lyrical direction of his thematic preoccupations. The expressive conflict underlying so much of his earlier work is absent, for his ambition is no longer to tell a story (or to narrate "imaginative links") but to illuminate a psychic state.

Another aspect of the theme of solitude is explored in "Mito" (Myth) from the same period—a poem that describes the disappointment of an adolescent, envisioned as a young god, as he crosses the threshold into manhood. The symbolic antecedents of this character's predicament are suggested in the poem's original title, "Teogonia" (Theogony), which also highlights Pavese's increasing fascination with mythology as well as his attempt to formulate a personal understanding of myth.[8] Here childhood is equated with the end of summer, a paradisiacal season when the boy, still unaware of death, perceived the mountains to touch the sky, the clouds to form clusters of grapes, the sun to be made of fire. All these illusions must pass with the rainy season of maturity when the divine youth becomes a mere man and must accept the tedium of mortal existence. This theme is foreshadowed in some earlier poems, but here it finds its fullest expression in the fusion of subjective meditation with the sensitive transformation of mythical insights.

Of the poems written during Pavese's exile in Brancaleone, only "Un ricordo" (A memory) deals with love. The core of the poem, however, evokes a profound sense of solitude:

> Non c'è uomo che giunga a lasciare una traccia
> su costei. Quant'è stato dilegua in un sogno
> come via in un mattino, e non resta che lei.
> Se non fosse la fronte sfiorata da un attimo
> sembrerebbe stupita. Sorridon le guance
> ogni volta.
>
> (*P,* 129)

> No man alive can leave a mark on her.
> The trace of everyone vanishes, dissolving like a dream,
> like a dream in the morning. Only she survives.
> Except for the instant that grazes her brow,
> she would seem taken by surprise. Her cheeks smile.
> Every time.

The second stanza develops the image of the woman's obstinate aloofness, suggesting a sphinxlike presence, both more and less than human. Consistent with Pavese's ambiguous portrayal of women, her voice is described as more masculine than feminine.

> Nemmeno s'ammassano i giorni
> sul suo viso, a mutare il sorriso leggero
> che s'irradia alle cose. Con dura fermezza

fa ogni cosa, ma sembra ogni volta la prima;
pure vive fin l'ultimo istante. Si schiude
il suo solido corpo, il suo guardo raccolto,
a una voce sommessa e un po' rauca; una voce
d'uomo stanco. E nessuna stanchezza la tocca.

(*P,* 130)

Not even the days accumulate
on her face, nor shift the faint smile
she casts on things. She does everything
with firm determination, always as though for the first time
and always fully down to the last instant. Her strong body,
her thoughtful gaze, are heard in a voice that is low and hoarse, the voice
of a tired man. And no fatigue ever touches her.

In the final stanza the destructive aspect of the woman's presence is deftly suggested, and the irremediable distance between lover and beloved is reinforced in the poem's concluding allusion to her enigmatic smile, suggesting a sinister, incomprehensible power. "Un ricordo" anticipates the mythic treatment of the female presence in Pavese's later poetry and in *Dialoghi con Leucò*.

Pavese's gradual surrender to lyricism in his verse was paralleled by a new surge of activity in short-story writing. With this outlet for his narrative needs, telling stories in verse was no longer a compelling necessity. The painful emotional crisis that Pavese experienced upon his return to Turin in 1936 also exerted a powerful impact on his creativity. For over a year he completely abandoned the professed ambition of his earlier poetics and began to write sentimental lyrics, voicing the pain of unrequited love. Although these poems were excluded from the Einaudi edition of *Lavorare stanca* and remained unpublished for many years, Pavese did not discard them. He carefully preserved them, together with a small number of lyrics in the same vein written slightly earlier, in a special folder bearing the title, *Poesie del disamore* (Poems of unloving), a title used for their posthumous publication.[9]

In a diary entry dated December 1937 Pavese signals the end of the period of grieving from which these lyrics emerged, observing with satisfied relief: "This year I tried again the poetry of self-indulgent release and overcame it" (*MV,* 69). In retrospect these poems seem not so much the product of a passing aberration as the indication of a whole new direction in the author's poetic activity that reached fruition in the subsequent decade. The tone of the *Poesie del disamore* is intimistic and self-searching. The imagery characteristic of Pavese's earlier period gives way to images used as mysterious presences, or landscapes overlaid with symbolic suggestions. In "Sogno" (Dream), the second-person singular—dominant in the tradition of love poetry since the thirteenth century and avoided by Pavese since the beginning of the *Lavorare stanca* cycle—finally makes its appearance in the direct invocation of the beloved.

The poems written during the late 1930s, which Pavese decided to include in the definitive version of *Lavorare stanca,* may be roughly classified into two groups: those that follow to some extent the narrative tendency of the early poems of the cycle (insofar as they have a strongly developed protagonist and unfold against the backdrop of a distinct physical setting), and those intimistic lyrics with a declared or implied first-person stream of consciousness that tend to voice the sentimental or existential predicament of the discarded *Poesie del disamore.* Even in the first group, however, a change from the flat, unequivocal narrative style of the *poesia-racconto* can be discerned. "Il figlio della vedova" (The widow's son), for example, is a mysterious, allusive poem set in the countryside, which offers nothing of the rustic realism seen in "I mari del Sud." The poem ostensibly describes a woman on the threshold of childbirth, a situation infused with an atmosphere of tension and mystery through the rhythmic repetition of the phrase "può accadere":

> Può accadere ogni cosa nella bruna osteria
> può accadere che fuori sia un cielo di stelle,
> al di là della nebbia autunnale e del mosto.
> Può accadere che cantino dalla collina
> le arrochite canzoni sulle aie deserte
> e che torni improvvisa sotto il cielo d'allora
> la donnetta seduta in attesa del giorno.
>
> (*P,* 154)

> Anything could happen in the dimness of the tavern.
> The sky outside could be full of stars,
> beyond the haze of the autumn fog and the new wine.
> One might hear the sound of hoarse songs from the deserted farms
> on the hill.
> It could happen that suddenly, under the skies of long ago,
> that little woman might reappear, seated and waiting for dawn.

A similar atmosphere of mystery is achieved in "La moglie del barcaiolo" (The wife of the boatman) in which dream, fantasy, and reality intermingle and overlap.

Even the landscape poems of the same period are invested with a new symbolic dimension, as well as a hint of the subjective lyricism present in *Poesie del disamore.* "Paesaggio VIII" (Landscape VIII) provides an example of how Pavese transforms a natural setting into a series of mysterious, mythical presences:

I ricordi cominciano nella sera
sotto il fiato del vento a levare il volto
e ascoltare la voce del fiume. L'acqua
è la stessa, nel buio, degli anni morti,
Nel silenzio del buio sale uno sciacquo
dove passano voci e risa remote;
s'accompagna al brusío un colore vano
che è di sole, di rive e di sguardi chiari.
Un'estate di voci. Ogni viso contiene
come un frutto maturo un sapore andato.

(*P,* 159)

Memories begin at evening,
with a breath of wind, to lift their heads and listen to the voice of the river.
The water,
in the darkness, flows as it did in the dead years.
In the silent darkness a rustling rises.
Old voices, old laughter go flowing by,
and with the murmur goes an empty color,
the color of sunlight, and river banks, and bright faces,
A summer of voices. Each face keeps,
like ripe fruit, the flavor of something gone.

In two of the last poems of the *Lavorare stanca* cycle Pavese realizes his full talents as a lyric poet: "Estate" (Summer) and "Notturno" (Nocturne). Both are love poems, and both address the beloved as "*tu.*" Yet in each poem the woman is completely fused with the landscape. More ethereal than physical, her presence is evoked in a series of expressions, movements, silences, and reflections:

La collina di terra e di foglie chiude
con la massa nera il tuo vivo guardare,
la tua bocca ha la piega di un dolce incavo

tra le coste lontane. Sembri giocare
alla grande collina e al chiarore del cielo:
per piacermi ripeti lo sfondo antico
e lo rendi piú puro.
   Ma vivi altrove
Il tuo tenero sangue si è fatto altrove.
Le parole che dici non hanno riscontro
con la scabra tristezza di questo cielo.
Tu non sei che una nube dolcissima, bianca
impigliata una notte fra i rami antichi.

(*P*, 163)

The hill with its earth and leaves contains
in its black mass your living look.
The curve of your mouth is like a gentle dip
between the distant slopes. You seem to play at being
the great hill and the clarity of the sky;
to please me you repeat the ancient setting,
and you make it purer.
But you live elsewhere.
Your tender blood was made in some other place.
The words you speak have no echo here
in the harsh sadness of this sky.
You are just a cloud, white and very sweet,
entangled one night among the ancient branches.

Abandoning the simple analogous imagery of his earlier verse, Pavese began to approach a symbolic allusiveness not entirely dissimilar to that of the hermetic poets. This is not a question of external influence, however, for Pavese arrived at his highly personal mode of mythical symbolism through the gradual discovery of his most authentic inner world. The self-conscious preoccupation with the external environment in the early years of the *Lavorare stanca* cycle gives way in the final period to unabashed introspection.

When Pavese reassembled the poems of the original Solaria edition for republication by Einaudi (a process that involved including some poems omitted from the first edition and adding several written since that time) he still insisted, in the name of clarity, on maintaining a rationalizing posture, now more than ever in contrast with the intimistic reverberations of his recent lyrics. Disregarding chronological order, he arranged the poems of *Lavorare stanca* into six thematic sections, which—he would have us believe—are connected by a unifying narrative thread. Although Pavese had disclaimed the usefulness or even validity of such a *canzoniere* in "Il mestiere di poeta," he now claims in the essay "Su certe poesie non ancora scritte" (On certain poems not yet written) that the poems of the *Lavorare stanca* cycle are united by a single thematic preoccupation:

> *Lavorare stanca* can be defined as the adventure of the adolescent boy who is proud of the countryside where he lives and who imagines that the city will be like the country. But in the city he discovers loneliness and tries to cure it with sex and passion; but they only uproot him and alienate him from city and country alike, leaving him in a more tragic loneliness that marks the end of adolescence. In this *canzoniere* I discovered a formal coherence, the evocation of completely solitary figures who are imaginatively alive insofar as they are bound to their brief time and place by means of the internal image. (*P,* 206)

The titles of each of the six sections of *Lavorare stanca*—"Antenati" (Ancestors), "Dopo" (Afterwards), "Città in campagna" (City in country), "Maternità" (Motherhood), "Legna verde" (Green wood), and "Paternità" (Fatherhood)—some intentionally ironic, focus on a particular facet of the declared overall theme. Yet this superimposed framework, as well as the author's repeated declarations on his own poetry, have led to considerable critical misinterpretation. Many critics have insisted on reading the poems of Pavese's first collection primarily in the light of what the author himself had to say about them, since Pavese's two critical essays seem to declare themselves as an essential tool for the reading and interpretation of the poetry.

One of the most influential critiques of *Lavorare stanca* was provided in Massimo Mila's preface to the 1961 edition of Pavese's collected poetry.[10] In this essay Mila, a distinguished musicologist and a personal friend of Pavese, claims to find the atavistic antecedents of the poet's "ternary rhythm" in the collective, Allobrogian unconscious of the peoples of northern Italy. Here the critic's "Celtic" thesis emphasizes Pavese's gifts as a narrative, epic poet, claiming that *Lavorare stanca* is the first attempt in recent history to give voice to the peasant civilization of Piedmont. With such a bias it is hardly surprising that Mila neglects the lyrical components of Pavese's first collection, announcing that there is no continuity of style or inspiration between *Lavorare stanca* and the poetry of the following decade (anthologized as *La terra e la morte* and *Verrà la morte e avrà i tuoi occhi*). He concludes, therefore, that these are separate and distinct seasons of the author's creative inspiration.

Italo Calvino's edition of Pavese's poems, *Poesie edite e inedite,* published by Einaudi in 1962, only a year after the appearance of Mila's essay, invites a radically different critical perspective. Calvino presents the poems of Pavese's entire career in chronological order (from "I mari del Sud" of 1930 to the English-titled "Last blues to be read some day" of 1950), and thus dismantles the framework that Pavese constructed when reediting *Lavorare stanca* in order to reinforce a deliberate poetic posture.[11] Each poem is carefully dated and annotated, and Calvino often provides alternative versions deciphered from surviving rough drafts. Calvino's critical edition thus enables the reader to observe the gradual evolution of Pavese's poetry, which moves from a contrived, though original, formulation of narrative verse to the adoption of simple, analogous imagery (the *poesia immagine* or *immagine interna*), and eventually to the discovery of a personal symbolism infused with mythic intuition. We can thus witness how Pavese moves from characters to presences, from storytelling to lyrical contemplation. The last poems of the *Lavorare stanca* cycle, when considered in this light, point forward in a continuous way both to the meditative lyrics of *La terra e la morte* (Earth and death), a small collection of poems written in 1946, and ultimately to the narrative symbolism of Pavese's mature novels.

Chapter Three
The Quest for Narrative Technique

Ciau Masino

Ciau Masino, Pavese's first collection of experimental stories, was written between October 1931 and February 1932 and published posthumously in 1968.[1] The desire for innovation that characterizes the earliest poems of the *Lavorare stanca* cycle is evident here also. *Ciau Masino* is unique in the Pavesian repertoire for both its extensive use of the Piedmontese dialect and its unusual structural features.

The collection is made up of fourteen narrative episodes. Half of these recount the adventures of Masino, a young middle-class journalist; the other half feature his proletarian counterpart, Masin. The Masino stories alternate with the Masin cycle, creating a double-edged narrative sequence where two lives and two contrasting social worlds are repeatedly presented for the reader's attention. In addition, each pair of stories (with the exception of the last) is followed by a poem. These six poems (two of which, "Mari del Sud" and "Antenati," appeared in *Lavorare stanca*) are written in the present tense by a first-person narrator. Thus they serve as a meditative pause between the more rapidly paced third-person stories of youthful adventure.

Pavese's fascination with parallels and antitheses that emerged in the thematic polarities of the first poems of the *Lavorare stanca* cycle is part of the dynamics at work in the steadily declining fortunes of Masino and Masin. Both characters start out with comparable resources of energy, ambition, and independence of spirit. We first meet Masino as he takes on an experiment in songwriting in collaboration with a Neapolitan musician, while Masin is introduced at the point when, discharged from military service, he begins attending night school in order to improve his education. Although each of the young men experiences failure in these initial situations, the results are more serious for the proletarian. Masin is soon expelled from school for challenging authority. Despondent because of this setback, he gets drunk, runs over a pedestrian, and is fired from his job as a test driver.

Leaving Turin in the wake of the fatal accident, and escaping prosecution only by virtue of the fact that the pedestrian he killed was himself intoxicated, Masin decides to move to the countryside in the episode entitled "La Langa." Though he expects better luck in a rural environment, he discovers that the peasants are as mean-spirited as their urban counterparts. In "La zoppa" (The lamelegged girl) Masin, outsmarted and defeated, goes to work as a chauffeur for a wealthy country family. Here too he experiences disappointment and alienation, and fails to establish companionship even with the family's disgraced alcoholic governess. After returning to Turin in "Ospedale" (Hospital), he falls in love with a fickle vaudeville dancer, Pucci, whom he marries in "I cantastorie" (Ballad singers) and by whom he is soon cuckolded. Going back to the Langhe in "Masin 'dla frôja" (Masin the guitar player), he decides to work as a wandering musician but is immediately tricked out of his newly acquired guitar by the sly peasant Talino, whom he had unsuspectingly befriended. He then wanders without food or money through the unfriendly villages of the Langhe until, weak with hunger, he begins to hallucinate. In "Carogne" (Jailbirds), Masin, now back in Turin, is arrested and found guilty of murdering his faithless wife. His story ends as he is transported to a penitentiary to serve a long sentence of forced labor.

The fate of Masino, Pavese's middle-class protagonist, is considerably less bleak. After his initial failure to launch himself as a lyricist, Masino appears in "L'acqua del Po" (Waters of the Po), where during the course of a boating trip on the river he becomes caught up in the tensions and insecurities that his friendships evoke in him. Next, in "Arcadia"—a retrospective episode recounting a moment from Masino's student years—he explores the excitement and dangers of the more lurid neighborhoods of Turin, only to recognize the alienation of his privileged position as a spectator. Later, in "Masino padre" (Masino as a father), he embarks on an absurdly unsuccessful courtship with a genteel, middle-class girl. In "Hoffmann" he goes on an outing in the Turinese hills with the friend who most inspires his admiration and envy. Then, in "Religiosamente" (Religiously), Masino experiences a dramatic inner conflict when he mistakenly assumes that this friend has drowned. In the concluding story, "Il mare" (The sea), Masino unsuccessfully tries out his bookish knowledge of American speech on an uncomprehending black sailor in the port of Genoa. Despite setbacks, however, Masino's future seems full of promise, for he has received a professional assignment as a foreign correspondent and is about to embark on a journey to America.

Masino's adventures have some parallels with those of Masin. Nevertheless, the bourgeois youth is generally called upon to test his wits against his peers or to struggle with his own inadequacies, whereas Masin's battle is often one against authority figures or the injustices of the social system. For Masino the struggle, though difficult, is not impossible, since at least on the material level he achieves some success. Masin's adventures, by contrast, follow a relentlessly destructive course.

Ciau Masino contains some autobiographical elements, especially in its range of settings and situations. Many of Pavese's favorite haunts in and around Turin—the banks of the Po and its tributaries, the crowded working-class restaurants on the city's outskirts, the nighttime world of cabaret and variety show performers—provide the background for the adventures of his protagonists. These settings were to become characteristic of Pavese's work. More important than these details of local color, however, is the device of the double protagonist itself. In this split character, whose capacity to merge as a single identity is suggested in the two almost identical names, the writer is able to present conflicting elements within his own complex sense of self-understanding. Thus the contrast between Pavese's identity as an introspective middle-class intellectual, self-doubting yet bound for success, and his simultaneous fantasy of himself as an urbanized peasant, heir to the instinctive and sometimes violent energies of his rural ancestors, is hinted at in the separate destinies of Masino and Masin. Yet, partly because Masino and Masin never meet within the frame of any single episode, the contrast between them lacks dynamic development. In subsequent works, Pavese created characters who function as foils to each other and whose differences are presented in a more dynamic manner. This tendency to create doubles or pairs is related to Pavese's stylistic predilection for binary oppositions, first witnessed in the thematic polarities of *Lavorare stanca*.

Whatever autobiographical qualities can be detected in *Ciau Masino,* there is little sentimentality or subjectivity in this work. Psychological development is limited, even in the case of Masino, whose inner life is depicted to a greater degree than that of Masin. Despite their recurrent misfortunes, the two protagonists are kept at an ironic distance at all times, and pathos is avoided. For these reasons *Ciau Masino* has a humorous and playful tone that is largely absent in Pavese's subsequent fiction.

Although a summary of the diverging fortunes of Masino and Masin might suggest a straightforward critique of class differences, the polemical bias of this work should not be overestimated. While it is true that *Ciau Masino* presents a more challenging attitude toward social realities than much of Pavese's subsequent fiction, his interest in his characters even here, as in *Lavorare stanca,* is more existential than sociopolitical.

The most striking innovation of *Ciau Masino* occurs on the linguistic level. These stories are unique in Pavese's work by virtue of the insertion of dialogue in various Piedmontese dialects. The text is also enriched with colloquial expressions and the occasional use of slang. Pavese's admiration of the seemingly spontaneous qualities of American literary language had already led him to invent a new discursive rhythm in "I mari del Sud" and now enabled him to attempt a more complex and radical experimentation with language in the stories of Masino and Masin.

Linguistic self-consciousness is one of the dominant features of this early work. Pavese repeatedly draws attention to the question of language and the problems of verbal communication. In many of the stories it is a linguistic difficulty that prompts the denouement. The opening episode, "Il blues delle cicche" (Cigarette butt blues), provides an example of this phenomenon. Here, the Turinese Masino attempts to set up a working relationship with Don Ciccio, a Neapolitan musician, for the purpose of composing songs together. This professional collaboration is undermined almost immediately by the difficulty of finding a mutually satisfactory language for songwriting. It is Masino's failure to resolve this problem that leads him to abandon the venture entirely. The struggle between the two men is brought to life by Pavese in the skillful use of dialogue written largely in dialect, with Masino using Turinese and Ciccio responding in Neapolitan.

Similarly, in "Congedato" (Discharged), the first story featuring Masin, the protagonist's expulsion from night school is triggered by a provocatively worded essay that parodies the rhetoric of historical textbooks. As Masin is ordered to leave the classroom he and his proletarian companions exchange comments in Turinese dialect, immediately accentuating the distance between the students and their officious Italian-speaking instructor. The scene is linked thematically with the final episode in *Ciau Masino,* where Masino discovers, during his vain attempt to practice his English with the black sailor, that the language of books is a world apart from the language of working men.

From the linguistic viewpoint, "La Langa," the second episode in the Masin cycle, provides one of the most dynamic examples of Pavese's pervasive preoccupation with the theme of language.[2] Here, as in the other tales of *Ciau Masino,* dialect is used only in direct speech or in the protagonist's interior monologue, whereas literary Italian is limited almost exclusively to the narrative framework. Each of the participants in "La Langa" reveals his geographical provenance as well as his position in the social spectrum through subtle nuances of speech. Masin himself speaks only in Turinese, with occasional recourse to contemporary slang. Don Rôss, his avaricious and unscrupulous employer, speaks mainly in the dialect of Santo Stefano, with some calculated shifts into Italian. Talino, the peasant who first befriends Masin and later tricks him, also shifts from one dialect into another in order to achieve his devious ends. Masin is first drawn to Talino when he hears him speaking in Turinese, a feature that distinguishes him from the other peasants. Gradually, as Masin's confidence is assured, Talino begins to lapse into Santo Stefano dialect. Finally when the peasant's trick is accomplished, his speech no longer reveals even a trace of Turinese dialect.

The virtuosity of Pavese's manipulation of dialect in this story, and the precision of his phonetic transcription of local nuances, is lost, inevitably, on the majority of his readers. Though "La Langa" provides a fascinating document of the use of regional dialects in a particular place and time, the problem of readership remains unresolved. Unless Pavese's readers possess the same multilingual range as his characters, their appreciation of the story is restricted, and the dialogues written in dialect retain a purely ornamental function in the text. In "La Langa," as well as in "Arcadia" in the Masino cycle, however, several turns in the plot are triggered within the dialogues so that at least a minimal comprehension of the dialects is required of the reader in order to follow the logic of events.

A more successful integration of dialect elements into the text occurs in the passages that indirectly report Masin's interior monologues. Here the meaning of regional or slang expressions can be deduced from the surrounding context: the use of *paco* rather than *contadino* for "peasant" is the most obvious example. Even more important than the insertion of these lexical elements into the main body of the narrative is

Pavese's adoption of a syntax that reflects the peculiarities of local speech.

In a seminal study of the *Ciau Masino,* Anco Marzio Mutterle discusses the evolution of Pavese's command of interior monologue, illustrating the writer's gradual mastery of the skill of integrating into passages dominated by the omniscient narrator lexical or syntactical elements that suggest the simultaneous presence of the consciousness of Masino or Masin.[3] Unimpressed by the claim that the importance of this early work lies in its implicit critique of class, Mutterle finds instead that within *Ciau Masino* there is a steady progress in thematic focus from outer to inner experience, from the objective to the subjective. He shows that this movement is due partly to Pavese's abandonment of sociolinguistic mimesis in favor of a subjectively nuanced narrative voice. The pattern can be more readily detected in the stories of the Masino cycle than in those that feature Masin.

The poems that alternate with the narrative episodes of *Ciau Masino* provide a puzzling juxtaposition with the rapidly paced adventures of Masino and Masin. They share with the stories the backdrop of Turin and the Langhe, which is filtered here in the lyrics through the subjective consciousness of the first-person narrator. Though recounted in the present tense, the poems evoke the power of memory and contemplation and reveal a sensibility that is in contrast with the more ironic tone of the stories. In these poems, the landscape of the Langhe countryside is transfigured through the memory of the narrator into a complex, mythic motif, very different from the treatment of the same landscape when filtered through the contemptuous perspective of Masin. Though the poems evoke the distinctive qualities of Piedmontese sensibility, overt transcriptions of dialect are avoided. Elements of dialect are obliquely reflected here, as in all the poems of the early *Lavorare stanca* cycle, through the syntax, the cadences, and the rhythms of speech. It is precisely in this direction that Pavese later found his most distinctive and authentic narrative voice.

The poems also have in common with the stories the recurrent theme of misogyny, giving a tenuous unity to the collection as a whole. In the narrative episodes, the misogynistic note is discernible in all the social settings described by Pavese, whether urban or rural, bourgeois or lower class. It is presented almost as a preexisting social mandate, rather than the expression of the protagonists' subjectivity. The image of women that emerges in the accompanying lyrics, however, shows greater complexity, ranging from a hint of decadent idealization in "Le maestrine" (The schoolteachers) to the stoic assertion of male supremacy in "Antenati" (Ancestors).

The problem of aesthetic unity was perhaps Pavese's strongest motivation for abandoning the project of *Ciau Masino.* He was still too close to the residual influences of his Crocean training to be able to move with confidence in experimental territory. Furthermore, he had not begun to attempt the expression of his most pressing existential preoccupations in narrative form. Yet the enterprise of this early work both taught Pavese the limits of his use of dialect for literary purposes and enabled him to explore a range of human types and situations within the territory that would become uniquely his own.

The Short Stories, 1936–38

Pavese's second period of short story writing began after his return from political detention in Brancaleone Calabro. Between 1936 and 1938 he produced fifteen stories in rapid succession, as well as many unfinished fragments. Unlike the narrative episodes of *Ciau Masino,* which were written during the most serene period of Pavese's life, the new stories grew out of a profound emotional and intellectual crisis and they reflect an urgent attempt to find a change of artistic direction. It is clear that Pavese regarded these works as experimental. Of the fifteen stories only one, "Primo amore" (First love), was published during his lifetime.[4] It was not until 1953, when Italo Calvino anthologized several of the other stories from this period under the title *Notte di festa* (Festival night), that the evolution of Pavese's narrative work during this crucial period could be studied and observed.

Even the earliest entries in Pavese's diary dating back to his detention in Brancaleone express some dissatisfaction with the strictures of his self-imposed stylistic principles and anticipate the shift from verse to prose. Echoing a judgment that is also implicit in "Il mestiere di poeta," he reports a pressing need to create a new point of departure that would enable him to cast off the stale techniques in which his writing had become enmeshed: "the halfhearted, compulsive reduction of every situation to . . . the image-story" (*MV,* 14). Furthermore, the tone of moral reflection regarding the creative enterprise briefly introduced in "Il mestiere di poeta" becomes more marked in the diary entries during the spring of 1935. Pavese now censured himself in a manner that is unequivocally moralistic, condemning his poetry as a series of superficial exercises that "merely present the spectacle of life, but not life itself." He thus proposed to "build in life and to build in art. To be, tragically" (*MV,* 35–36).

The aesthetic crisis that led Pavese to begin his journal in Brancaleone was followed upon his return to Turin by a severe emotional crisis, triggered by his personal difficulties with Pizzardo. At this juncture, the aesthetic meditations in the journal gave way to the fragmented but spontaneous expression of pain, and many entries combine elements of moral and psychological self-questioning with the search for new forms of expression. Implicit in these meditations is the notion of the moral and therapeutic possibilities of artistic endeavor. It was thus as much in an attempt to sublimate a personal sense of humiliation and loss as to explore a new narrative technique that Pavese wrote his first fully developed short story on the subject of human solitude.

The narrator of "Terra d'esilio" (Land of exile)—loosely based on Pavese's experience in Brancaleone Calabro—is a northern engineer who has been sent to "the very bottom of Italy" on a professional assignment. Soon after his arrival in the village, he attempts to dispell his sense of alienation by making contact with Otino, another northerner. Otino, who shares the narrator's contempt for the southern village, is a political prisoner serving a sentence of internment for having assaulted a Fascist guard. Despite this sentence, however, Otino is not politically committed. His crime was an act of revenge against the man who had seduced his wife. He is still smoldering with fury and obsessed with his wife's betrayal. When, finally, he learns that she has been murdered, he observes that his deepest regret is that he has been deprived of the opportunity of killing her himself. In this character Pavese fuses the themes of isolation and misogynistic rage. Otino's sentiments are reechoed in those of Ciccio, an aging vagabond whose eccentric appearance is a familiar sight in the villages of the region. Ciccio, we are told, had in reaction to his own wife's desertion "abandoned everything: work, home, dignity, and had wandered for a year scavenging along the coastline, without knowing what he was looking for" (*R,* 141). He functions in the text as a grotesque exemplification of the extremes to which solitude and betrayal can drive a human being.

While the narrator stands at a distance from the anger and explicit misogyny expressed by the two other men, he shares with them the conviction that he is chronically incapable of fitting into society. He will always be an outsider, and in his awareness of this condition there is a tone of embittered resignation. The sense of a shared destiny does not, however, lead him to friendship or solidarity with Otino or the crazed Ciccio, for he is intrinsically incapable of companionship.

The plot of "Terra d'esilio" is tenuous, tracing in a linear way the condition of the narrator's monotonous existence during his stay in the South. Pavese's purpose is more to illuminate his character's internal state than to weave a tale of action or of intrigue. Yet the tone remains free of the excesses of subjectivity, except in a few instances where the narrator's self-pitying reflections become heavy-handed and repetitious. The language here retains nothing of the rough experimentalism of *Ciau Masino,* and is closer to the "calligraphic" conventions of contemporary narrative prose, especially to the classical aspirations of the once-rejected *prosa d'arte.*

In the stories that followed Pavese drew less on the precise circumstances of his autobiographical experiences while offering an increasingly complex exploration of the theme of human solitude. In the ironically entitled "Viaggio di nozze" (Honeymoon), the motifs of isolation, the inability to love, and the refusal to grow up are explicitly linked. The story is structured as a remorseful memory of the narrator Giorgio, who describes a trip taken to Genoa years earlier with his wife, Cilia, now dead. The cause of Cilia's death, though never explained, seems connected with Giorgio's insistent habit of "rejecting reality for daydreams" and with his painful vocation for solitude. In the account of their unhappy "honeymoon," Giorgio's quest for the kind of isolation that will offer the illusion of infinite freedom and potential is juxtaposed with Cilia's wearying solicitude and anxiety. This contrast between the man's rejection of adult preoccupations and the woman's unrelenting demands is one of the major motifs in Pavese's early repertoire of misogynistic themes.

The crisis of "Viaggio di nozze" is prompted by the narrator's fear that his wife might achieve a small measure of happiness—impossible for himself—in their being together. Having accompanied her on a trip to Genoa, he leaves their hotel in order to wander alone around the harbor at night. The story comes to an abrupt conclusion as Cilia later confronts Giorgio with the pain of his abandonment of her in Genoa. Crudely underlining the reality of their separation, Giorgio harshly dismisses his wife's tears. "I've always been alone," he tells her. "I didn't enjoy myself in Genoa either and I'm not crying" (*R,* 166).

"L'idolo" (The idol) is related thematically to "Viaggio di nozze," but with a role reversal. This time it is Guido, the male narrator, who plays the part of the unrequited lover, and the story of his emotional addiction is recounted in the first person. The story begins with Guido's chance ~~chance~~ reunion with Mina, his lost love, during a visit to a brothel. Although at first he fails even to recognize her, his old passion is soon reawakened and he pursues her with a self-destructive intensity, despite her insistent rebuffs. When Mina finally announces her intention of marrying someone else, Guido is momentarily shattered, crying himself to sleep as he had done as a child. He now perceives Mina and her husband as "two grown-ups with a secret," and concludes: "a boy can only watch them from a distance, unaware of the joys and sorrows that make up their lives. Now that I have grown old and have learned to suffer, Mina no longer exists" (*R*, 296). The failure of love in this story is thus linked with the weaknesses and immaturity of the male narrator, as much as with the aloofness of "idol" he has chosen to love.

With "Suicidi" (Suicides), Pavese reiterates the misogynistic elements in "Viaggio di nozze" while minimizing the theme of remorse and sentimental regret in order to create a more cogent and at the same time more perverse portrayal of the male narrator. In the contrast between the victimized woman and her cold, contemptuous lover, Pavese sets up a classic sadomasochistic situation, characterized in this case by emotional rather than physical abuse. The originality of "Suicidi" lies less in its treatment of this commonplace theme than in the device of using a story within the story to suggest elliptically the ultimate fate of the narrator's lover. Pavese's tale of an exemplary suicide, taken directly from his memory of the suicide of his childhood friend Baraldi, is introduced into the narrative without additional commentary, almost as a diversion from the main theme. It is only at the abrupt conclusion of "Suicidi" that its function in bringing the hapless woman to the inevitable act of self-destruction falls into place.

"Amici" (Friends) develops the theme of male antagonism toward women through a dialogue between two old friends who have been reunited after a long separation. To the dismay of Rosso, recently returned from the war in Ethiopia, his friend Celestino expresses a domesticated acceptance of life's routines and the necessity of conjugal commitment. The returned soldier, still suspended in a state of adolescent restlessness and desire, is appalled at the other man's surrender of youthful freedom. This is the first of Pavese's stories to express the idea that women serve to destroy the more important bond between male friends.

In "L'intruso" (The intruder) Pavese subordinates the theme of misogyny to the more universal theme of solitude and self-willed alienation from society. Its two protagonists are prisoners who have been assigned involuntarily to the same cell. Lorenzo, the older man, perceives life itself as a prison, and prefers solitary incarceration to any manner of contact with other human beings. Despite the young narrator's attempts to achieve a truce that will allow both men to live together in greater tranquillity, Lorenzo savagely protects his isolation. Finally, he achieves his ambition of solitary confinement through an outbreak of violence for which he is rewarded by being removed from the shared cell. Lorenzo's attitude, however, has already begun to make some cruel sense to the narrator, who has just received a hostile letter from his wife, causing him to reflect bitterly: "That morning I saw myself as though trapped under glass, no longer a prisoner of walls and bars, but isolated in the void, a cold void that the world knew nothing about" (*R,* 180).

Pavese attempts a different type of narrative in "Misoginia" (Misogyny), which develops an atmosphere of tension and suspense despite an almost total absence of plot. The setting is a remote mountain hotel near the French border, where two mysterious travelers, a man and a woman, take refuge overnight before attempting a clandestine border crossing. The story is narrated in the third person, through the inquisitive perspective of Giusto, the innkeeper, who makes arrangements with a guide to help the couple enter France. Though he never discovers their identity or understands the motive for their frightened behavior, his evaluation of their situation is summed up in his probing query: "All this for a woman?" Pavese's central thematic preoccupation of the period, explicit in the title of this story, is otherwise elided here, emerging only in the innkeeper's ultimately unanswered question to the unknown traveler.

"Carogne" (Jailbirds) develops the theme of solitude and misogyny within a framework of more ambitious narrative scope. The prison setting is reminiscent of the penultimate episode of *Ciau Masino* (which bears the same title), as well as the more recent "L'intruso." After the initial introduction of various characters in the prison, the focus of the narrative shifts to Rocco, a new prisoner who has been assigned to a solitary cell. Rocco, who emerges as protagonist of "Carogne," has been arrested for the murder of his rival in love. As the result of the warden's carelessness, however, he manages to escape from jail almost immediately. Propelled by the urgent desire for revenge, he sets out to find

Concia, the woman who betrayed him. The encounter between the two lovers forms the crucial episode of the story. During his dramatic altercation with Concia, Rocco gradually becomes convinced of the woman's fundamental shallowness and falsity. After a brief, crudely executed sexual interlude, he abandons his intention of violent revenge. Concia's shifting emotional responses enrage him beyond his ability to confront her. While it was possible for him to murder his male rival, the falsity of Concia's character—as he perceives it—now disarms him, making his anger against her seem absurd. Yet this awareness does not liberate him from his inner pain, and he abandons her, burdened less by anger than by a profound contempt. The scene serves to illustrate in a dynamic way Pavese's conviction of the incompatibility of male and female consciousness. In the final sequence of "Carogne" Rocco returns voluntarily to the prison and silently lets himself in. His choice is clear: he prefers the solitary confinement of a prison cell to the company of the faithless Concia. In this act of choosing solitary confinement as an act of will, as a statement of his existential predicament, Rocco is sharply reminiscent of Lorenzo in "L'intruso."

"Temporale d'estate" (Summer storm) is the most violent of Pavese's early stories, and describes the rape of a young woman and her drowning during a storm. The misogyny expressed in many of the stories of the period receives its most graphic and brutal expression in this work. Through the use of an impassive third-person narrator Pavese keeps at a distance the subjective world of the characters while highlighting weather and landscape. The true protagonist of the story is the storm itself. Pavese's evocation of the fury of wind and water gradually builds an atmosphere in which the episode of human violence appears to develop in accordance with a rhythm of cosmic inevitability. This theme of predetermined violence was to play a major part in Pavese's later work, where it is accompanied, however, by cathartic elements that are completely absent in this story.

In "Notte di festa" (Festival night) Pavese's provides a more powerful and moving example of his narrative talent. Like "Temporale d'estate," this is a relatively long and complex story, narrated in the third person, which suggests the influence of irrational, cosmic forces on human behavior. Yet despite its initial intimations of violence, it concludes on a note of meditative serenity.

"Notte di festa" unfolds against a backdrop of the Langhe countryside in summertime, on the feast of a local patron saint. In the powerful opening scene the director of a rural boarding school—a priest referred to throughout the story as "il Padre"—supervises three adolescent boarders involved in the task of spreading manure around the farmyard. While they work, the wind carries in their direction the sound of carnival music from a nearby town, much to the irritation of the priest who fears its lure for the boys who earn their keep with grueling labor on the farm. Against this background of festive music and the priest's stern admonitions, the boys dodge splashes of the steaming manure with the rhythmic movements of a demonic dance.

The juxtaposition of the priest and one of the boys, Biscione, ("viper") is rich in symbolic resonance. The priest is one of Pavese's most memorable rustic types. Despite his clerical title, he is essentially a primitive, prerational peasant, attached to the agrarian landscape with primordial commitment and respect. He presides sternly over the process of spreading the manure, showing less concern with the well-being of the boys in his charge than with the demands of nature. Only Biscione, the toughest of the boys, actively challenges the priest's cruelty. The others perform the tasks assigned to them in sullen submission. Reminiscent of the spirited runaways of *Lavorare stanca,* Biscione is motivated by the dream of a life unburdened by harsh responsibilities and unending toil. For the priest, the boy's restlessness presents a threat to his own needs of controlling and cultivating nature. The tension between the two leads to Biscione's attempt to murder the priest in his sleep later that evening; but the priest wakes up in time to discover and admonish the boy, submitting him to a penitential exercise.

Another important juxtaposition is set up between the figure of the priest and that of the cerebral, repressed young teacher, referred to simply as "il Professore." In the story's opening scene the priest's contempt for the distant music that invades his hardworking world is contrasted with the teacher's fascinated response to the festive noise. The teacher, lacking the priest's elemental connection with the land, is prey to the enticement of the *festa.* Later, lured to the village by the sound of the music, this customarily withdrawn young man, now fortified by wine, encounters the sad, yet sensuous wife of a lion tamer. The woman, introduced earlier in the narrative as the object of the boys' erotic fantasies, seems drawn to the teacher because of a surfeit of carnality in her own life. The timid, odorless presence of the teacher offers her a respite from the filth and stench of the lions and the crude insensitivity of her husband. It is through this meeting that the teacher fully experiences the spirit of the festival night, which exerts on him a kind of catharsis, opening him up to a more joyous perception of the surrounding world. Only the initial moments of this encounter, however, are described in the narrative. The rest is elided.

In the concluding section of the story the priest confronts the teacher upon his return to the farm in the early hours of the morning. The priest, already absorbed in his customary tasks, responds in a disparaging way to the younger man's awed perception of the nocturnal landscape. The contrasting tensions of this episode recall the concluding lines of "I mari del Sud," juxtaposing the themes of activity, unending toil, and the necessary control of nature, with the themes of passivity and the aesthetic contemplation of the natural world. In the poem, the tension between these antithetical motifs remained deliberately unresolved. In "Notte di festa," on the other hand, it is the teacher's altered vision of things in the wake of the *festa* that prevails in this final episode and is reflected in the lyrical description of the nocturnal landscape, where earth, hill, and sky appear to mingle and overlap.

Pavese's skillful interweaving of landscape, characters, and mythic themes in this story points forward to the distinct narrative style of his later work. Elements that appear at first to be purely descriptive tend to acquire, with repetition, a special allusive power. With "Notte di festa," Pavese was able to incorporate some of the strategies of his poetic technique into the rhythm of his prose narrative, so that individual consciousness no longer dominates the text but is fused with the mythic revelations of landscape. Significantly, the theme of misogyny, pervasive in all of the more psychologically oriented stories of the period, is almost completely absent in "Notte di festa." This story is unique within Pavese's repertoire for its presentation of a sexual encounter as a genuine release from personal solitude and as the path to a serene contemplation of cosmic destiny.

The only other story from this period that ranks alongside "Notte di festa" in its artistic maturity is "Primo amore" (First love), which Pavese published later in *Feria d'agosto.*[5] Narrated in the first person, it describes a boy's coming of age in the Langhe countryside during the summer holidays. This rural setting serves to reinforce the magic and the terror of his sexual discovery. Like many Pavesian protagonists, the boy, Berto, is juxtaposed with a stronger, wiser counterpart, Nino, the son of a genteel country family and the brother of Clara, a blond girl with whom Berto is secretly in love. Through Nino, Berto also comes to know Bruno, a slightly older, unscrupulously promiscuous youth who works as a chauffeur for Nino's family. Berto's discovery of Bruno's sexual exploits coincides with the birth of a calf on the farm, an event that causes the boy a mixture of horror and awe. The fact that animal births resemble human birth appalls him and leads him to contemplate in a confused way the bestial nature of human sexuality. The ambiguity of his discoveries is accompanied by a strong sense of transgression and confusion. Through skillful manipulation of dialogue and ellipsis Pavese suggests the complexity of Berto's reaction to the revelations of sexuality.

In the story's climactic episode, Berto, Nino, and a local boy go together to spy on Bruno while he is involved in a secret sexual encounter. Through the window of a shed Berto watches the white, nude body of Bruno's companion, only to realize that the woman is none other than Clara, Nino's sister. The revelation of Clara's nakedness coincides with Berto's loss of innocence and the necessary abandonment of his childish idealization. In the wake of this traumatic incident the three adolescent onlookers attempt to sublimate an overwhelming sense of confusion and anger in an outbreak of physical violence against each other. The episode, which for Berto is an important rite of passage, thus ends with a scene of bloodshed and tears.

Another important though ambivalent motif in "Primo amore" is that of male bonding. Friendships among males feature in most of Pavese's works, and these relationships are juxtaposed with the complex tensions that characterize the association between men and women. Berto measures himself against Nino and against the boys of the surrounding countryside. They both look to Bruno as a model of masculine behavior. Yet all these attachments are highly ambiguous and combine elements of attraction as well as of explosive resentment. Berto and Nino are drawn together in the end not only by their mutual fascination with sex and their mutual confusion about the discovery of the trysting lovers, but also by virtue of the bloodshed and the scars incurred during the tussle with each other. When, in the concluding lines, Bruno attempts to help Berto to reconcile his differences with Nino, Berto's response is one of relief, a sensation that is intensified by the knowledge that Clara and Nino are still closely attentive to each other. It is with the elliptical image of this triangular attachment that the story concludes, in a peculiarly ambiguous and open-ended way that became characteristic in Pavese's narrative works.

"Il campo di grano" (The wheat field) contains some of the elements of "Primo amore"—the rural myth, the awakening to sexuality, the sensitivity of an adolescent consciousness. It is nevertheless narrated in the first person by a young girl. Born in the country and transplanted to the outskirts of the city as an adolescent, the girl belongs neither to the country nor to the city, and yet equates her transition into independent adulthood with the assumption of an urban identity. Her father's insistence on cultivating wheat in the field in front of their house mortifies her, reminding her of her rural origins. Her shame and anger intensify as she becomes emotionally involved with a young racing cyclist, who eventually abandons her. The central image of the wheatfield is skillfully evoked as an allusive, symbolic presence, suddenly and mysteriously destroyed during the night of the cyclist's abandonment of the girl. "Il campo di grano," which ends abruptly without further disclosure, shows Pavese's increasing mastery of a repertoire of personal mythic themes expressed along the lines of a binary opposition: city and country, adulthood and innocence, hope and disillusionment.

The only other story from this period narrated by a female voice is "Le tre ragazze" (The three girls), also introducing the theme of a girl's coming of age. Through the experience of her sexual awakening, Lidia realizes the necessity of personal freedom above and beyond romantic attachment. Reminiscent of the prostitute in the early poem "Pensieri di Deola," Lidia is one of Pavese's strong, independent women for whom solitude is not a burden but a rational choice. Though she manifests a degree of cynicism, she remains, on the whole, considerably more sympathetic than the male narrators, for whom isolation brings disfiguring characteristics. Paradoxically, it was in the characterization of strong female figures that Pavese, though fundamentally a misogynist, most frequently reflected the elements of his ideal self.

If Lidia corresponds emblematically to the positive side of Pavese's struggle with the notion of solitude during this period, it is Berto, the central character of "Jettatura" (The evil eye), who emerges as her most forceful counterpart, providing an almost grotesque exemplification of a life destroyed by the burden of unchosen isolation. In this story, which is almost Pirandellian in its atmosphere, the pathetic, middle-aged Berto is briefly befriended by Gigi, his youthful fellow worker at a bookstore. To Gigi, who narrates the story, the balding, round-shouldered Berto seems more dead than alive. Though his behavior seems inoffensive, everything about him excites disgust. Gigi discovers that Berto has failed to establish a relationship with a woman and that he has resigned himself to a life of isolation and defeat, finding some small pleasure in the books he borrows surreptitiously from the store where he works. Far from expressing compassion, Berto's colleagues grow increasingly hostile toward him, until he is finally dismissed for his habit of borrowing books in secret. In the meantime, the narrator has discovered that what repels him most profoundly in Berto is the possibility of finding in the other man a reflection of himself. This is the negative power, alluded to in the story's title, which excites the loathing and secret terror of Berto's fellow workers. It is a power generated entirely by the fear of self-recognition.

Though slight, this story is an important example of Pavese's attempt to express the deeply problematical circumstances of his emotional life during the period. The external details of *Jettatura* do not correspond to autobiographical realities, but the psychological material is clearly rooted in the writer's state of dejection in the wake of his abandonment by Pizzardo. Pavese attempts to gain aesthetic distance from the grotesque figure of Berto by setting up two separate characters, narrator and protagonist. The younger Gigi does not, however, provide a sufficiently strong contrapuntal presence. The story is little more than a stylized sketch of an extreme case of existential isolation, and seems to have been written almost in the spirit of a cautionary tale.

Il carcere

Developing the central theme and situation from "Terra d'esilio," Pavese wrote his first novel in 1938. Originally entitled *Memorie di due stagioni* (Memories of two seasons), the novel was eventually retitled *Il carcere* (The prison), highlighting the symbolic aspect of the protagonist's solitude.[6] Though it remained unpublished for many years, the novel finally appeared in 1948 in the same volume as *La casa in collina,* under the joint title *Prima che il gallo canti* (Before the cock crows).

Stefano, the protagonist and narrator of *Il carcere,* is condemned to a political detention in a southern village for a crime that is never explained in the narrative. Despite his sentence, Stefano seems indifferent to politics. He is presented devoid of any previous history. The roots of his isolation and uneasiness thus remain mysterious. The plot simply follows his stay in a village modeled on Brancaleone Calabro, charting his tedium and his unsuccessful relationships with the inhabitants until, quite unexpectedly, he receives the news of his release.

Within the span of the narrative Stefano attains a growing self-awareness and becomes particularly conscious of his tendency to isolate himself emotionally from others. Two of the women in the village become a part of his life, and his relationship to each of them reveals much about his character and his ongoing psychological torment. Almost immediately after his arrival he initiates a sexual relationship with Elena, the woman who functions as his housekeeper. Though he perceives her as a pathetic figure, already past her prime, he cannot resist her docile availability. His reactions to her are ambivalent. While she offers the possibility of sexual release, he feels an acute sense of revulsion for her physical proximity. Yet he continues to accept her sexual favors, until her efforts to domesticate him and to turn his squalid residence into a comfortable dwelling place drive him to a state of extreme irritation. When she explicitly assures Stefano that she wishes to be his *mammina* (little mother), he responds with inordinate revulsion and displeasure. Yet, while Elena may be perceived by Stefano as a maternal figure, she also emanates an ambiguous erotic threat. Particulars of her physique are recorded in a manner that conveys Stefano's confused attraction. It is only after he has totally rejected her that he can offer her his only token of compassion, murmuring to himself in solitude: "I pity you, little mother."

The tension between Stefano's chosen solitude and the pull of sexual need is also evoked in his fantasies about a local girl, Concia. Pavese's account of this elusive relationship is skillfully drawn through the use of the "image-story" technique. The girl is presented in the initial sequence as a goatlike creature who moves through the hilly terrain with the sure-footed, nimble gait of a young animal. Subsequently, almost all the images associated with Concia evoke some form of nonhuman life.

From the beginning, Stefano thinks of her in connection with the vivid red geraniums displayed on the terrace of the house where she lives. The flowers, as well as the earthen jar full of water that she carries on her head from the well, express some of the mysterious magnetism that she holds for him. Pavese sets up these links in a scene that is perhaps too forced in its exposition of the "image story" technique. In this scene Stefano finds Concia's water jar on the wall in front of her house and raises it "by its hip-like curve" to his lips. The water has "an earthy flavor, sharp to the teeth" which reminds him of goats. It also has a quality that is "both wild and sweet, bringing to mind the color of geraniums."

In this passage, which constitutes a Pavesian epiphany, an affinity is set up between disparate elements: the goatlike Concia, the earthen jar, the water, and the potted geraniums on her balcony. Its imagistic force is diminished, however, when the narrator intrudes with the heavy-handed observation that "there was a relationship between the geraniums and the girl." This draws attention to the presence of the author and to the technical effects he wishes to achieve.

Stefano's relationship with Concia remains purely on the level of his imagination. When he actually comes face to face with the girl, he is as tongue-tied as an adolescent. It is clear that he desires her only as a fantasy object, and his most vivid perceptions of his feeling for her are when he is alone, daydreaming in his solitary hut. This passion can endure only because Concia does not offer the disconcerting physical availability provided by Elena.

The only other female figure in the novel is that of Annetta, the prostitute, to whom Stefano pays a visit, more out of deference to local custom than active desire. When he finally finds himself in Annetta's presence, realizing the absurdity of his situation, he pays her and leaves. He perceives the prostitute neither as mother nor lover but as a fleshy, childlike creature. Since she fails to inspire the elements of erotic conflict that characterize his perception of the other women, Annetta is completely desexualized in Stefano's imagination.

The relationships that Stefano forms with the men of the village are also problematic. From the beginning he recognizes some slight degree of affinity with Giannino, whom he joins one morning at dawn to go quail hunting. This episode, however briefly drawn, constitutes one of the rare moments of contentment in Stefano's sojourn in the alien village. Yet Stefano feels ambivalently about Giannino's intrusion into his solitude, and reaches a level of peace and acceptance of the friendship only when Giannino himself has been imprisoned on charges of raping a minor. Recognizing the other man's status as an outcast and a prisoner, and protected from his presence by virtue of their mutual state of detention, Stefano finally acknowledges the importance of Giannino's friendship, a friendship that is, paradoxically, based on solitude.

With the men of the local tavern Stefano also builds up a gruff, measured camaraderie. His status as a political prisoner as well as his innate distaste for social relationships precludes the development of friendships here. His most problematic relationship during the period of his detention, however, is not with one of the local men, but with another outsider, a fellow political prisoner whom he never meets. Whereas Stefano's own political sentence is something of an irony, the man who is detained in the older section of the village, halfway up the hillside, is still actively committed to the ideas that led to his arrest and exile. When Stefano receives a letter from the other man, a curt plea for solidarity, he simply chooses to ignore it, despising the crude style in which the message is couched. Nevertheless, his renunciation is not without anguish. A kind of envy enters his thoughts about the other man, referred to throughout the narrative as simply "the anarchist": "Stefano envied even the anarchist stuck over there where he could see the plains, horizons, and the coast looking like a tiny toy across this stretch of openness, and the blue patch of the sea in the distance. Everything would have for him the beauty of an unexplored country, like a dream, whereas he himself saw merely the squalor of the narrow streets and windows, the few hovels rising straight up over the abyss, and he felt ashamed of his own cowardice" (*PG*, 90). Later, when he realizes that the anarchist is not only a man of action, but also one who possesses the ability to connect with other human beings, his bitterness increases: "Thinking about him, Stefano began to imagine another race of beings, with an inhuman temperament, raised in cells—a subterranean people. And yet that being, who played with children in the town square, was in fact simpler and more human than himself" (*PG*, 90).

The character who provides the grotesque projection of the protagonist's secret sense of identity is the half-insane outcast, Barbariccia. Here is another human being imprisoned in the solitude of his own mind, for whom alienation from others is an unalterable fact of existence. Though the link is not explicitly drawn, the figure of the demented vagabond presents an important reflection of Stefano's self-understanding. The willful squalor of his dwelling place, which Elena's well-meaning efforts can never fully eradicate, is one of the most obvious points of connection between Stefano and Barbariccia. So too is the open, unpacked suitcase at the foot of his bed—a stubborn statement of his transcience and his unwillingness to acknowledge even temporary roots.

On the linguistic level, *Il carcere* is far removed from the experimentalism of Pavese's early prose. Like many of his short stories from this period, the novel reveals a surprising acceptance of the refined, literary style of the *prosa d'arte,* which he had originally shunned. No attempt is made to re-create a sense of place through the introduction of dialect or popular speech. Even the dialogue of the southern peasants is rendered in classical Italian. Pavese already seems in the process of a more conscious rejection of naturalism in favor of a kind of symbolic impressionism committed to evoking a mental state rather than recounting a series of objective events.

In his study of Pavese's language Anco Marzio Mutterle has pointed out that the predominant feature of the stylistic texture of this first novel is its extremely limited field of lexical and imagistic choices.[7] *Il carcere* contains an abundance of similes or metonymic images, most of which suggest affinities between the world of nature and the world of human experience. According to Mutterle, Pavese's insistent use of analogies presupposes the unacceptability of the connections and combinations that normally form the basis of the development of a narrative text. Many of the images in *Il carcere,* for example, seem to anthropomorphize the protagonist's surroundings, particularly the sea and the houses of the village. Mutterle has pointed out that these images do not serve to ground Stefano in a clear spatial relationship with the physical world, but rather to create a sense of vagueness and transparency. Since the spatial references of the protagonist's surroundings are constantly undermined and dematerialized by images that evoke indeterminacy, it is clear that this narrative is not a naturalistic or mimetic text, but the reflection of an obsessive psychic state.

The tenacious quest for similarities and analogies in the narrative suggests a perhaps unconscious doubt in the epistemological validity of such links. Pavese's use of symbolism in this early period attempts to create the impression of a definitive statement. This crystallization, as Mutterle terms the phenomenon, serves to exorcise and transform psychic material into literary artifact. But the result is neither truly therapeutic nor artistically cogent. Pavese's obsessions are simply organized in the text. They are not sublimated. The extremely selective range of his rhetorical choices—especially his frequent use of an analogy and metonomy—gives a forced effect, sometimes bordering on the stereotypical.

The most insistently repeated image in *Il carcere* is that of a prison cell. Stefano perceives the sea as "the fourth wall of his cell" (*PG,* 9). The patch of sky seen through his window becomes "a prisoner's sky" (*PG,* 14), and while surrounded by companions in the village tavern, he sees himself as "alone and precarious among these temporary people, painfully isolated by invisible walls" (*PG,* 17). Eventually, the mountains, the village, the room, the light, and the air itself are associated with the imagery of physical imprisonment. A casual encounter is described as a "voluntary prison" and even an open door serves to remind Stefano of a cell. This overwrought elaboration of a single central concept eventually destabilizes the image of imprisonment, so that it becomes synonymous in the most general way with the confused consciousness of Stefano himself.

Stefano continually wants to be elsewhere. While enjoying the sexual favors of Elena he desires to be with Concia. He accepts people and situations only insofar as they can become integrated into the patterns of his perceptions and thus create a background for his obsessions. He is prone to a sense of dissociation that obliges him to focus his imagination on a situation from which he is currently removed. Thus, the sea, "if seen while [Stefano is] thinking about something else, was as beautiful as it had seemed in his early days [there]" (*PG,* 22). This dissociation is related to the tendency in the Pavesian protagonist to search for his own identity by establishing a point of reference for his personality in another figure. In *Il carcere,* the protagonist arrives at a sense of self-revelation through the development of his relationship with Giannino. This occurs, however, only after Giannino himself has been imprisoned. Now Stefano is finally able to identify with the other man and at the same time is no longer obliged to tolerate his company.

The use of parataxis, so widespread in the early work of Pavese, is not the indication of a spontaneous, "realistic" contact with things. On the contrary, it is complementary to the situation of his protagonist, an outsider in the world, to whom reality presents itself in disconnected sequences, without meaningful hierarchies. The evocation of an absurdist world view through parataxis in this novel is reinforced by the supersaturation of analogy and metonymy in the text.

Whereas the normal function of the image in narrative is revelation, the result here is one of increasing abstraction and vagueness. The final impression of Stefano's account of his experience is one of an optical illusion. This effect was set up early in the narrative when Stefano "realized that the game of life could vanish, just like the illusion that it was." This destabilization and dematerialization of experience seems to be the only way that Stefano, or his creator, can deal with unresolved emotional material within the span of the novel. Thus everything can be turned through artifice into a vanishing trick, so that Stefano's world becomes "so minute and absurd that all he has to do is to put his thumb in front of his eye to hide it all away" (*PG,* 30).[8]

Chapter Four

The Evolution of Symbolic Imagery

Paesi tuoi

Pavese wrote his second novel, *Paesi tuoi* (Your part of the country),[1] between June and August of 1939. It was published by Einaudi in 1941 as the inaugural volume of a new series of contemporary fiction supervised by Pavese himself. Although his only previously published book, the Solaria edition of *Lavorare stanca,* had received little critical attention, the appearance of *Paesi tuoi* brought him instant notoriety and acclaim. Emerging as it did at the height of Fascist repression, it represented a shocking departure from the tone of mainstream culture. Though the response of some reviewers was favorable, Pavese did not escape virulent attack from the Fascist press. This reaction was prompted by the novel's coarse, colloquial style as well as its violent and unflattering depiction of rural life. These elements clearly subverted the official image of Italy's "progressive and magnificent destiny" that the Fascist regime was seeking to propagate. On the other hand, however, Elio Vittorini, one of the first major literary figures to recognize the novel's ground-breaking importance, observed in a letter written to Pavese on 3 June 1941 that "three or four books like this every year are what we need to get rid of the age-old misunderstandings that enable so many false books to be written and accepted."[2]

At the time of the novel's publication Pavese was known primarily as a critic and translator of American literature. It is not surprising, therefore, that *Paesi tuoi* was scrutinized from the outset for possible American influences, an approach that subsequently enjoyed considerable popularity among his critics. The names of Caldwell, Faulkner, Anderson, and Steinbeck were cited in connection with the novel, and Pavese himself intervened to add the name of James Cain to the list.[3] Other critics, avoiding this Americanist approach, have regarded *Paesi tuoi* principally as an early manifestation of neo-realism. Both of these critical approaches—the Americanist and the neo-realist—are essentially reductive, neglecting the work's complex stylistic links with earlier Italian literary influences, as well as its continuation on a much broader canvas of one of the dominant aesthetic tasks of *Lavorare stanca*: the attempt to create a symbolically allusive narrative through the recurrence of key images.[4]

The countryside is the dominant landscape of *Paesi tuoi*. This is not the alien southern territory of *Il carcere,* but the familiar hill country of the Langhe region already present in Pavese's poetry as well as in some of his short fiction, particularly "Notte di festa." It is nevertheless a landscape observed through the narrative perspective of an outsider, with a corresponding absence of sentimentality. The vision of the Langhe in this work is highly stylized—some would even say Americanized—reflecting an insistence on rural violence that Pavese had come to associate with the contemporary American novel.

This harsh portrayal of peasant life, accompanied by an implicitly fatalistic world view, is also reminiscent of Giovanni Verga. In a letter written some five years after *Paesi tuoi* Pavese obliquely acknowledged his debt to *verismo* (*L,* 454).[5] Yet the influence of D'Annunzio, who offered a more dramatic and ultimately more romantic view of the countryside, should not be discounted in the novel's combination of eroticism and violence. *Paesi tuoi* transcends these residual echoes of *verismo* and the decadence of D'Annunzio, however, to create a new narrative vision that incorporates some of the intuitions already developed in the poetry of *Lavorare stanca*.

In writing this novel Pavese sought to weave the themes of human solitude and quest with the image of a violent and mystically charged agrarian world. The theme of solitude, developed quietly through the creation of Stefano's interior world in *Il carcere,* receives a more complex and fatalistic treatment here. With *Paesi tuoi* Pavese attempts to evoke the revelation of human solitude through a tale of suspense and bloodshed in a primitive rural setting where irrational human actions are connected with the forces of the natural world in a powerful and mysterious manner. Elements of this vision had already emerged as early as the poem "Il dio–caprone," written in 1933, and in his recent story "Notte di festa." From the moment of his first discovery of Frazer's *The Golden Bough* in the early 1930s Pavese had been fascinated by its revelations concerning the issues of myth and primitive consciousness. His formal knowledge of anthropology and ethnography had developed little by 1939, the year in which *Paesi tuoi* was written, although he was by now also familiar with the works of the ethnographer Lucien Lévy-Bruhl. Furthermore, his personal meditations on myth had not yet reached the maturity of thought subsequently acquired after his study of Vico and Károly Kerényi. Nevertheless, the mythic, "magical" component of the agrarian landscape is of crucial importance to the novel's inspiration. It is invoked in the narrative through the recurrence of key symbols, giving the work its unique rhythm and atmosphere.

The plot of *Paesi tuoi* unfolds in a straightforward, linear manner. It begins as the narrator, Berto—a young Turinese mechanic—is released from prison along with his cell mate, Talino, a peasant from the Langhe region. Talino attempts to persuade his companion to accompany him back to the family farm for the harvesting season, hoping in this way to ensure some protection from the wrath of his father. Talino insists that he is innocent of the crime for which he was imprisoned—the arson of a neighboring farm—thus presenting himself to Berto as a victim of circumstance. Berto initially rejects this offer, since Talino fails to inspire his trust. Nevertheless, upon discovering that his own friend and accomplice, Pieretto, is himself in prison, Berto realizes that his resources are limited, and after a brief sexual interlude with Pieretto's girlfriend, he decides to take the train to the Langhe with Talino. During the course of their journey through the countryside Berto begins to realize that he is entering a strange and baffling territory. The encounter with Talino's family serves to reinforce this impression. Vinverra, Talino's father, is an authoritarian, brutish presence absorbed only in the needs of the land. Vinverra's wife and four daughters, who function almost as beasts of burden, are entirely subject to his dominion. Once he has settled in on the farm, Berto's uneasiness begins to mount. Having discovered that Talino had lied about the arson, he becomes aware of a vague and pervasive sense of threat. Partly in an attempt to escape from his own uneasiness, Berto begins to pursue Talino's youngest sister, Gisella, who seems "the least cowlike of the lot." He eventually seduces her in the fields, only to realize that Talino is the jealous guardian of Gisella's sexual attentions and that the scars on her body have been caused by her brother's possessive rage. During the work of the harvesting, Talino's fury explodes when Gisella refuses him a drink of water. He stabs her in the neck with a pitchfork and runs away. During the long vigil during which Gisella lies dying in her bed, the tasks of the harvesting are resumed, taking preeminence over the loss of a single human life. Berto is forced to reflect on the strange ways of the peasant family, the violence as well as the silent acquiescence that led to Gisella's death, and the general sense of surrender to the will of nature and the needs of the land.

Pavese establishes the contrast between city and country in *Paesi tuoi* not only through juxtaposition of an initial urban episode with the rural landscape that dominates the remainder of the narrative, but more pervasively through Berto's perplexed responses to the unfolding revelations of the agrarian world. The contrast between the two poles is always mediated through Berto's stream of consciousness, where the urban point of departure, though alluded to only occasionally, is constantly implicit. The juxtaposition of country and city does not, however, constitute a simple dichotomy of good and evil, but rather provides Berto, the narrator, with a series of bewildering revelations that ultimately lead to the perception of his own alienation and solitude. It is in the technical elaboration of this city-dweller's "discovery" of the violent irrationality at work in the countryside that some of the most important aesthetic issues of this novel lie.

The language of *Paesi tuoi*—always attributed to Berto's voice—has a crude, paratactical rhythm, replete with coarse expressions and ungrammatical turns of phrase that excited much critical comment when the novel first appeared. It is here, in the narrator's language, however, that the novel's departure from realism can be immediately observed. Instead of the mimetic transcription of Turinese elements into the text—a technique never again attempted after *Ciau Masino*—Pavese fashions a kind of dialect-inflected Italian intended to evoke the general rhythm and feeling of working-class Turinese speech. His intentions are summarized in a letter to Tullio Pinelli, to whom he had shown the manuscript: "As for the language . . . it is something other than naturalistic impressionism. I didn't write in Berto's voice, word for word . . . but translated his thoughts, his perplexities, his mockery into the words he would have used if he had been speaking Italian. I wasn't interested in showing how Berto speaks when forced to speak Italian, but rather how he might speak if his words were transformed by dint of some Pentecostal intervention into Italian" (*L*, 358–59). In the same letter Pavese explicitly articulates his vision of the novel's symbolic importance: "This work is a symbol where characters and setting are the *means* of narrating a little parable, which is the ultimate basis of inspiration and interest: the 'journey of the soul' in my Divine Comedy."

Despite Pavese's denial of naturalism and his insistence on the symbolic dimension of the novel, the opening chapter of *Paesi tuoi*—the only section set in Turin—is narrated in a realistic, nonallusive manner. Geographical orientation is achieved by means of minimal topographical references, and the atmosphere of the city is briefly evoked. The episode between Berto and Michela in her working-class apartment is incisively drawn, and its complex psychological tensions resonate through the perspective of Berto's mysogynistic contempt in a style reminiscent of Pavese's short fiction of the same period.

With the description of the journey from Turin to Monticello, Talino's village in the Langhe, changes begin to occur in the narrative texture as Berto reports his initial reactions to the foreignness of rural experience. In the brief description of Talino walking through the country town where both men wait for another train, there is an obvious increase in stylization almost to the level of caricature: "Talino forged ahead, bumping into people, parting his legs to let dogs pass through without even bothering to wipe his neck with the red handkerchief that fell in a triangle on his shoulder" (*PT,* 17). This stylization of character description is consistent with the subsequent evocation of the peasant world in the novel. On a less immediately apparent level, however, the same scene in the country town also signals the introduction of key images, which through frequent recurrence will gain an important allusive significance, thus banishing the impression of a realistic tale of adventure: "But what fine peppers the women were selling! Then we came to the watermelons and I began to feel thirsty" (*PT,* 17). Throughout the remainder of the novel, the images of fruit and water emerge repeatedly in connection with Talino's sisters, while the motif of thirst is linked both with bloodshed and sexual desire.

Soon after this early scene in the country market, the single most recurrent symbol in *Paesi tuoi* is introduced: the association of the hills with female breasts. As Berto arrives at Talino's village, one of the first perceptions is the breast-shaped hillside: "I turn around and again I see the hill I'd seen from the train. It had grown and it really looked like a woman's tit, completely rounded at the sides and with a tuft of trees darkening the tip. And Talino laughed slyly, like a fool, as though he were really looking at a woman showing him her breast" (*PT,* 21). At other moments in the narrative Berto's attention is drawn back to the same image. In the scene where he is about to touch Gisella for the first time, for example, there is an initial allusion to the feminine contours of the hill: "From where I lay I could see the first hill, scorched and bare—it was all vineyards up there—and at the top of it the nipple that was so good to look at" (*PT,* 35). Pavese clearly intended to establish with this central image the sexual power of the rural landscape.[6] Its recurrent presence gives a corresponding symbolic resonance to other details in Berto's environment: the well, the store of apples, and ultimately the pitchfork that Talino uses to kill his sister.

Almost simultaneously with the introduction of these key symbols into the narrative, Berto is described as experiencing a sense of disorientation. His feelings of fear and distrust appear at first to reflect merely the suspicious contempt of a city-dweller for his rural counterparts, as when, for example, he mutters to himself in the rural market town: "Keep an eye on them! You're at the mercy of these people from now on" (*PT,* 17). Soon afterward, Berto's report of his arrival at Monticello, Talino's village, reflects a more unsettling sense of disorientation and strangeness: "I had been looking around carefully, so that if I needed I could find my way back and hop on a train. But the train, the track, and the station had completely disappeared. 'I'm really in the country,' I say to myself. 'No one will ever find me here'" (*PT,* 21).

The city-dweller's perceptions of Talino's family are evoked in a manner that serves to break down further the novel's initial impression of a realistic narrative. The details of the women's dark, coarse appearance border on the grotesque. From Berto's viewpoint as an outsider, the distinction between the animal and the human order in the countryside becomes blurred. In their physical closeness with nature, the peasants manifest a primitive instinctuality that both fascinates and repels the city-dweller, though his ambivalence is barely articulated. Pavese's stylized depiction of these characters recalls the goatlike allure of Concia and the unkempt wildness of Barbariccia in *Il carcere.* In *Paesi tuoi,* however, the women are frequently linked with the image of fruit. Gisella, in particular, is associated with apples and with water, which Berto imagines to possess the flavor of cherries. It is in her fruitlike aspect that Berto perceives Gisella to be different from her brother Talino, and this antithesis is at the root of his attraction to her. Thus the images of fruit and water, associated with women, emerge in juxtaposition with the violence and bloodshed instigated by men, although the juxtaposition is not fully apparent until the novel's climax.

As tensions begin to build in the story, the image of blood suddenly emerges in Berto's fantasy. Observing Vinverra walk toward him in the village square, the city-dweller begins, inexplicably, to think of bloodshed: "Watching him come toward me in the sunlight I had the idea that shedding blood in the countryside makes less of an impression than in the shadow of a house in Turin. Once I had seen it on the streetcar tracks after an accident, and it was terrifying. To think of someone bleeding while bent over the stubble in a field seemed more natural, like a slaughterhouse" (*PT,* 71). Although the "naturalness" of bloodshed in the countryside is one of the major themes of *Paesi tuoi,* the elaboration of this motif sometimes draws attention too overtly to the technical effects that Pavese is striving to create. Such is the case with the detail of the bowl of blood that Berto notices on the kitchen table during a family meal. This image is first inserted into a passage which functions as a flash-forward, foreshadowing an atmosphere of tragic suspense: "Back home we found the rabbit and the stewed peppers, and some nice *polenta* Gisella had turned out on the board. I remember it as now, because later on that evening nobody had time to cook anything and I ate two hunks of it cold and it seemed to taste like blood, and my teeth were chattering, because just in front of me on the table I could see a bowl full of blood, and I could feel my heart in my mouth, colder than the *polenta*" (*PT,* 113). Later, after the tragedy, he observes the bowl of blood again, realizing that the others have forgotten it. Although the image has a powerful impact when it first appears, it loses its effectiveness with repetition.

Apart from the images of blood, water, and fruit, the related motifs of wheat, earth, and fire are also interwoven throughout the novel, suggesting the inexorable cycles of growth and destruction that transcend human will and understanding. In the novel's crucial episode, where Talino stabs his sister in the neck with the pitchfork, Pavese combines the elements of blood and water against a backdrop of harvested wheat, reinforcing the suggestion of a link between violence and agricultural fertility: "Then Gisella let the bucket drop and the water flooded my shoes. I thought it was blood and jumped aside. Talino jumped aside too and we heard Gisella's voice come gurgling up in her throat: 'Holy Mother!' And then she coughed and the pitchfork dropped away from her neck. . . . Gisella was coughing and vomiting blood, and the mud was dark with it. Then we lifted her, with myself holding her legs, and carried her over against the stack of wheat" (*PT,* 78–79). When Berto returns to the scene after the tragedy, however, the image of blood reappears with a loss of impact as Berto's meditations intrude on the description: "In the doorway you could still see big spots of blood. What's so strange about that, I thought, every day the streets soak some up. But looking at it and thinking that the muddy mess was Gisella's warmth ebbing away, I went cold as well" (*PT,* 84). It is at such moments that Berto's thoughts betray the presence of his author. Although the language of *Paesi tuoi* has a crude, unlettered ring, the perceptions attributed to Berto occasionally reflect Pavese's literary preoccupations.

One of the strongest criticisms of this work has been articulated by Giorgio Bàrberi Squarotti, who claims that the details of the plot function simply as a pretext from the persistent elaboration of sexual symbolism. Thus although the novel purportedly delineates a journey of personal discovery—a motif characteristic of Pavese's mature work—Bàrberi Squarotti points out that Berto's experience is one of exploration rather than discovery, recounted with excessive recourse to metaphoric language.[7]

The language of *Paesi tuoi* remains highly allusive, and its obsessive tensions are not worked out with sufficient resolution on the level of psychological characterization. The novel nevertheless contains some extraordinary passages in which landscape and atmosphere are unforgettably evoked. One such passage is the episode in the moonlit night while Berto waits outdoors for Gisella and is rewarded instead with the apparition of a goat. More powerful still is the account of Gisella's slow agony, juxtaposed with allusions to the unrelenting work outside in the torrid sunshine. In this concluding sequence Berto begins to articulate with considerable psychological impact complex feelings of rage, compassion, and sorrow. Berto expresses his grief for the dying Gisella with a mixture of denial and desperate hope: "If she isn't dead, then maybe she can hear them threshing the wheat. Maybe she'll remember that and it will send her to sleep. At this point she's no longer in pain" (*PT,* 90). Later, he tries to quell his thoughts by telling himself his grief is pointless: "That's enough. It isn't up to you now. The more you think about her, the more dead she is" (*PT,* 91). Berto's feelings of empathy and sadness for the dying Gisella are clearly in contrast with his tendency to objectify women earlier in the novel.

If indeed Berto has undergone any growth in the course of his experience in the countryside, it emerges chiefly in the evolution of his attitude toward women. In the opening chapter he encapsulates the crude, unmitigated misogyny that permeates much of Pavese's previous work. This first emerges in Berto's sexual encounter with Michela, Pieretto's girlfriend. The ambiguity of Berto's attraction to Michela is reminiscent of Stefano's treatment of Elena in *Il carcere.* His seduction is prompted purely by physical appetite, unadorned by feelings of compassion or friendship, and he makes little effort to conceal his contempt for Michela while enjoying her sexual availability. He is also pleased later on at the thought that she may have suffered guilt and remorse because of her infidelity to his friend Pieretto. The incident of Berto's complicity in a sexual betrayal for which he sees the woman to be principally responsible introduces some important elements into the narrative that will emerge in the crucial moments in the novel. It is significant that Michela is the lover of Berto's close friend, Pieretto, just as Gisella turns out to be the lover of Talino, also Berto's friend. The triangularity of these situations has a peculiarly Pavesian ambivalence, and has led some critics to detect a hint of repressed homoeroticism.

Nevertheless, Berto's attitude toward women fluctuates in the process of his move from city to country. "Women don't need to go to jail to betray a friend," he observes after his encounter with Michela (*PT,* 13). Later, after his arrival in the Langhe, he observes that the only thing that does not change between country and city is the trickery of women. And yet, almost from the start, he perceives Gisella both as a sly seductress and as a helpless victim. When he meets her for the first time, she disappears immediately into a shed with Talino. Although Berto can no longer see Gisella, he imagines her playing with her brother: "Talino was running after that little devil in the cow-shed. They were grabbing at each other. I knew it" (*PT,* 25). This initial allusion to the incestuous tensions between Gisella and Talino is followed by a reference to the hillside, which briefly catches Berto's eye and prompts the thought of Talino's alleged arson. Thus a tenuous link is created in Berto's consciousness between Gisella's seductive playfulness and the violence wrought on the landscape. In another episode, describing an incident later the same day, Berto watches Vinverra beating Gisella as a punishment for her angry response to a humiliating joke played by Talino. Here she appears less a sly seductress than a pathetic victim of cruelty: "Everyone gave a cry, for Vinverra had taken off his belt and was hitting Gisella as if she were shoe-leather. But Gisella did not run away; she buried her face against Adele's side, and yelled and squirmed like a snake, while Adele sheltered her baby with her arm. . . . If I had been twenty years old and in Gisella's place, I'd have shown that old man a thing or two" (*PT,* 28).

Implicit in the fact that Gisella does not defend herself and that the others do not attempt to protect her, either during this incident or later when she is attacked by Talino, is the implication of perceived culpability. There is also the suggestion, however, that within this rural family there is a common, if unconscious, perception of Gisella as a sacrificial victim, and an acceptance of tragic destiny at a level that Berto, the outsider, cannot understand.

The change in Berto's sensibilities at the end of the novel is unusual in Pavese. Generally, the Pavesian protagonist, though capable of insight, is not rendered more compassionate as the result of his experience. Nevertheless, Berto, who initially perceived Gisella as scarcely human ("the least cowlike of the lot"), is moved through the experience of his own solitude and alienation to contemplate the human tragedy before him. When Gisella lies in the throes of suffering, he begins to suspect that the entire community tacitly conspires to delay the arrival of help from the outside world, and his sensibilities revolt. His protest has a certain poignancy, though there are no further clues that Berto has achieved a greater moral or emotional awareness than he possessed at the outset. The tragedy serves above all to confirm his disgust with the mysterious powers of the countryside and to reinforce his sense of identity as a city dweller. He finally tells himself: "Your place is Turin" (*PT,* 91), recapitulating the typical Pavesian antithesis between city and country, between the pole of rational experience and the pole of the *selvaggio,* the primitive, violent forces in rural life.

La bella estate

In a diary entry for 1 January 1940 Pavese dismissed the achievements of the two novels he had already completed, maintaining that they offered nothing but the proof of his ability "to will a style into being and sustain it" (*MV,* 156). His unresolved preoccupations with the issues of naturalism and narrative technique continue to find expression in his diary in the early months of that year, even as he had already begun work on his new novel, which initially bore the title *La tenda* (The curtain).[8] The novel, which was later to be retitled *La bella estate* (*The Beautiful Summer*), was finished by June but did not appear in print for several years. It was finally published in 1949 in a volume bearing this new title, along with two subsequent novels, *Il diavolo sulle colline* (*The Devil in the Hills*) and *Tra donne sole* (*Among Women Only*).[9]

La bella estate, written in the spring of 1940, belongs to the group of early fiction that Pavese himself later described as naturalistic (*MV,*

342). It is the story of a working-class girl's coming of age recounted against a backdrop of Turinese interiors. While the author's presence sometimes intrudes too blatantly on Berto's narrating consciousness in the previous novel, Pavese was more attentive to the elision of his own personality in this work. Ginia, the young protagonist through whose perspective the narrative unfolds, is the most fully realized character in the Pavesian repertoire up to this point. Her inner world is elaborated with compelling force and poignancy, and she embodies a range of Pavese's absorbing existential preoccupations.

Though not as symbolically saturated as *Paesi tuoi, La bella estate* attempts nevertheless to invest surface elements with symbolic weight through the recurrence of carefully chosen images. This is essentially a story of a sentimental education in which the urban setting is portrayed as the repository of both adult understanding and bitter disillusionment. In Pavese's preceding work, the city generally represents a place of maturity, responsibility, and action, and is frequently contrasted with the wild, uncivilized forces of rural experience.[10] Yet, even in his earliest poem, "I mari del Sud," the city also presents the threat of the unknown, as well as the ambivalent allure of alien, yet fascinating energies.

At the outset of the story, Ginia is a sixteen-year-old dressmaker's apprentice who, though impatient for adulthood, is also nostalgic for the carefree abandon of adolescence. Through her friendship with the slightly older Amelia, an artist's model, she is introduced to a group of Bohemians and painters, who encapsulate for her the sophistication and maturity to which she aspires. The first crisis of her initiation comes from her confrontation in the artist's studio with the reality of nudity. Realizing that her friend Amelia undresses for painters as a matter of course, Ginia attempts to accept nudity as a practical, occupational necessity, and to separate this idea from the terror she secretly experiences at the thought of exposing her own body to the gaze of others.

Almost immediately Ginia falls in love with Guido, one of Amelia's artist friends. Forcing herself to overcome her sense of inhibition, she decides to yield to him. The moment of sexual initiation, though traumatic, does not change her childlike reactions to the world. Her greatest inhibition continues to be the obsession with nudity, and throughout the painful development of her relationship with the largely indifferent Guido, she refuses to reveal her nakedness. Finally, as a desperate ploy to recapture her lover's faltering attentions, she agrees to pose for a painting in the nude. This important surrender of her nakedness, however, is also witnessed unintentionally by another visitor to the studio, Guido's friend Rodrigues. Deeply disturbed by the presence of a casual observer, and already wounded by Guido's behavior, Ginia finally acknowledges the loss of her adolescent illusions. The hard-edged independence of the cynical, bisexual Amelia now seems the only plausible option open to her. In the concluding lines, she turns to Amelia and announces that she is ready to accept her leadership: "Let's go wherever you want. Bring me with you" (*BE,* 83).

In contrast with the rural summer landscape in which the violent tensions of *Paesi tuoi* unfold, this gentle, melancholy tale develops against the backdrop of a bleak Turinese winter. References to darkness and cold abound, and summer exists only in the domain of Ginia's fantasy. Yet the novel's sunny opening paragraph, as well as the title itself, provide an important key to the thematic threads of Ginia's story. It has been pointed out that summer in *La bella estate* is a "mythical background, a fairy-tale point of reference of regrets and impossible expectations."[11] This background immediately comes to life at the start of Ginia's narrative: "At that time, every day was a holiday. We girls had only to go out of the house and cross the street to start acting crazy, and everything was always so wonderful, especially at night, that when people got home dead tired they still hoped that something would happen, that a fire would break out, that a baby would be born in the house, or even that day would suddenly break and they could go on walking and walking as far as the open fields, even as far as the other side of the hill" (*BE,* 9).

The temporal emphasis of the novel's opening words, "At that time," clearly sets the initial scene at a distinct distance from the moment of narration. Having thus established the "pastness" of the past, Ginia's breathless surge of memories provides a contrapuntal reference for the main body of the narrative, which records in slow detail the wintry evolution of the girl's coming of age. This is the first of Pavese's novels in which the themes of memory and yearning establish the tone of the narrative, and in which youth is mythicized as a privileged, magical moment. The theme of the holiday, the *festa,* which is a recurrent motif in Pavese's work, is connected specifically in this novel with the "beautiful summer" of youthful innocence and abandon. Thematically, therefore, *La bella estate,* with its focus on the transience of youth and the loss of illusion, is closer to the preoccupations of late romantic and decadent literature than either of Pavese's two earlier novels.

The use of the stream-of-consciousness technique in this novel is both more conventional and more internally consistent than in *Paesi tuoi.* Abandoning the device of the first-person narrator, Pavese constructs a third-person account that corresponds at all times to Ginia's point of view.[12] The narrative reflects a corresponding limitation of lexical and syntactical range, and a certain mimetic attention is paid to the psychological realities of the protagonist's world.

Although the emotional and cultural distance between Pavese and his protagonist is greater here than in either of the two previous novels, the characterization of Ginia is ultimately more layered, more nuanced than that of his male protagonists. In *La bella estate* Pavese was first able to embody his psychic obsessions in a character who on the surface bore little resemblance to himself, and was thus able to attain a less cluttered, more intense orchestration of those themes and images without the distractions of other autobiographical elements. Elio Gioanola claims that in this novel Pavese attains "the first integrated process of transferring his intimate anguish and obsessions into realistically probable characters and into a clearly defined environment."[13] The important characteristic of Ginia for Pavese is not her femininity but her immaturity, her incompleteness as an adult human being. Her struggle throughout the narrative is to attain maturity, to learn how to live as a grown-up, but in the end she yields to what she perceives in her defeat as her destiny, that of a perpetual adolescent and a victim of circumstance. Ginia's character in this respect is merely the narrative extension of the adolescent figures who populate *Lavorare stanca,* those runaway boys who are permanently caught up in a game of avoidance and escape.

The theme of solitude, articulated at the outset of *La bella estate,* is the most important motif throughout the narrative. As the novel begins, Ginia appears to derive great pleasure from her moments of isolation. Before her involvement with Guido, she develops the habit of drawing the curtains in her apartment, blocking out noise and light, in order to enhance her sense of solitude. Her goal, like Lidia's in the early story "Le tre ragazze," is to achieve an independent detachment that will set her apart from the pathetic neediness of the other young women in her environment. But with the loss of innocence Ginia is obliged to abandon the illusion of joyous self-sufficiency. Her experience of solitude is transformed into anguished isolation. After the episode in which she finally removes her clothes in Guido's studio, she begins to recognize this transformation on an emotional level: "'Ginia, may I?' she heard Amelia ask near the curtain. Ginia clutched the curtain and didn't answer. 'Let her be,' she heard Guido say; 'she's stupid.' Then Ginia began to cry in silence, holding on to the curtain" (*BE,* 87).

The curtain in Guido's studio that serves first to conceal Rodrigues, Ginia's inadvertent voyeur, and later to protect Ginia herself from the scornful incomprehension of the others, has a central symbolic function in the novel's development of the theme of solitude. The original title of the novel—*La tenda*—reinforced the absolute importance of this image, which weaves together the motifs of sexuality, shame, and the loss of identity. Like the image of the breast-shaped hill in *Paesi tuoi,* the curtain recurs in the narrative at important moments in the protagonist's process of discovery. It is behind this curtain that Ginia is first seduced by Guido, in a space that seems to be at first warm, inviting, and removed from the rest of the world. But the curtained bed in which Ginia exchanges her innocence for the knowledge of adult experience is fraught with ambivalent associations as the illusion of intimacy yields to the awareness of a profound separateness and alienation.

The concept of sin, unarticulated before this point in Pavese's works, recurs at several points throughout the novel and is always associated with sexual activity. When Ginia learns that Amelia has syphilis, for example, she immediately equates her friend's misfortune with moral retribution for a life of promiscuity. This judgment is followed by the concern that everyone involved in sexual activity might deserve such a fate. Amelia herself tells Ginia that "the Lord punishes," adding that she hopes that the woman who contaminated her will be struck blind in retribution. The question of Amelia's own morality holds an ambivalent fascination for Ginia. While she finds herself repelled at the older girl's ease in appearing naked in front of men, she also envies that same self-confidence, associated as it is in her mind with the acquisition of adult ways. When Amelia offers Ginia a sexual kiss, and later confesses to an erotic infatuation with her, Ginia does not recoil. Amelia's behavior, though violating conventional taboos, excites the curiosity of one who aspires to exploring the ways of adult sensuality while still experiencing the reticence of the uninitiated.

Ginia's sense of sin, which is existential rather than religious, is reflected most often in her obsessive fear and fascination with nudity. The games of hiding in the darkness, under blankets, or behind curtains are linked with the fear of recognizing her own altered identity in the reflection of Guido's gaze. At many points in her narrative Ginia surveys herself in mirrors, and eventually rehearses her nakedness in front of her solitary reflection, trying to imagine how Guido would see her. The topos of the male gaze is an important one in the novel's repertoire of images. It is associated with the coming of age, the loss of Edenic innocence, and the acquisition of a sense of shame.

Although the city is the dominant environment in *La bella estate,* the country is also present as its antithetical pole. It is significant that Guido is a peasant by birth, and that he leaves Ginia to return to the countryside during the course of the narrative. Guido, though an educated, urbanized youth, draws his inspiration from the countryside he loves, and owes to this place a visceral sense of loyalty and belonging. He shares with other peasants in Pavese's work the tendency to perceive the countryside in sexual terms as well the habit of regarding women as inferior to the landscape itself. After Guido has seduced Ginia he tells her: "There is no girl as beautiful as a hill" (*BE,* 73). He also observes that she is "not summertime," a season he associates with the landscape of his rural birthplace. Claiming that he feels happy only while on top of a hill, Guido tells a fellow painter about a plan to paint a landscape resembling a naked woman: "Guido was talking about the hill he wanted to paint, and said that he had in mind to treat it like a woman lying down with her breasts exposed to the sun, and to give it the moisture and the flavor of a woman" (*BE,* 75).

The most striking image of the countryside in *La bella estate* is provided in Guido's scheme to paint an enormous landscape that will cover the entire wall of his studio creating a *trompe l'oeil* effect, thus giving form to the cherished rural world of his imagination. This fantasy of nature as an artifact, as an illusion to be created by her seducer in the very space where she has been forced to surrender her own illusions, is as close as Ginia will ever come to the countryside in the course of the novel. Like the "beautiful summer" of her brief adolescence, the rural landscape belongs to the domain of irretrievable dreams and forms no part of her destiny.

Stylistically, *La bella estate* is not as daring as *Paesi tuoi,* and is closer in some respects to the stories written at the end of the 1930s. Pavese does not attempt to re-create the working-class nuances of Ginia's speech, and the use of vocabulary echoing dialect variations is absent in this novel.[14] Also absent are the odd syntactical transpositions that created such clamorous critical reaction upon the publication of *Paesi tuoi.* Parataxis is, however, still extensively used, and the four-part paratactical sentence occurs frequently in this novel.[15] Though the accumulation of these breathless paratactical constructions gives the sense of Ginia's manner of feeling and thinking, the structure is not as ambitiously handled as it is in the earlier novel, where stream of consciousness and the account of external action mingle in the same sentence.

The language of the novel succeeds, however, in echoing the staccato quality of the protagonist's fragmented attempts to communicate with others, thus juxtaposing the emotional richness of an intense inner world with the clumsiness of her conversational resources. What is most striking and innovative in the linguistic texture of *La bella estate* is the appearance of what would become the characteristically Pavesian non sequitur, of dialogues that seem to be recorded with one ear, providing an echo of the inanity and subversive inconclusiveness of day-to-day conversation. In subsequent years the profusion of the literature of the absurd made this motif something of a cliché, but at the time when Pavese's novel was first written it constituted a striking technical insight. It functions with particular effectiveness in this novel to offset an occasional echo of lyrical sentimentality.

La spiaggia

In November of 1940, Pavese began the composition of *La spiaggia* (*The Beach*), which expands on the theme of an earlier short story, "Villa in collina." It seems to have been undertaken more as a diversion than as a project with specific literary goals. The manuscript was completed in January 1941 and appeared soon afterward in installments in the magazine *Lettere d'oggi.*[16] Published by Einaudi only in 1956, this novel was for many years among the most neglected of Pavese's works. The author's own scathing dismissal of *La spiaggia*—published posthumously in the essay "L'influsso degli eventi" (The influence of events)—seems to validate the lack of critical attention devoted to the novel: "*La spiaggia* . . . that novel of mine which is neither violent nor lower class nor 'American'—and which, fortunately, few have read—is not a chip off the monolith. It amounts to a distraction, which I would be ashamed of if it made a difference. It is what one might call a straightforward search for style" (*SL,* 224).

The novel has, however, been reevaluated in recent years, and by now it is apparent that *La spiaggia* holds a crucial place in the development of Pavese's fiction, reechoing elements from previous works and reflecting the quest for a narrative voice in which the development of atmosphere and recurrent symbols take precedence over the conventional development of character and plot.

A publicity note that Pavese sent to *Lettere d'oggi* at the time the novel was first printed provides an interesting summary of the work, in the light of the author's ongoing struggle with the idea of naturalism and psychological allusiveness:

> This last novel represents an effort to transcend naturalism by building up psychological atmosphere. It deals with the friendship of two young men and the wife of one of these, who manages simultaneously to separate and bring together the two friends. Nothing extraordinary happens. Around them the little world of the beach resort is suggested by dialogues made up of resonances, rather than [visually] represented. Four men gravitate around a woman and their private worlds are perceived as . . . an uneasiness that transcends the facts. (*L,* 415)

Pavese's summary highlights the centrality of ambivalent interrelationships within the development of a story in which "nothing extraordinary" seems to happen, and also suggests the importance of a second, more elusive dimension to be sought above and beyond the obvious details of the plot.

Though the events recounted in *La spiaggia* are few, the narrative is richly nuanced with mood, dialogue and setting. The two principal male characters are the anonymous narrator and his longtime friend Doro, who has married an upper-middle-class Genoese woman named Clelia, and moved with her to her own city. As the story begins, the narrator alludes to his estrangement from Doro in the wake of his friend's marriage and disappearance to Genoa. After this lapse in communication, it is Doro who takes the initiative in attempting to revitalize the friendship. Doro invites his old friend to join him for a brief visit to his native village in the hills, and later for a trip to the seaside. Their journey to the countryside involves a night of riotous carousing in the company of two village friends, culminating in a drunken serenade outside the home of some local women. These bacchanalian antics are brought to an abrupt end with a roar in the night and the sound of a pistol shot.

After this brief, animated rural episode the atmosphere and tempo of the novel undergo a complete transformation, as the narrator accompanies Doro home to his summer house on the Genoese coast. It is here that the friends will spend the rest of their vacation together in the company of the alluring and enigmatic Clelia. Pavese makes skillful use of elliptical dialogue to evoke the languid atmosphere of the seaside resort, highlighting the vacationers' quest for pleasure, their idle secrets and uneasy silences. The focus of the narrator's attention is the suspicion of unspoken tensions between Doro and Clelia. Without resolving the mystery, he becomes the uneasy confidant of both. He also begins to associate with several of the couple's other friends at the resort and eventually meets up with one of his own former students, Berti, whom he introduces to the group. The activities of this small community take on a predictable, almost monotonous rhythm, which is uninterrupted even by an accidental injury sustained by one of the women friends of Doro and Clelia. Guido, the middle-aged sensualist of the group, tries to make an argument for an amoral, hedonistic way of life where women exist only as objects of gratification. The narrator listens to the different preoccupations of Doro, Clelia, and Guido without much resistance or argument. His own growing fascination with his friend's wife is evidenced only in the most elliptical manner. Though jealous of both Doro and Clelia, he especially resents the woman's self-sufficient solitude. Clelia's superficial cordiality masks an emotional aloofness, and she coolly manipulates the attentions of Doro, the narrator himself, and the adolescent Berti who has also become infatuated with her. Psychological tensions begin to build until Clelia suddenly realizes that she is pregnant and decides to return to Genoa with her husband, leaving the narrator alone with the still smitten adolescent, Berti.

Like *La bella estate,* this novel charts the evolution of the protagonist's experience of solitude, discovered in the process of coming to terms with the adult world. Though already thirty years old, the anonymous narrator of *La spiaggia* seems still poised on the threshold of maturity. The novel thus gives voice to the motif of the perpetual adolescent, the spectator doomed to remain at a state of arrested growth and obliged to witness the adult experience of others from an insurmountable existential distance. All the minor characters in the story serve only to provide a foil for the central figures, Clelia and Doro, who as a couple appear to be inscrutable and inaccessible. The fact that they constitute a couple is a source of both fascination and dismay to the narrator. For him, their fused identity as well as the uneasy tensions that are generated between them present a mysterious magnetism, which he struggles repeatedly to decipher and to come to terms with.

Armanda Guiducci has described this novel as "a little jewel of misogyny," pointing out, however, that the misogyny is mediated through the highly attractive and ambiguous figure of Clelia.[17] In the idle, supposedly carefree world of the bourgeois seaside community, the presence of women continually casts a shadow. It is the women, with their moods, their accidents, and their emotional needs who spoil various outings, days at the beach, and evenings on the dance floor. Clelia draws attention to herself like a siren, but then deflects communication with her perpetual air of ambiguity and elusiveness. The narrator is jealous of her intimacy with the sea, with which she seems to enjoy a sensual connection. As in *Il carcere,* the sea here is not perceived by the narrator as a friendly presence. His reference to the "empty sea" suggests its lack of reassuring resonance. Like the sea, Clelia is vague, enigmatic, and restless. Her otherness is total. Yet she generates a sense of shame. The scene that follows the revelation of her pregnancy brings into focus the almost pathological dimension of Pavese's perceptions of femininity: "Clelia came out of the bedroom, and asked who was there. She gave me a smile, almost apologetically, and put her handkerchief to her mouth. 'Do I disgust you?' she said" (*S,* 62).

The slow-moving sequences at the seaside with their melancholy conclusion constitute two-thirds of the novel and present a sharp contrast with the animation of the earlier rural episode. This earlier moment functions as a glimpse of the narrator's lost paradise: a world of male camaraderie, of uninhibited mirth where women simply do not exist except as the imagined audience for a farcical serenade. It also creates an atmosphere of implicit nostalgia throughout the subsequent episodes and gives an ambivalent poignancy to the narrator's obliquely stated infatuation with his friend's wife. Nevertheless, the confrontation with Doro's "exile" into the world of marriage and adulthood represents an important moment of passage for the narrator. The joys of uninhibited friendship and the reassurance of male bonding have vanished as completely as Ginia's "beautiful summer."

The texture of *La spiaggia* is not as symbolically overwrought as that of the three previous novels. At moments the style seems to approach a kind of social realism, but this impression is undercut by the persistent recurrence of a symbol that functions as a mysterious refrain, giving a sense of rhythmic allusiveness to the narrative. Shortly after his arrival at the seaside resort, the anonymous narrator discovers a "thick twisted olive tree" outside the window of his lodging, "growing inexplicably right in the middle of the pavement."[18] As though recognizing retrospectively the private symbolism of the olive tree, the narrator remarks: "It's perhaps the best thing that I can conjure up from the entire summer" (*S,* 19). Like the ancient village in *Il carcere,* the breast-shaped hill in *Paesi tuoi,* and the curtain in *La bella estate,* the image of the olive tree is repeated in a rhythm that reinforces Pavese's central thematic concerns. It is less aggressively recurrent, however, than the dominant symbols in the other novels, and its link with the external events of the narrative is less bluntly spelled out. From the start the tree is linked with the countryside, which is explicitly the domain of Doro. Yet it is also more frequently linked with the narrator's unspoken love for Clelia, and thus becomes in a sense a key to the triangular situation to which the narrator alludes, but never explicitly acknowledges.

The tree also signals the existence of another triangle, since the adolescent Berti is referred to as a young man "who lives in the street with the olive tree" (*S,* 25). Berti's earliest signs of infatuation become apparent in a scene under the olive tree, and this is also the site of two episodes in which he attempts to confess his feelings to the narrator, as well as the eventual discussion of the departure of Clelia upon the discovery of her pregnancy. Since Berti functions as a specular image of the narrator, and the young man's blatant infatuation with Clelia serves to mirror the narrator's own unspoken passion for his friend's wife, the olive tree symbolizes in both cases the growth of unpredictable and unrequited feelings that have sprung up on what seems to be dry, barren terrain. The narrator obliquely suggests that a more appropriate setting for such a strangely vibrant tree would be the countryside, a location associated in this novel with sensual enjoyment and bacchanalian abandon. It is fitting to the novel's symbolic rhythm that the tree appears at the very conclusion of the story, highlighting the themes of loneliness and impossible erotic attachment by linking them once more with the presence of the same image: "In the meantime we had arrived in the alley, and the sight of the olive irritated me. I began to understand that nothing is as uninhabitable as a place where one has been happy" (*S,* 64).

This dominant image serves an almost Proustian function in the narrator's recounting of personal memories, evoking a sense of nostalgia through the adoption of a privileged image from the irretrievable past. But its more important function is the transformation of this privileged memory into an allusive symbolic cadence that enriches the otherwise slight tale of a summer vacation at the seaside. It was precisely while writing this novel that Pavese was beginning to articulate his ideas on memory and myth in preparation for the stories and essays that later formed the important collection *Feria d'agosto*.

On another level this novel is significant as Pavese's first sustained exploration of the bourgeois environment, a world he regarded with considerable ambivalence and fascination. Yet there is no attempt to analyze or describe that world in depth, and the social theme is of much less importance here than the evocation of mood and atmosphere, the ebb and flow of conversation, and the concealment of emotion signaled by the recurrent, emblematic allusions to the olive tree.

Chapter Five

The Articulation of a Poetics of Myth

Feria d'agosto

During the years of Italy's active involvement in World War II, Pavese's diary reflects an increasing preoccupation with the issues of myth, ethnology, dreams, and aesthetic theory. His initial discovery of Frazer's *Golden Bough* in 1933 had prompted an ongoing fascination with ethnology, anthropology, and myth. Though he had read Lévy-Bruhl in 1936, Pavese's interest in these diverse fields did not evolve into a systematic study for some time. In the early 1940s, however, he began to reread Vico, along with the works of Jung and Freud, paying particular attention to *Totem and Taboo.* He also discovered the novels of Thomas Mann, and read with interest the poetry of Rainer Maria Rilke. At approximately the same time Pavese was introduced to the ethnological works of Kerényi, Leo Frobenius, Mircea Eliade, Paula Philippson, and Bronislaw Malinowski. The body of writing that he produced during this period—anthologized as *Feria d'agosto* (August festival)—reflects his growing absorption with myth and remains of seminal importance to an understanding of his development as a writer.

Furio Jesi has provided the most thorough analysis of the diverse influences that inform *Feria d'agosto* and Pavese's later work. He suggests that the majority of Pavese's ethnological sources are rooted in the poetic sensibility of late nineteenth-century Germany rather than in a tradition of rigorous scientific inquiry.[1] Jesi establishes a link between the works of Kerényi and Frobenius, who formulate similar concepts of childhood, with the poetics of Rilke and the followers of Nietzsche in general. He also claims that Pavese, along with the generation of German expressionists, became heir to the late-romantic concept of childhood as an era of unrepeatable experiences, a paradigm of knowledge that is accessible to consciousness through memory. Furthermore, he demonstrates the link between this late-romantic myth of childhood and the thematic fascination with death, equated with a return to prenatal experience.

However marked these influences of the late-romantic imagination on Pavese's study of ethnology and myth, the importance of Vico as a contrasting model should not be underestimated. It was precisely during the period that Pavese was preparing the mythic meditations of *Feria d'agosto* that he was rereading Vico's *New Science.* This is reflected in a 1943 diary entry, which points to Vico as the only writer in the Italian tradition who was capable of perceiving the countryside above and beyond the restrictions of the Arcadian convention (*MV,* 243). Pavese had already come to regard Vico as the founder of all mythological scholarship and the first philosopher to recognize the connection between myth and man's essential need to give names to the things that surround him.[2] Like Vico, he perceived the poetry produced in the modern world as a manifestation of the survival of the once all-pervasive power of myth. Later, in an essay written not long before his death, Pavese was to reecho Vico's perception of the link between myth, religion, and poetry: "The religious moment, which is by now completely transformed or subsumed into other spiritual activities, manifests itself at this point in time only in the works of the imagination" (*SL,* 317).

Essential to Pavese's subsequent treatment of myth is the Vichian notion of a parallel between each individual's experience of childhood and the psychology of the earliest epoch of humanity. Like Vico, Pavese envisaged childhood as a reflection of the primitive world, in which contact with immediate reality was direct and instinctive, and the perception of the savage and the sacred forces in nature was marked with spontaneous emotion. This perception, largely lost to the modern era and forgotten by the child who has grown to be an adult, survives, however, in poetry and in mythology, and can be recaptured by the adult in rare instances of sharp recall. From this concept Pavese developed his notion of the "ecstatic moment"—illustrated in many of the stories of *Feria d'agosto*—which is not without a convergent influence from the late-romantic sensibility.

With the exception of the 1937 story, "Primo amore," *Feria d'agosto* was written between 1941 and 1944. Though some of Pavese's most memorable short fiction appears in this work, *Feria d'agosto* is not simply an anthology of short stories. In addition to several conventionally structured stories, it contains brief meditations on poetics, myth, and creativity, as well as a number of lyrical prose fragments, some of which have dreamlike elements bordering on the surreal. *Feria d'agosto* is divided into three sections, bearing mythically allusive titles: "The Sea," "The City," and "The Vineyard." The three-part division does not constitute, however, a clear-cut separation of the stories and essays by virtue of specific thematic elements, since the themes and images dominant in one section reappear inevitably in the others. A common thread running through the work is the concept of childhood as a privileged period in which fundamental perceptions take place that will unconsciously mold the individual throughout subsequent experience. This theme is explored both in the narrative portions of the collection and in the lyrical or theoretical essays. Closely linked with this is the concept of the uniqueness of the landscapes of youth, particularly the magical experience of life in the countryside with its still untamed, primitive energies. Through memory, each individual can discover and clarify myths that are rooted in the perceptions of early youth. In the essays of the final part of the collection Pavese explicitly links the creation of poetry and art with the discovery of the artist's personal myths through childhood memories.

In "Del mito, del simbolo e dell'altro" (On myth, symbol, and other matters), Pavese attempts to provide a new definition of myth:

> Myth is, in short, a norm, the shape of a fact that has happened once and for all, and draws its value from this absolute uniqueness which raises it beyond the sphere of time and transforms it into revelation. For this reason it always occurs in the beginning, as in childhood: it is timeless. Say that one day, who knows when, a man appeared in the hills of your region and inquired about willow trees and wove a basket before going on his way. This man would be the simplest and most genuine hero of the civilizing process. His revelation of an art would be mythical, insofar as the gesture had an absolute uniqueness, had no present or past, but grew out of a sacred eternity that is the paradigm of all weavers of willow branches. (*FA,* 140)

Essential to the creation of myth is this almost religious sense of a uniqueness, an atmosphere that is capable of investing the ordinary with the metaphysical: "[A myth] is a unique, absolute event, a concentration of vital powers from a sphere beyond the ordinary, and as such it casts an aura of the miraculous on everything that presupposes or resembles it" (*FA,* 141).

The child, who lives in a world of myths in the making, has no conscious realization of what is taking place in the psyche, since at this stage of his existence he "has better things to do than to give a name to his state." Yet, in this nonreflective period, the child is moved to ecstasy by words, fables, and fantasies, which he cannot distinguish from the concrete world around him: "At that age, fantasy strikes [the child] the way reality does, as objective knowledge and not as invention" (*FA,* 141–42). His subsequent experience of the world is mediated through the memory of these moments in which his imagination was stirred. Pavese thus concludes that "there is no seeing things for the first time," since perception is always filtered through memories, fantasies, or words. It is experiencing things "for the second time" that the individual can trigger the revelation of primal memories and the source of personal myth.

In the same essay Pavese also spells out the moral function of the writer in relation to his myths: "The life's work of every artist and of every human being is . . . an unending effort to reduce his myths to clarity. . . . He must never hold himself back from the most rigorous attempt to reduce them to clarity, which means to destroy them. Only whatever is left over after this effort . . . can have value as a basis for living" (*FA,* 142–43). This passage is vital to an understanding of the poetics at the basis of this collection and most of Pavese's subsequent work.

The opening story, "Il nome" (The name), sets the tone of *Feria d'agosto,* presenting the experience of children in the countryside, their contact with nature and animals, and the discovery of secret forces at work in the landscape that have the power to infiltrate the human realm. The narrator, a young boy, joins his friends hunting snakes in the rugged hills. Here he experiences for the first time a mysterious sense of uneasiness and transgression. A magical power seems to invade the atmosphere as the mother of one of the boys, Pale, yells out her son's name to the listening landscape. To the children's horror the boy's identity is thus exposed to the earth and to the animals, yielding to nature some vital information that may also be the source of power and dominion. These fears and intuitions are experienced by the children in the most spontaneous and primal way, since they have an immediate understanding of the natural world that adults have already lost.

"Il campo di granturco" (The corn field), a short lyrical meditation also from the book's opening section, repeats the motif of childhood as a privileged, visionary moment and shows how adult perceptions are rooted in the unique experiences of early life. It introduces the theme of "unique places"—the locations that inspire the creation of personal myth—interwoven with the motif of return. Pavese's formulation of these connected themes is influenced by Vico's contempt of mythically charged locations, places invested with special power when first perceived through the eyes of a child or through the eyes of a primitive human being. This initial, privileged perception becomes the forgotten "first time," through which all subsequent perceptions of the same place are mediated, evoking a powerful, recurrent sense of magical revelation. The child's first enchanted sight of a cornfield is transformed into a universal vision of "the corn field" that will permanently influence his perceptions and memories.

"Una certezza" (A certainty) examines the metaphysical nature of a phenomenon that occurs in the course of everyday life: an involuntary trancelike state that has the capacity to transport the individual above and beyond the turmoil of ordinary experience into a realm of timeless detachment. This experience originates somewhere deep with the self and provokes "an atmosphere which you seem to have within you rather than around you, a great abyss of air, nothingness, of possible events and thoughts that surge up from the depths of your being" (*FA,* 89–90). "Una certezza" makes a strong statement on the value of these moments of meditative ecstasy which seem to reveal the inadequacy of all worldly actions and ambitions in comparison with the pure contemplation of "this wonder, this void." It thus places a greater value on the contemplation of the inner self than on active participation in the everyday world. Pavese claims that his adult perception of reality is limited to a mere reflection of what he perceived during boyhood. Through his memories of that earlier period, he realizes that his imaginative world was shaped entirely by childhood experience (*FA,* 90).

The indelible power of the places and experiences of childhood is also examined in "La Langa," (The Langhe countryside). Here the anonymous narrator, in returning to his village in the Langhe, comes to acknowledge the fundamental link between his deepest sense of identity and the contours of his native countryside. He finds that the physical act of return simply confirms that he already possesses that landscape engraved within his being. In the process of his journey he achieves an awareness of the ineluctable power of early life in determining the fate of the individual, and is led to observe that "our entire destiny is already stamped in our bones before we reach the age of reason" (*FA,* 18). The explicit note of fatalism that emerged during this period reappeared in many of Pavese's subsequent works.

To illustrate the juxtaposition of man and boy, and the sense of magical revelation that this encounter can provoke, Pavese attempts a brief experiment in narrative surrealism. "Colloquio del fiume" (Conversation by the river) presents in a dreamlike vision the meeting of an adult man with his childhood self. The dialogue that ensues is depicted as a conversation between two distinct people and resonates with a poignant awareness of transience and loss (*FA*, 166).

The stories in this collection that evoke the discoveries of childhood and adolescence are among Pavese's most successful short fiction. In "L'eremita" (The hermit) a young boy's fascination with Pietro, a rural hermit, is shared to some degree by his father, narrator of the tale. The figure of the hermit—"a blond, hairy giant"—seems at first to reintroduce the earthy protagonist of the early poem "Paesaggio I." "L'eremita" is not, however, the story of this hermit, but rather the tale of a complex relationship between a father and his adolescent son. A particular pathos is achieved through the first-person narrative device, which filters the boy's yearning for adventure and escape through the observations of the older man, whose own nostalgia for youthful experience, though never stated, is always implicit. At the conclusion of the story, set during the festivities of late summer, it is the hermit who literally obliges the boy to walk on his own feet and to relinquish his childlike fantasies and dependencies. This event is reported with ambivalent sadness by the father in his account of the harvest celebration: "The memory of that night that we came back is in my heart like Nino's childhood. The songs, the exhaustion, the excitement under the moonlight had an unreal, sad effect on me. I almost love that Pietro; one would think *I* was the child" (*FA*, 34).

The most powerfully poetic vision of the world of childhood is achieved in "Il mare" (The sea), the title story of the book's opening section, which, like "L'eremita," is characterized by a marked sense of place. Here, the adult narrator looks back on a childhood adventure, when he and his friend Gosto had set out on a journey through the Langhe hills with the expectation of catching sight of the sea. The story is filled with familiar Pavesian motifs, the hills, vineyards, bonfires, and country festivals of the Langhe, as well as the exotic lure of the faraway ocean. The boys' journey begins spontaneously, as though prompted by some magical power, after the excitement of a farm being burned during a wedding. The image of the fire has a mythic allusiveness that colors the entire narrative and is repeated in the bonfire at the story's end. Various moments of the boys' adventure are evoked in rich descriptive detail, with each element contributing to the general symbolic fabric of the story: the initial moonlit journey through the hills, the encounter with a wandering beggar, the continuation of the walk in unfamiliar territory under the hot sun, and, later, the narrator's discovery of a peasant festival, with bonfires, music, and dancing.

There comes a moment in the journey when Gosto becomes weary of the effort, and despairing of ever being able to catch sight of the sea, decides to go home. The narrator, however, for whom the sea is simply a pretext and the quest itself is everything, resolves to continue. Implicit in this scene is the boy's undaunted yearning for a sense of the absolute: "For me it no longer mattered that I might not see the sea beyond Cassinasco. It was enough to know that the sea existed behind the slopes and villages so that I could think about it as I walked along among the hedges" (*FA*, 74). He is finally rescued in a state of hunger and exhaustion by Candido, a peasant clarinet player, in whose company he spends the final night of his journey. In the concluding scene they participate together in a farmyard festival with bonfires, music, and dancing. Candido has gradually been transformed into a father figure, providing for the adolescent a sense of serenity and peace.

The discovery of sexuality is perceived in Pavese's fiction as a deeply disturbing intrusion into the magical world of childhood. This theme, which is central to "Primo amore," also occurs in some of the other stories of this collection. The adolescent narrator of "La giacchetta di cuoio" (The leather jacket) describes the painful change wrought in a cherished male friendship when a woman appears on the scene. Ceresa, the man who had been the object of his affection and admiration, easily succumbs to the charm of the seductive Nora, much to the perplexity of the young narrator. The boy perceives the relationship between Ceresa and Nora as a threat to his own most valued friendship. The woman's sensuality inspires in his uninitiated imagination an uncomprehending sense of repugnance. This emotional reaction is conveyed with great incisive power in the allusion to the whiteness of Nora's flesh, a motif echoed elsewhere in Pavese's work. Despite the boy's contempt for Nora, he soon becomes an involuntary accomplice to the woman's infidelity to Ceresa, as he agrees to take her on a boating trip during which she becomes involved with another man. Though aware of Ceresa's subsequent jealousy and suspicion, he is powerless to prevent Ceresa's vengeance. The boy attempts to eavesdrop on the lovers' quarrel by lingering at the boathouse one night, but does not learn until the following day that Ceresa has strangled Nora and dumped her body in the river. Unlike the fatal violence in "Temporale d'estate" and *Paesi tuoi,* the murder here is presented obliquely through a perspective of adolescent incomprehension and dismayed innocence.

"Fine d'agosto" (End of August) reechoes the theme of adolescent innocence that pervades "La giacchetta di cuoio," though this story is narrated from the viewpoint of a sexually initiated adult. It has as its center a typically Pavesian epiphany: the narrator's sudden vivid reliving of childhood experience triggered by a gust of wind in the August night. In his ecstatic recapture of the most cherished sensations of his past he becomes aware that the difference between the man he has become and the child he was then is connected with the adult acquisition of sexual experience. For this narrator, as is always the case for Pavese's protagonists, the initiation into sexuality has meant a profound sense of loss. Suddenly, a spontaneous contempt for all women, even for Clara—the woman at his side—possesses him, leading him to conclude with bitterness that women alone have the power to "transform the faraway scent of the wind into the scent of flesh" (*FA,* 14).

The story that perhaps shares most in common with Pavese's short fiction of the late 1930s and which repeats the characteristic juxtaposition of country and city is "La città" (The city). It presents a first-person account of a young man's difficult transition from the country to the city, from adolescent fantasy to adult reality. Though written in a more naturalistic vein than many of the other stories in *Feria d'agosto,* it also weaves together the mythically charged themes of identity and alienation, the contrast between city and country and the necessity of fidelity to one's origins.

One of the most striking thematic preoccupations to emerge in *Feria d'agosto* is that of the *selvaggio*: the mysterious irrationality and violence at work in the rural landscape. This theme—which received its first extensive treatment in *Paesi tuoi*—is central to "Le feste" (Festivities) where it is interwoven with the story of a mysterious bay horse. While evoking a rich portrait of characters and locations of rural life, the narrative reaches its climax with the burning of a farm and the murder of the horse's owner. As the hillside farm burns down in a gigantic fire that dominates the landscape, the horse charges off into the woods and disappears forever. The mythic presence of this animal survives, however, in the collective consciousness of the local peasants: "The people . . . say that the horse roams through the woods, and on certain days they hear it passing by on the crests of hills" (*FA,* 136). The image of the fire, repeated in the festive bonfires elsewhere in this collection, is reminiscent of Talino's irrational act of arson in *Paesi tuoi* and foreshadows the tragic conflagration of *La luna e i falò.*

"Una storia segreta" (A secret history), the powerful and complex story that concludes the collection, also gives a prominent place to the theme of the *selvaggio.* Here it is interwoven with many of the other characteristic motifs of *Feria d'agosto*: the privileged moment of youth relived through adult memory; the sense of ecstasy induced by unique places singled out during childhood; the lure of the sea and of life in the city; the inevitability of return to the places of youth; the sense of visceral belonging to the landscape of one's origin. The story begins as the adult narrator who looks back with affection and longing on the events of his rural childhood. The central figure in his recollection is Sandiana, a vigorous young woman from a remote rural area who came to live with his widowed father during the narrator's boyhood. Rather than becoming a stepmother, Sandiana attained the stature of a wild earth-mother, introducing the boy to the mysteries of the countryside, amusing him with stories and gossip, and accompanying him on journeys through the surrounding landscape. With the introduction of this evolving relationship between the boy and the woman the narrative abandons its linear progression, moving back and forth in time, alternating between narrative account and meditative monologue. The woman functions not only as an initiator of magical mysteries, but also as a key to many themes and symbolic motifs the story weaves together.

The death of the narrator's father, which emerges in the central part of this story, is of great interest in its interweaving of the theme of human mortality with the notion of the *selvaggio* and the perceived timelessness—akin to the eternity of death—that characterizes the state of childhood:

> When, years ago, my father died, I found in my grief a sense of calm I had not expected but had always known. I went to the church and the graveyard. . . . I felt that my father existed now as some wild element, and no longer needed to wander around day and night to tell me. It is true that the church had swallowed him up, but the church, too, goes no farther than the horizon and my father had not changed underground. From body and blood he had become a root, a root among the many roots that survive in the earth after the plant is cut away. . . . Now I began to feel my father present in everything. . . . I could not imagine him closed within his coffin in the narrow tomb. . . . [He] began to accompany me everywhere. He went before me

on the hilltops, he wanted me to be a boy. In the places which he had made his own I would stop for him; I felt he was a boy. (*FA,* 179)

For the narrator of "Una storia segreta," the dead father was first transformed into a "wild element"—a root, surviving in communion with the earth itself. Later, his presence manifested itself indiscriminately in everything, until it became part of the narrator himself during his walks in the countryside. In the text, this fusion of identities is explicitly connected with the state of boyhood, characterized by an intimate contact with nature and an intuitive sense of the oneness and timelessness of being.

At other points in *Feria d'agosto,* the lure of the abyss and the surrender of adult rationality to the wildness of nature are treated in less positive vein, and are equated with a self-indulgent regression to a subhuman state. This judgment is implicit even in "Nudismo" (Nudity), a lyrical meditation that evokes the sensual mysteries of sunbathing in a wild and secluded spot. The abyss is symbolized here by the image of a semistagnant water hole where the narrator loves to immerse himself during long hours of solitary sunbathing. The ecstasy of tanning his naked body, which already approaches the color of a wild creature, leads to a long meditation on the meaning of nudity and the encroachment of culture upon nature. "Nudismo" concludes, however, on a note of ambivalence: "Every day I find life here, but then I stretch out, my body blackened, like a dead man" (*FA,* 165).

This notion also appears in "Mal di mestiere" (Job sickness), which provides one of the most striking statements of Pavese's underlying dualism. The essay opens with a description of a personal temptation: the desire to merge with the forces of the landscape, and to become one with "rock, humidity, manure, sap, wind." This rapturous fusion with nature is evoked in a language which echoes, as Calvino has pointed out, the overblown stylistic tensions of D'Annunzio's work.[3] Yet Pavese makes a simultaneous claim that the surrender to the ecstatic and the relinquishing of human rationality involves considerable moral danger. The attraction of the *selvaggio* or the abyss is the same as that of animal instincts, "like drunkenness or murder" (*FA,* 164–65).

"Mal di mestiere" thus reflects Pavese's concern that he might have begun to overindulge in the irrational, a scruple that is repeated in his diary on 8 February 1944 (*MV,* 259). In the perceived dichotomy between the physical realm and the world of the rational intelligence, between adulthood and boyhood, between responsible action and instinctive reaction, Pavese is echoing an age-old dualism, rooted perhaps in his early religious training. This essay takes a strong moral position on the necessity of keeping one's mental faculties uncontaminated by the seduction of the senses. Significantly, Pavese expresses the inappropriateness of a surrender to the irrational in sexual imagery: "There is even something obscene in this. It is the same as abandoning oneself to sex and wanting to narrate all its secret sensations" (*FA*, 157). Only through memory can the direct experience of the senses be clarified and humanized. He concludes from this that "the most reliable reservoir of symbols is that of childhood; remote sensations that have been stripped bare . . . of all material residues and have assumed in the memory the transparency of spirit" (*FA*, 157).

According to the dualistic perspective articulated by Pavese, adulthood and childhood are antithetical states. During early life "reality received us as it receives seeds and stones. . . . But the secret history of everyone's childhood is in fact made up of the wrenching and pulling that tore us away from reality until . . . through the use of language we came face to face with things and learned to contemplate and value them" (*FA*, 157). The adult can look back on the wealth of childhood sensations, but he cannot and must not attempt to relive that unmediated instinctual state: "On the contrary, we must make every attempt in the other direction, which means to reject whatever remains of that base nature . . . to reject it in order to rediscover it. But there is little that adult life can add to the treasure of childhood discoveries. What we can do instead is to bring to light those primordial forms and contemplate their value, like the shape of roots which the soils of our daily lives has continued to nourish" (*FA*, 157).

Memory, language, and—by implication—poetry are thus presented as the tools of the rational spirit and the best protection against the temptations of the abyss. Nevertheless, though Pavese implies at many turns that the function of poetry is essentially a cognitive one, his own basic position remains ambivalent. While making a claim for the necessity of clarity and rationality, the essays that dominate the final section of *Feria d'agosto* are characterized by an increasingly ambiguous language, often yielding to a tone of sensual lyricism. It is precisely in this unresolved tension that the unique energy of the entire anthology lies.

Pavese's ideas on myth and the irrational in the meditations and stories of *Feria d'agosto* do not constitute a coherent philosophical statement. They are intuitions, elaborated in a variety of ways and with occasional inconsistencies, that serve primarily to form the basis of his personal poetics. With this work Pavese consolidated his belief that the source of all art lies in personal memories, which can be repeatedly scrutinized and explored for new insight and inspiration. There is thus a vital connection between Pavese's vision of the importance of childhood experience and the narrowness of the range of themes that he was driven to explore in his writing.

Dialoghi con Leucò

The spiritual crisis that beset Pavese during his stay in the monastery in Monferrato toward the end of the war led him to reexamine the meaning of religious faith. His diary entries provide sporadic clues to this process. Given his longstanding interest in myth and symbol, it is not surprising that he was tempted to explore the "rich, symbolic reality" of Christianity. Yet to accept this faith would mean "to enter into the world of the supernatural." Up to this point he had viewed his own metaphysical quest for myth and symbol as a manifestation of the psychological rather than the supernatural, and had defined this path as "Protestantism without God" (*MV,* 249). While living with the priests at the monastery he began to read the New Testament and to examine various works of theology and religious history accessible to him in their library. He now began to perceive a link between his own search for ultimate meaning through symbol and the possibility of a faith in the Absolute.[4] On 9 January 1944 he summarized his experience of the previous year in these terms: "A strange rich year. It began and ended with God, with prolonged assiduous meditation on the primitive and the savage. . . . It could be the most important year of your life so far" (*MV,* 270).

Pavese's metaphysical quest seems to have stopped short of a wholehearted religious conversion. His "assiduous meditation on the primitive and the savage" and his explorations of symbolic reality ultimately led him in a different direction. The countryside of Monferrato, especially the mountain of Crea, had an enduring effect on his imagination and sharpened his commitment to the exploration of mythic revelation. He later acknowledged the crucial impact of the period he had spent in the region: "Myth is a discovery you owe to Crea, to the summer and the two winters you spent there. The whole mountain is imbued with it" (*MV,* 280).

The study of ethnology and psychoanalysis had prompted Pavese to reexamine classical literature for the wealth of its mythological insights. He found in Vico the confirmation of his own intuitions on the link between myth and primitive psychology. In the novels of Thomas Mann he also found the idea that mythology is not an arbitrary set of esoteric images, but a timeless reflection of the human psyche. His growing interest in the classical world as the crucible of the European imagination heightened his appreciation of the city of Rome, to which he returned just after the war in order to reorganize a branch of the Einaudi publishing house. This was a difficult but busy period in Pavese's life. The memory of his friends who had died as members of the Resistance caused him considerable grief and uneasiness. While he earnestly devoted himself to new political commitments and professional responsibilities, he simultaneously began to work on what was to become his own favorite among his books: *Dialoghi con Leucò* (*Dialogues with Leucò*), a collection of lyrical meditations presented in the form of dialogues. The book was composed over a period of a year and a half and was published by Einaudi in 1947. This is stylistically and thematically the least accessible of all of Pavese's works, and was not a popular success. Nevertheless, he remained personally attached to it, choosing it for the inscription of his last words before ending his life.

Dialoghi con Leucò introduces characters borrowed from Greek and Roman mythology to discuss the existential issues closest to the writer's heart. This is the only one of Pavese's works that is not set in familiar contemporary locations and where landscape is dematerialized into metaphor. Narration is virtually abolished, and characters become merely the expressive outlet for a dense tapestry of ruminations and ideas. Pavese's dialogues differs in tone from his major model in the genre, Giacomo Leopardi's *Operette morali*. His purpose was not to set up a dynamic exchange of philosophical insights, but to provide a framework for the expression of his most pressing existential problems and anxieties.

It was in *Dialoghi con Leucò* that Pavese invested most of himself, emotionally and intellectually. He began this work during his relationship with Bianca Garufi, a fellow worker at the Einaudi office in Rome. The inclusion of the nymph Leucothea in the title dialogue of *Dialoghi con Leucò* was a calculated allusion to the Greek translation of Garufi's first name, Bianca, and several of the dialogues contain private references to the events of their passionate but short-lived relationship. This autobiographical dimension of the work has generally been ignored by critics.[5] Pavese attempted to disguise the highly personal, intimate nature of its inspiration through the device of classical characters and mise-en-scène. In a preface to the first edition of the book he offers a self-justifying explanation of the complex mythological apparatus: "Had it been possible, we would have done without so much mythology. But we are convinced that myths are a language, a means of expression; not arbitrary, but pregnant with symbols that, like all languages, have a special significance that can be expressed in no other way. . . . Here we have contented ourselves with Hellenic myths, in view of their understandable popularity at the present moment, and their immediate and traditional acceptability" (*MV,* 281).

Eugenio Corsini claims, however, that Pavese's recourse to the Greek context is explained by other reasons. While not denying that the primary inspiration of *Dialoghi con Leucò* sprang from Pavese's need to clarify his own myths, Corsini claims that Pavese's introduction of the ancient Greek world into this work was an attempt to endorse his personal quest with the seal of an indisputable heritage.[6] Despite its setting, *Dialoghi con Leucò* is as much a testimony to Pavese's decadent sensibility as to his classical heritage. His rereading of the ancient authors and his interpretations of the classical texts—even the work of Herodotus and Homer—were always shot through with the illuminations of a late romantic worldview.[7]

The dialogues can be divided into three groups.[8] The first of these groups is influenced by Pavese's rereading of Frazer's *Golden Bough* and deals with themes of the earth and of primitive life. These central motifs have already been reflected in the symbolic substructure of many of his earlier works: fertility, the harvesting of crops, ritual bonfires, and the tribute of bloodshed. The second group is more directly concerned with themes of classical mythology, and gives central focus to the struggle between the forces of the Titanic age and the order of the Olympian gods. These classical themes are mediated through the influence of Nietzsche and through Pavese's relatively recent study of the works of Kerényi and Philippson. A third group focuses on Pavese's own most pressing existential questions and seems to validate the rational, human struggle against the limitations of destiny and the pull of the instinctive. These three groups are not thematically as distinct as this schematization might suggest, for many of Pavese's most characteristic preoccupations recur consistently throughout the work.

Lorenzo Mondo has pointed out that two opposing conceptual positions can be gleaned in the *Dialoghi,* often coexisting within the same dialogue. On the one hand, there is the "mythological" thrust, which holds in high esteem the world of primitive, irrational energies, the period of childhood and early memories. Juxtaposed with this is the rationalist position, which upholds mature action, progress, the present rather than the past.[9]

Almost all the themes contained in *Feria d'agosto* recur in the dialogues, where the classical format is intended to bestow on them a timeless perspective. The motif that dominated *Feria d'agosto,* the difficult passage from childhood to maturity, emerges here also and is found in the central group of dialogues where it is transposed on a mythical plane into the passage from the Titanic world, characterized by chaos and irrational forces, to the era of the Olympian deities with its rationality and commitment to order. Essential to Pavese's delineation of the realm of the Titans—also referred to as the "monsters"—is his concept of the *selvaggio,* already elaborated in *Feria d'agosto.* This vision of unmediated instinctuality that survives as the basis for all existence is evoked in *Dialoghi con Leucò* with a degree of ambivalence, sometimes reflecting nostalgia for a lost era, and at other times implying a sense of horror and condemnation.

The characters who speak within Pavese's dialogues are most often minor deities or humans, although some of the major deities are also represented. Several of the characters express a yearning for the ancient instinctive universe. In "La Chimera" (The chimera), Sarpedon describes Bellerophon's lament for the time of the ancient monsters when men "could violate the limits," unlike the new age wherein he must wear the "bewildered look of one who is nothing any more and yet knows everything" (*DL,* 17). Similarly, in the opening dialogue, "La nube" (The cloud), Ixion, a youth not yet fully of age, protests at the idea of submitting to the limits imposed by the advent of the Olympian deities when he has been accustomed to living with the freedom of the natural elements.

The negative power of the instinctive world is encapsulated in the terrifying female figure who appears in "La belva" (The wild beast). In this and several of the other dialogues Pavese attempts to sublimate his intimate struggle with sexuality and misogyny through powerful mythic imagery. Endymion speaks of his meeting in trancelike sleep with "the cruel virgin, the one who goes by on the mountains." This frightening apparition "has no name" and "has many names"; it evokes the destructive, incomprehensible threat of the *selvaggio.* In his manuscript notes Pavese associates the beast-goddess with Artemis, who, strictly speaking, belongs to the Olympian rather than the Titanic world. Her image in this dialogue, however, is clearly linked with the overwhelming ferocity of the ancient monsters. Her power, like that of the entire world of the *selvaggio,* is against action, against rational or self-determined movement of any kind. She commands Endymion with chilling words: "You must never wake again . . . you must never act again" (*DL,* 53). Echoing the theme of misogyny in his earlier writing, Pavese describes the voice of the beast-goddess as "hoarse, cold, and maternal."

In "La madre" (The mother) Pavese presents an equally terrifying vision of irrational female power. Here the maternal relationship is described as an ancient link with cruel, primeval forces. Meleager—whose mother determined his death by deliberately placing a fatal brand in the fire—tells Hermes: "In everyone's flesh and blood the mother roars." His anguish is mixed with a tragic irony: "Hermes, you should have seen her eyes. You should have seen them from the time of my childhood, you should have felt how familiar they were, how they were fixed on my every move, my every gesture, for days, for years, until I felt sorry for her and was afraid to offend her." Hermes points out that the baffling cruelty of the mother's eyes is to be found in the eyes of all women: "And if you find these eyes again—and they are always to be found—the woman who has them is once more your mother. . . . No man can escape the destiny that has been marked for him by fire at the moment of his birth" (*DL,* 54).

Pavese portrays the world of Titanic powers as a realm beyond moral judgment. In "I ciechi" (The blind), Oedipus, still reigning as king of Thebes, asks the sightless Tiresias if the gods are to blame for his blindness. Tiresias tells Oedipus that too much importance is given to the Olympian deities, latecomers to the world, whose presence cannot change the nature of the "rock." A recurring image in these dialogues, the rock represents the world of the Titans, a place where death did not exist, where hierarchies were unknown. With the advent of the Olympian gods, language was invented and names were given to things. Things, in turn, became "words, illusion, menace." Altered by the word, the world now presented obstacles against the immediate experience of physical life, of the earth itself. Language created the possibility of moral interpretation. According to his understanding of the natural forces of the universe, however, Tiresias knows that if a child were to drown in a river in the course of his cheerful play, neither the child's death nor his pleasure should be attributed to the gods: "[They are responsible] for neither the one nor the other. Something has happened, which is neither good nor bad, something which has no name. Later the gods will give it a name" (*DL,* 21).

It is Tiresias who states that sex is the most ancient of the powers of nature and the essence of the Titanic world. Sex precedes morality and language. The conscious discovery of sex thus coincides with the difficult transition from the happy spontaneity of instinctive life to the painful understanding of maturity, a moment that is also linked with the awareness of mortality. The serpent is used here as a combined image of sex and death, in an obvious echoing of the Edenic myth: "When it flattens itself out on the earth, you have the image of sex. In it there is life and there is death" (*DL,* 22).

In "La strada" (The road) Oedipus reappears, blinded by now and wandering the roads of Greece with an anonymous beggar. His greatest lament is not that he had been deprived of his sight, but that he had no knowledge or control over his destiny: "I would prefer to have been the most wretched and pathetic man provided that I could have willed what I actually did." His query about human fate evokes the sense of determinism at the core of the Pavese's own deepest fears: "What are we if even the most secret desire of your blood existed even before you were born and if everything had already been said?" (*DL,* 66).

In contrast with the bitter regret of Oedipus is the attitude of the beggar who accompanies him on his perpetual wanderings. This man has abandoned everything, choosing to transform his life into a quest and a journey. His words to Oedipus reflect a heroic serenity: "And even if I didn't find the Sphinx and if no oracle spoke for me, I've enjoyed the life I had. You were my oracle. You have overturned my destiny. To be a beggar or a king, what does it matter? We have both lived. Leave the rest to the gods" (*DL,* 67). The beggar's destiny has thus become his wandering. His freedom lies in his willing acceptance of nakedness and poverty. Oedipus, too, begins to recognize the nature of freedom based on the pursuit of a personal destiny. The image of the road thus becomes an emblem of human endeavor, which Oedipus eventually acknowledges as "perhaps the only thing which is truly ours" (*DL,* 67).

Oedipus introduces the idea of the consoling power of language: "Certainly, when we speak, something is calmed in our hearts." The beggar adds: "Speaking helps us to find ourselves." These themes are connected with Pavese's conception of the power of poetry to bring "order where there is chaos." Language and poetry are thus the positive legacy of the Olympian age, of rationality and human maturity.

The anguish of man's powerlessness to determine the consequences of his own actions and desires is echoed in "Il lago" (The lake). The once mortal Virbius, who as the youth Hippolytus was saved from death and rendered immortal, finds that the timeless world into which he has escaped has its own unrelenting tedium. "I need a voice and a destiny," he tells Diana. "I ask to live, not to be happy" (*DL,* 109). The irony of his state is that he had unwittingly desired the fate from which he cannot escape. His story reveals a paradoxical futility: "Once, when I was still a boy, I thought I only needed to travel beyond the mountain, to keep on traveling, and that beyond the mountains, far away, where the sun went down, I would arrive at a child's land of morning, a land of hunting and eternal games. A slave said to me: 'Watch out for what you desire, little one. The gods always grant it.' It was this. I did not know that I wanted death" (*DL,* 107). This blind circularity of all human aspirations and endeavors forms the tragic core of *Dialoghi con Leucò*.

The concept of determinism is treated with an unexpected twist in Pavese's version of the Orpheus myth. In "L'inconsolabile" (The inconsolable) Orpheus recalls the crucial moment in which he was about to lead Eurydice out of the underworld: "We were climbing the path through the wood of the shades. The Cocytus, the Styx, the boat, the laments were already far behind. . . . I could feel behind me the rustle of her step. But I was still down there, and I still had this coldness around me. I thought that one day I was going to have to come back. That what has happened will happen again. I thought of my life with her, how it used to be. That one more time it would come to an end. What has been will be" (*DL,* 77). Because of his realization that he is doomed to repeat the same anguished path, Orpheus deliberately abandons his endeavor to rescue Eurydice. His journey to the underworld is thus transformed into a mission to claim his own destiny.

One of the most poignant meditations on human destiny is evoked in "Schiuma d'onda" (Sea foam) by the dead Sappho, who has been transformed into a wave for all eternity. Though her earthly existence had been a continual struggle of desire and suffering, the self-destruction she had sought at her own hand did not bring relief but only the tedium of unchanging, eternal awareness. Sappho, too, had realized that her poetry was a gift with which she could hope to transform the awareness of her destiny, but it had not been enough. It had not enabled her to transcend the torture of desire. She tells the nymph Britomartis: "I have never been happy. Desire is not song. Desire destroys and burns, like the snake, like the wind." Then, asked if she envies the apparently serene but unsmiling Helen of Troy, Sappho responds: "I envy no one. I wanted to die. To be someone else is not enough. If I cannot be Sappho, I prefer to be nothing" (*DL,* 49). The proud restlessness of her unrelinquished identity now makes it impossible for her to enjoy what Britomartis describes as the smiling life of eternity.

In *Dialoghi con Leucò* the finality of death is sometimes perceived as a form of freedom, to be envied even by the immortals. The perpetual, impassive smile of the gods—a recurrent image throughout this work—is a contrasting form of death, an eternal stasis. Perceived by humans as an image of the perfection to which they aspire, this smile corresponds to the annihilation of the individual self.

Pavese observed in his diary while writing *Dialoghi con Leucò*: "In these dialogues men would like to have divine qualities and the gods would like the qualities that belong to men" (*MV,* 306). What the gods envy most is the power of the imagination, the same power that enables humans to endure the limitations of destiny and mortality. Observing the unique irony of the human situation, Dionysus tells Demeter in "Il mistero" (The mystery): "All their richness is death. It forces them to strive, to remember and to make provision" (*DL,* 152). The transforming power of language is crucial in this human struggle with destiny. Dionysus describes the ability of humans to name things and to invent meaning and rhythm: "They have a way of enriching life by giving names to themselves, to things, and to us. . . . Wherever they expend their efforts and their words, rhythm, meaning, and rest come into being." To this, Demeter concedes: "They know how to give us names that reveal us to ourselves, and they snatch us from the heavy eternity of fate to give color to our days and to our landscapes" (*DL,* 151).

The power of language, illusion, and myth is also a major theme in "Il diluvio" (The flood). Here the Satyr describes to the Hamadryad the imaginative resourcefulness of humans in the face of the terror of mortality: "They know how to tell stories, these mortals. Their future lives will depend on how much their imagination has been stirred by the terrors of this night. They will be wild beasts, rocks, and trees. They will be gods" (*DL,* 159). The tree nymph, however, cannot understand the human need for illusion and self-deception. She asks the

Satyr: "Why can't they understand that it is in fact their fleeting mortal lives that make them precious?" While she is envious of the human experience of death, the Satyr reminds her that men, in turn, are envious of the immortals: "[Those humans] who live through a series of unforeseen, unique instants do not appreciate their value. They would prefer to have our eternity" (*DL,* 159).

If humans are envied by the Olympian deities, their peculiar mortal values also come to the attention of the Titanic forces. In "Le muse" (The muses), Mnemosyne tells Hesiod: "I love to be where men are, though I stay at a distance." As the source of memory dear to men's imagination, she discovers that she has been incorporated into the human process of self-discovery and self-construction. Hesiod confirms her unique importance, echoing Pavese's poetics of memory: "You give names to things, which make them different, unheard of, yet dear and familiar to us like a voice long silent" (*DL,* 164).

Continuing an age-old tradition, Pavese uses Odysseus as a symbol of mankind. This human hero conquers the attention of the immortal Calypso and Circe in "L'isola" (The island) and "Le streghe" (The witches). Calypso tempts him with the prospect of gaining immortality, with the possibility of abandoning earthly struggle for the tranquil stasis of eternity. But Odysseus, in his humanness, has recourse to an experience unknown to Calypso. He has the ability "to see a country and to shut his eyes to create illusions." In this lies the richness of the inner life of the imagination, unknown to the gods. The destiny of men is tempered with fantasy and poetry. Through the power of words, Odysseus manages one evening to share some of that inner life with Circe, who later recounts the experience to Leucothea: "He told me to sing, and singing I set myself at the loom and I turned my hoarse voice into the voice of his home and his childhood. I softened it, I became his Penelope." To Leucothea's question whether anyone laughed at this scene, Circe replies: "No one laughed, Leucò. That evening I too was mortal. I had a name: Penelope. That was the only time that I dared to look, unsmiling, on my fate and lower my eyes" (*DL,* 115–16). Man's advantage over the gods is most clearly articulated by Pavese in the figure of Odysseus, who towers in vitality and fantasy over the empty smile of Circe.

The process of writing *Dialoghi con Leucò* served its purpose in enabling Pavese to scrutinize his own myths and monsters. It provided him with no reassuring answers to his deepest existential concerns on the issues of destiny and free will, but it seems clear from several of the dialogues that it brought him, at least on an intellectual level, to a greater acceptance of his own humanness. This was perhaps why the book remained of such special importance to him.

Dialoghi con Leucò presents a peculiar mix of styles. There are moments when the language of the dialogues achieves a clear, unforgettable lyricism. Its underlying rhythm is based loosely on a ternary cadence similar to the early poems of *Lavorare stanca.* Other rhetorical devices also lend a distinctly poetic flavor, such as the use of assonance and refrain. The repetition of classical proper names throughout the work has a purely incantatory effect, giving prominence to music and rhythm over meaning. In contrast with the generally refined tone of the language in *Dialoghi con Leucò,* dialect structures are not absent even in this work. These function at specific moments to lighten the despairing bleakness of the existential themes.[10] Furthermore, a tone of ironic absurdity is also inserted in the short introductory notes to each dialogue. These introductions often undercut the tragic seriousness of the characters' subsequent pronouncements. The self-mocking sarcasm of the authorial comment on Sappho is the most extreme example of this strategy: "That Sappho was a lesbian from Lesbos is regrettable, but much sadder is the dissatisfaction that made her throw herself into the Aegean sea" (*MV,* 46). These stylistic variations not only contribute to the work's unique texture and rhythm; they also compound the difficulties of comprehension, a problem that Pavese was eventually forced to acknowledge and in which he took some stubborn satisfaction.

Chapter Six

Between Myth and History

From *Fuoco grande* to *Il compagno*

For the first two years of the postwar period, Pavese's writing reflects a marked degree of internal conflict and self-questioning. The work that he most valued and the one that occupied most of his attention during this period was *Dialoghi con Leucò,* but he was also involved in a number of other projects that seemed to lead in different, and sometimes opposing, directions. Though his imagination drew him increasingly toward the mythic, a sense of duty arising from his recent affiliation with the Communist party led him simultaneously toward political activity.

The first work to emerge during this period was a small group of love poems inspired by Bianca Garufi, written toward the end of 1945 and published under the title, *La terra e la morte* (Earth and death).[1] The poems are imbued with the allusive, mythic atmosphere also developed in the dialogues. Here, too, the female figure merges with the elements of nature, and has a mysterious, sphinxlike power:

> Hai viso di pietra scolpita,
> sangue di terra dura,
> sei venuta dal mare.
> Tutto accogli e scruti
> e respingi da te
> come il mare. Nel cuore
> hai silenzio, hai parole
> inghiottite. Sei buia.
> Per te l'alba è silenzio.
>
> (*P,* 168)

> You have a face of carved stone
> blood of hard earth
> you come from the sea.
> You gather everything, look it over
> and cast it away,

like the sea. In your heart
there is silence, swallowed
words. You are dark.
For you the dawn is silence.

Yet even within the context of this intimistic collection, a direct image of the bloodshed wrought by the recent historical struggle emerges in a short poem that begins:

Tu non sai le colline
dove si è sparso il sangue.
Tutti quanti fuggimmo
tutti quanti gettammo
l'arma e il nome.

(*P*, 169)

You do not know the hills
where the blood was shed.
All of us fled
All of us threw down our rifles and our names.

Then, in a few graphic strokes, the poem evokes the death of a resistance fighter and his subsequent transformation into a "blood-soaked rag." This violent image is charged, however, with an aura of myth that transcends the specific historical reference and is similar to the treatment of bloodshed and violence in *Dialoghi con Leucò*.

The most interesting outcome of Pavese's relationship with Garufi was the experimental novel they began writing together in the early months of 1946, each contributing alternate chapters corresponding to the point of view of a male and female protagonist. Though the novel was abandoned, still unfinished, some months later, it was eventually published by Einaudi in 1959 with the title *Fuoco grande* (Great fire). The chapters contributed by Pavese have an element of the mythic atmosphere he had developed in the poems of *La terra e la morte,* although there are also traces of a more flamboyant lyrical prose, reminiscent of the novels of D'Annunzio. The landscape against which this contemporary story unfolds is that of southern Italy, the ancient Magna Grecia, evoked here with greater sensual resonance than in *Il carcere.* Against this background the theme of the *selvaggio* emerges with great power, encapsulated in the premature death of a child and in the suppressed history of an incestuous relationship.

Silvia, the female protagonist, exudes—through the perception of her male counterpart, Giovanni—some of the mysterious elemental energy attributed to the woman of *La terra e la morte.* The theme of return—Silvia's return to her dying child and to her incestuous stepfather—has a particularly decadent poignancy in its implicit conjunction of sex and death. This work presents one of the most extreme statements of Pavese's thematic association of the rural world and the subterranean forces of violent sexuality. The device of alternating two separate first-person narrators gives the novel an effective contemporary ring and builds a rhythm of mounting tension and suspense, despite occasional lapses into mannerism. Although Pavese never stated why he abandoned the project of this novel in the early summer of 1946, it is easy to surmise that the increasingly strained personal relationship between Pavese and Garufi made further literary collaboration difficult if not impossible. It is also clear that, apart from the simultaneous composition of *Dialoghi con Leucò,* many other often conflicting concerns were demanding his attention.

In 1945 Pavese began to contribute articles of general cultural interest to the Communist daily *L'Unità* and the journal *Rinascita.* His essays voice the need for commitment, for moral renewal, and for a new humanism. "Ritorno all'uomo" (Return to man), published in *L'Unità* in May 1945, provides the first statement of his objectives: "Words are our craft. We say this without a trace of irony or hesitation. . . . Words are delicate things . . . and yet they are made for man, not man for them. It seems to all of us that we live in a time when it is necessary to restore words to the bare, solid clarity that they possessed when man created them for his own use." As if already anticipating the accusation of populism,[2] Pavese raises the issue of intellectual condescension immediately: "We do not go out toward the people, because we already are the people and nothing else exists. If anything, we go out toward man. Because this is the obstacle, the barrier to be broken: the solitude of men, our own solitude and that of others. . . . This new style is to be found in this" (*SL,* 198).

In "Di una nuova letteratura" (On a new literature), published in *Rinascita* a year later, Pavese describes the self-imposed isolation of writers and intellectuals in a passage that seems to echo a self-indictment:

> To attend to our work we have to isolate ourselves, and not only in the material sense. The effort we have to make to listen deep within ourselves tends to

destroy many bridges to the outside world and makes us lose the taste for sharing, for living together, for the cordial company of fellow humans. . . . Though the reason we did this was to begin to understand and possess reality with greater depth, the result is that we have enclosed ourselves in a fictitious world that rejects reality. (*SL,* 218)

Nevertheless, he expresses his reservations about the opinion that a writer must abandon his isolation in order to throw himself into the midst of active public life. For Pavese, a different kind of balance should be sought, since writers cannot be motivated simply by an abstract sense of duty ("no one makes love for reasons of duty or theory"). Here Pavese seems to be attempting to justify his aloofness from the demand for ideologically committed art, an issue that was to become of increasing importance. He betrays a hint of sarcasm in his allusion to the contemporary novelists who had moved away from a personal narrative style in favor of the aesthetics of social realism. In order to preserve artistic integrity, Pavese claims, "the novelist, poet, or 'worker of the imagination' must above all accept destiny and find harmony within himself" rather than follow externally imposed dictates (*SL,* 219).

These issues reappear in "Dialoghi col compagno," a series of four articles published in *L'Unità* from 1 May to 11 July 1946. The articles are structured as dialogues between Pavese and various working-class characters. Echoing his previous resolve to avoid the current vogue for fiction mechanically reflecting political ideals, Pavese tells his proletarian comrade: "In our job . . . we don't decide to write in a certain way, to speak for a certain class or for certain interests. We could do it, but that would be to sell ourselves, even if the buyer is indeed the working class" (*SL,* 227). Though the writer's work does not have to offer the direct reflection of a political position, Pavese claims that the writer's life must nevertheless be rooted in solidarity and action: "If the writer is a man of talent, he must at all costs want life to be better, happier and more just. He must make every effort not to stop at this simple need, and so he must work with others and take part in the struggle" (*SL,* 232).

These articles reveal numerous inconsistencies and ambiguities. Despite the repeated affirmations of the integrity and independence of his artistic interests, the condescending tone of the "Dialoghi col compagno" betrays a naive and miscalculated eagerness to please. Pavese's uneasiness in the active ranks of the PCI is all too apparent. An essay written soon afterward and published posthumously echoes the same uneasiness. Pavese begins the essay affirming his resolution to reject the pressure to write fiction with a marked sociopolitical content: "I doubt that I will paint large frescoes of society. I will not retell anyone's experience of prison or life underground" (*SL,* 221). He then evaluates—with more than a hint of self-justification—his own contribution over the years to the cultural resistance to fascism, pointing out that while many of his contemporaries were hiding out in the ivory tower of hermeticism, he was dealing in his poems and novels with "peasants, laborers, sand-dredgers, prostitutes, convicts, working women, and adolescents." The essay also alludes defensively to his earlier interest in American literature and emphatically denies an excessive American influence on his own fiction. Pavese concludes with a significant insight on his own creative history: "I am convinced of the basic and lasting unity of everything that I have written or will write . . . a unity of themes and vital interests—the monotonous stubbornness of someone who is sure that from the very first day he touched the true, eternal world, and there is nothing more that he can do other than go around the same great monolith, taking pieces off, polishing them, and studying them under every possible light" (*SL,* 223).

The same theme of creative "monotony," essential to Pavese's self-understanding, is repeated in his journal during the same period: "We have nothing in common with travelers, experimentalists, or adventurers. We know that the surest and fastest way of becoming awed is to stare fixedly at the same object" (*MV,* 282). Yet the same journal entry makes a statement about the noncognitive value of art that seems to contradict his claims in the newspaper articles: "Poetry is not a sense but a state, not understanding but being" (*MV,* 282).

Political ideology held no real interest for Pavese. During the same period his diary reveals a historical pessimism and a lack of trust in the humanizing possibilities of culture. This is in contrast with the confident tone of his simultaneous public statements. He felt that while human self-interest could be subsumed into dangerous national myths, it could never be exorcised by the illuminations of learning and culture. "It is stupid that some ethnologists think that one has only to bring the masses in contact with the cultures of the past and of the present for them to gain understanding and tolerance and for them to abandon racism, nationalism and bigotry" (*MV,* 283). In a self-critical letter written to a friend in November 1945, however, he confessed his shame in the fact that he had "to make an effort to listen to politics" (*L*, 508).

It was in this mood of ambivalence with regard to the burning issue of social and political involvement that Pavese embarked on writing *Il compagno* in late 1946. Pablo, the protagonist of this "political bildungsroman" (*L*, 146), narrates a story of precisely the sort that Pavese had denied, some months earlier, the need to tell. The novel, which is set in 1936 at the height of fascism, traces Pablo's gradual evolution from an idle lower-middle-class existence to active participation in the anti-Fascist struggle.

The first half of *Il compagno* is set in Turin and reintroduces many of Pavese's characteristic locations and social situations. Pablo appears at first to be a typical Pavesian protagonist, an aimless young man without any sense of commitment who feels a vague dissatisfaction with his life. Though he works occasionally in his mother's tobacco shop, he spends much of his time playing the guitar in the restaurants and taverns of the city's outskirts, a habit that has earned him his Spanish nickname, Pablo. The most important figure in his life at the outset is his friend Amelio, a confident, self-determined young man whom Pablo perceives to be the opposite of himself. Even after Amelio becomes paralyzed as the result of a motorcycle accident, his strength of spirit remains intact. At Amelio's bedside, Pablo meets Linda, a young Turinese dressmaker who was with Amelio the night of his accident. Gradually, Pablo succumbs to Linda's seductive charm and drifts away from his friend. Nevertheless, Amelio continues to hold an emblematic importance in Pablo's consciousness.

Though Linda seems at first to offer Pablo salvation through love, he is deluded when he realizes that she is also being pursued by Lubrani, a sly, middle-aged entrepreneur. The relationship between Linda and Pablo gradually collapses as Linda yields to the temptation of Lubrani's wealth and power. In these characters Pavese encapsulates some of the manipulation and petty ambition of Fascist society. Unable to bear the fickleness of Linda's behavior, Pablo finally decides to leave Turin.

The second part of the novel begins as Pablo moves to Rome, following the suggestion of Carletto, an anti-Fascist comedian whom he befriends. It is in Rome that Pablo begins to undergo a dramatic change. He takes a job as a mechanic at a bicycle shop and makes friends with a group of impoverished performers and actors. He then seduces his employer, Gina, a young widow who offers him a more steadfast affection than Linda. His growing awareness of political realities evolves through discussions with mechanics and truck drivers, and eventually through reading a bundle of political literature that Carletto gives him to get rid of. The encounter that leaves the deepest impression is with a militant Marxist, Gino Scarpa, a veteran of the International Brigades in the Spanish Civil War. From the conversations with Scarpa, Pablo begins to realize the shallowness of his own existence, and he decides to commit himself to the clandestine Marxist cause.

A brief reunion with Linda who makes a visit to Rome serves as a kind of temptation, testing his newfound dedication to a life of responsible action. Nevertheless, he is able to surrender his attachment to Linda. In the meantime, he learns that his old friend, the crippled Amelio, has been imprisoned for his involvement in anti-Fascist activity, and begins to realize in retrospect that Amelio had been politically active even before his accident. Pablo's subsequent imprisonment functions as the final seal of his ideological conversion. Unlike the use of the prison motif common in Pavese's other works, implicit in Pablo's incarceration is a stoic sense of purpose and commitment. The jail sentence raises Pablo symbolically to the level of his long-admired friend, Amelio. His eventual release is experienced as a true liberation, rather than as a lateral transfer (like Stefano's in *Il carcere*) into the ongoing imprisonment of an alienated existence.

Critics are unanimous in their appraisal of the superiority of the first half of the novel over the second half. It has been suggested that the novel fails in the second half because the setting is no longer the cherished city of Pavese's youth, but the unfamiliar and sentimentally neutral environment of Rome.[3] Yet this hypothesis is not altogether convincing. What creates the difficulty in the second part of the novel seems to be the attempt to transform the flawed Pablo into an unequivocally positive character.

Pablo's story is emotionally compelling only in the Turinese episodes where he is beset by insecurities, loneliness, and a nameless existential uneasiness. In these episodes the narrative acquires the full range of nuances characteristic of Pavese's prose. There is a keen sense of place, evoked through random allusions to the damp, foggy atmosphere of the city and its surrounding areas and to the nighttime haunts of Pablo and his companions. The narrative retains some of the mythic resonance of the earlier novels. In his passive restlessness and inability to find happiness in love, Pablo follows the usual inner path of the Pavesian protagonist. His struggle is conveyed with a sparse, incisive economy, without grand gestures or forced crises. With the onset of his political conversion, however, there is a marked change in narrative mood.

A foreshadowing of Pablo's eventual political direction is unobtrusively prepared in the first half of the novel, with a few unelaborated clues that allude to Amelio's activism and the introduction of Carletto, the anti-Fascist comedian. In the second half, as the subject of Pablo's changing consciousness moves into the foreground, the political theme becomes a dominant thread and is woven into the narrative with visible effort.

Pablo's growing political awareness is portrayed through his meetings and discussions with workers and militants. The orchestration of these scenes has a heavy-handed quality, with occasional stylistic lapses into propagandist cliché. Pablo suddenly develops a moral sensibility at odds with his history in the earlier part of the novel, and his insights—in their abruptness and precision—ring false. The characterization of Pablo loses emotional authenticity the more he is invested with the role of exemplary comrade. Pavese's forceful, virile personalities are credible only on condition that they retain a marginal position and do not occupy the psychological foreground of the narrative. While the figure of Amelio retains an incisive resonance, the transformation of Pablo into his mirror image seems absurd. Pavese's strength is not in the creation of strong personalities whose actions will carry forward the plot, but in evoking environments, atmospheres, memories, and moods in which the tensions of the flawed protagonist can be reflected without the need for narrative resolution.

Pablo's conversion lacks plausibility, since he comes to it in an intellectual way, by research and discussion. No economic deprivation or direct experience of exploitation led him to this moment, only a vague need for distraction from the wounds of sentimental rejection. It is a bourgeois conversion, springing from velleity rather than need. His sudden activism is also improbable since he is contemplative, rather than active by nature.[4] His dreamy digressions, stirred by the things in his environment—whether the smell of the sea or the taste of fruit—are always at odds with the outgoing militant mood he is supposedly in the process of acquiring.

There is an absence of genuine joy in Pablo's dedication to the class struggle, much as Pavese's own acceptance of political commitment was joyless and forced. It has been observed that although Pablo may believe himself to be a proletarian, "his gestures, his actions, his boring and ineffective manner of speech glaringly reveal the abstract intellectual roots from which he springs."[5] Pablo's ultimate discovery of his working-class identity is excessively idealized, as was noted by Giorgio Bassani in his negative review of this novel: "As for these quiet, proud, sober, independent, naturally refined, sentimentally pugnacious Communists, we must frankly admit that we never met them in Italy."[6]

Giorgio Bàrberi Squarotti has pointed out the intellectual tensions at the heart of Pavese's decisions to create a proletarian hero.[7] Like many middle-class intellectuals of his generation, Pavese romanticized the working class. *Il compagno* presents the world of the proletariat as an absolute metaphor of the positive—as a source of deliverance from all unrest and discontent. According to classical Marxist understanding, however, this romantic image of the proletariat is problematical, since the working class is by definition oppressed and in need of liberation.

In *Il compagno* Pavese's tendency to portray the Manichean dichotomy between good and evil is transferred from spirit and matter to an opposition of bourgeois and proletarian forces, of fascism and Marxism. This reflects in a starker and less nuanced tone the dualistic opposition of the ancient monsters with the forces of reason and light in *Dialoghi con Leucò.* There is an implicit correspondence between the metaphor of the bourgeois world with its corruption and exploitation in the novel and that of the Titanic powers in the dialogues. It is significant that in both works the exorcism of the old powers is carried out through the use of reason and language. Once again Pavese proposes the rational process as the only salvation in the face of evil. Pablo achieves his change of consciousness by means of an intellectual conversion, without any direct emotional experience of poverty. It is not surprising that his commitment to the class struggle remains a purely cerebral endeavor. As Doug Thompson suggests, Pablo's involvement in the anti-Fascist cause "does not extend as far as the humanity that it must embrace if it is to have a truly progressive meaning in the history of mankind."[8] The memory of the absent Amelio, now his comrade in the struggle, provides a rare note of emotional resonance in the novel's concluding pages.

This connection with Amelio, which attempts to provide a narrative link with the earliest part of the novel, is ambivalently charged and seems to belong to some other level of the discourse than the purely political. Amelio's full significance in his friend's consciousness is not clear. The scene, early in the novel, in which he offers to show Pablo his maimed legs has a certain sexual ambiguity, which is more striking, however, in Pavese's earlier draft of this novel. This ambiguity is echoed in reverse later on through Pablo's allusions to Gina's masculine ways. His devotion to Amelio's memory, coupled with the residual suggestions of that early scene, provides an interesting counterpoint to the evolution of the misogynistic themes in the novel.

The motif of feminine infidelity is dominant in *Il compagno.* Linda, the Turinese woman who breaks Pablo's heart, constitutes the liveliest characterization in the novel. She is invested with the function of sexual betrayal, an almost compulsory component in Pavese's fiction.[9] It should be noted, however, that Linda's betrayal of Pablo was preceded by Pablo's own betrayal of Amelio, and it is the memory of Amelio that is dominant in Pablo's mind at the end. The exorcism of the pain of betrayal is achieved by Pablo through his dedication to the abstract notion of Man, while he maintains his misogynistic attitudes to the end. His feelings toward women are decisive: "That evening I knew that women didn't matter" (*C,* 115). "What Linda shouted at me—that for me a woman was only a plaything—was really true" (*C,* 122).

An interplay of reversed mirror images has been noted in the two parts of *Il compagno.*[10] Thus Rome becomes the specular opposite of Turin, and Pablo's behavior there is the reverse of his behavior in Rome. In the hard-working city of the North he is idle, selfish, and ill-at-ease. In Rome, a city he finds dominated by an atmosphere of laziness and leisure, he becomes industrious and politically committed. Similarly, the worldly, feminine Linda is the specular opposite of Gina, the hard-working, independent widow who offers herself unconditionally to Pablo in Rome. While Pablo and Amelio are opposites in the first half of the book, they begin to resemble each other in the second half. Thus Pablo's guitar, his ubiquitous prop in the early part of the novel, is eventually replaced with books, a motif reminiscent of the description of Amelio on his sickbed, surrounded by newspapers and notes.

Pavese was not completely satisfied with the style of *Il compagno,* criticizing its asthmatic phrasing and its jagged progressions, which he compared to "an electric charge" (*MV,* 322). There are too many disparate energies at work in the novel. The first half promises to go in the direction of an existential tale, but the second half becomes an exemplary parable of political conversion. The psychological rhythm of the concluding half of this novel is unlike that of Pavese's other works, in that it develops in a steadily optimistic direction, leaving the protagonist in the final pages substantially altered in a positive way by his experiences. The more typically Pavesian novel, however, builds an ebb-and-flow progression, exploring the protagonist's existential state, describing some of his transformations, but ultimately leaving off in much the same way as the story began.

There are elements even in *Il compagno* of keenly evocative power, reminiscent of the prose of *Feria d'agosto.* Such, for example, is Pablo's description of his first sight of the sea on a trip to Genoa. But these moments are more frequent in the novel's first half than in the second. Also more dominant in the first half is the use of the leitmotiv of Linda's silk scarf, emblematic of the woman's elusive feminine charm. The recurrent use of this image acquires a mythic function and is one of the few examples of the image-story technique used by Pavese in this novel.

The major stylistic triumph of *Il compagno* is its mastery of dialogue, wherein the nuances of a psychological situation are captured through the non sequiturs, silences, and evasions typical of ordinary conversation. Echoes of dialect and of popular speech are present in these dialogue sequences, though the use of dialect is excluded from Pablo's narrative.

This novel constitutes Pavese's only sustained attempt to produce ideologically committed art. It was, however, a novel that pleased virtually no one, least of all his comrades on the Left. After this experience Pavese became aware more than ever of his limits and strengths, of the "monotony" of his deepest inspiration, and he went on to explore his mythic insights in the great novels of his artistic maturity.

La casa in collina

La casa in collina (*The House on the Hill*), one of Pavese's most powerful and enduring novels, was written between September 1947 and February of the following year. It was published in 1948 along with *Il carcere* in a single volume with the title *Prima che il gallo canti* (Before the cock crows). This collective title refers obliquely to the themes shared by both novels: the painful inability to relinquish isolation and self-interest in the face of the struggles of others, and the lonely remorse of the uncommitted.[11] Both novels draw to some extent on Pavese's personal experiences during fascism and the war, and reflect in their protagonists a similar unwillingness to join in the active Resistance movement. But whereas *Il carcere* is set in the relatively tranquil environment of political detention in the South, the action of *La casa in collina* unfolds in war-torn Piedmont between the summer of 1943 and the autumn of the following year, incorporating allusions to the fall of Mussolini, the armistice, the establishment of the Salò Republic,[12] and the escalation of the Partisan struggle.

This is the first time that Pavese attempted to deal directly in his fiction with the overwhelming violence of recent history. Yet even in its first paragraph, the documentary potential of *La casa in collina* is modified by the mythic nuances of Pavese's vision and style: "Even in the old days we used to mention the 'hill' as we might have talked about the sea or the woods. I used to go back there in the evenings from the town when it grew dusk, and for me it was not simply a place like any other; it represented an aspect of things, a way of life" (*PG*, 97). The novel thus opens with the hills—specifically the hills above Turin—and ends with the hills of the Langhe, the birthplace and final refuge of the narrator. This cyclical movement, along with the insistent recurrence of the image of the hill throughout the narrative, provides a clue to layers of meaning beyond the purely documentary.

La casa in collina has continually been discussed in terms of its historical content, and has been described on the one hand as "one of the few great novels that the Resistance inspired"[13] and on the other as a "betrayal of the Resistance."[14] But Pavese's inspiration in writing the novel was not motivated by documentary intentions or political ideals. After *Il compagno* he had permanently abandoned the attempt to write purely ideological fiction. The perspective on the war in *La casa in collina* is filtered through the sensibilities of its introspective protagonist, a self-confessed coward, who, perhaps by virtue of his position as an uncommitted outsider, ultimately comes to contemplate the futility of bloodshed and the tragic loss of life on both sides. Pavese's refusal to exalt the Partisan martyrs over the Reppublichini in his depiction of the Resistance was a point of controversy for many of his comrades on the Left.[15] By now convinced that ideology cannot justify terror, he conveyed that vision in the novel, risking incomprehension and the hostility of his critics. At a time when it was easier to divide the world into heroes and villains, Pavese chose to create a protagonist who reflected his own complexities and self-division and his own ambivalence in the face of commitment.

Corrado, the narrator of *La casa in collina,* is reminiscent of Corradino, protagonist of "La famiglia"—an unpublished story written in 1941 that served as a rough sketch for much of this novel. Central to the development of the earlier story was the crucial dilemma of Corradino's relationship with Dino, his unacknowledged son, a dilemma that reflected the broader issues of isolation and human commitment. Although "La famiglia" lacked a political-historical dimension, *La casa in collina* combines the central existential questions of the earlier work with the motifs of political struggle and historical powerlessness. This historical dimension is evoked through a vision of bombings, deportation, and bloodshed, and is juxtaposed with the immutable, subterranean powers of the hill.

As the novel begins, Corrado has moved to the Turinese hills to escape the air raids in the city, while still commuting to the city school where he works as a teacher. In his new lodgings his needs are taken care of by Elvira, a middle-aged spinster who treats him with a mixture of maternal solicitude and repressed erotic desire. Corrado resists the woman's attachment, preferring the company of his dog, Belbo, and the wild but familiar presence of the surrounding landscape. Corrado has a natural vocation for solitude, and the circumstance of war have provided him with an alibi for his living apart from others: "All the war did was to remove the last scruple I had about living alone, consuming the years and my own heart" (*PG,* 98). His exploration of the uncultivated areas of the hillside offers him not only a respite from the war-ravaged city but also inspires the retrieval of early memories. It is thus in this landscape, pulsating with the hidden forces of the *selvaggio,* that he calls into being his lost childhood identity, creating a curious psychological split reminiscent of "Colloquio del fiume": "I was rediscovering myself as a boy in order to have a companion, a colleague, a little son. . . . We were alone together, the boy and I. I relived the discoveries of the old days" (*PG,* 99).

Even in the hills, however, Corrado cannot avoid human contact. Among a group of evacuees from the city he discovers Cate, a woman he had broken up with some years earlier when her emotional demands had become too much for him. With Cate is the seven-year-old Dino, whom Corrado realizes may be his own son. Though dreading the truth of his responsibilities, Corrado befriends the boy, while Cate—aware of Corrado's self-centered weaknesses—refuses to confirm the child's paternity. Cate has grown from the awkward girl of Corrado's memories into a strong, responsible adult who challenges him with some ruthless insights into his deficiencies as a human being.

As the clandestine Resistance begins to form after the official fall of Mussolini, Cate and her companions associate themselves with the Partisans. Corrado, with customary diffidence, remains aloof, though he recognizes that the war had finally invaded even his cherished hillside domain. After the arrest and deportation of Cate and others, he takes refuge in a monastery at Chieri, where Dino is also offered sanctuary. There is a brief moment when he hopes for the deliverance offered by religious faith, though he acknowledges that his motives spring from the deepest cowardice: "I wanted . . . an anesthetic, the certainty of being well hidden. I didn't want the peace of the world, only my own peace" (*PG*, 185). Eventually he realizes that his physical safety is not assured even in the monastery, and he decides to risk the long journey home to his native hills in the Langhe. In the meantime Dino has run away to join his friends in the Resistance.

Corrado's path back to the hills of his birthplace is a vision of horror. Along the way he witnesses the infernal destruction of war and contemplates the dead on both sides—Partisans as well as the soldiers of the new Fascist republic—with equal terror and dismay. The sacred landscape of his childhood memories has become a theater of death. Although he has always known that the "ancient indifferent heart of the earth" broods under the surface of the hillside, there is no escaping the violence wrought by men. The landscape will eventually absorb the bloodshed and continue its timeless existence, but Corrado cannot escape his own limited humanness, his mortality and subjection to the domain of time and history. He is thus forced to relinquish the quest to retrieve his lost childhood and its illusion of oneness with the instinctive, indifferent forces of the hills. Yet he achieves, through the surrender of illusion, the ability to feel compassion.

The story is narrated by Corrado from the temporal standpoint of the ongoing war. Though he has by now arrived at his parents' house in the Langhe, he no longer believes in the possibility of a completely safe refuge. The comments in the present tense that interrupt the story at various intervals are generated from this narrative moment, located sometime during the autumn of 1944. It is significant that Pavese chose to set the entire story within the span of the unfinished war, evoking on a symbolic level Corrado's enduring powerlessness over both the violent forces of history and his own yearning to recapture the timeless domain of childhood.

La casa in collina has often been perceived as Pavese's most autobiographical work, not in its depiction of specific events but in its evocation of Corrado's existential struggle. It has been suggested that this novel offers more intimate self-revelation than even *Il mestiere di vivere.*[16] Corrado is clearly the narrator closest to Pavese's own temperament to emerge up to this point, and is developed with greater compassion and complexity than the two earlier "intellectual" protagonists, Stefano, the narrator of *Il carcere,* and the anonymous narrator of *La spiaggia.* Corrado reflects Pavese's perennial conflict between the need for human commitment and the desire for solitude; between misogyny and the striving for love; between his metaphysical yearnings and his ambivalent attempts at political involvement. It has also been pointed out, however, that Cate, Corrado's sharpest critic in the novel, is also invested with a marked autobiographical component.[17] Her harsh comments on Corrado's passivity and aloofness echo much of Pavese's merciless self-flagellation in *Il mestiere di vivere.* Yet Cate is not simply the abstract expression of Pavese's ruthless superego. She also possesses the vivid autonomy of other positive female types, from the vignette of Deola in *Lavorare stanca* to the sustained portrait of Clelia in *Tra donne sole.*

Despite the underlying elements of autobiographical inspiration, *La casa in collina* avoids the psychological focus of a confessional novel. Corrado's existential journey, from an illusion and isolation to ultimate clarity and compassion, is narrated in a series of symbolic connections and mythic intimations. Pavese's mastery of the technique of symbolic realism is the culmination of the experiment he embarked upon with the prose of *Feria d'agosto.* The psychological tensions are fused with mythic themes in a more successful sublimation than was achieved in *Dialoghi con Leucò* or even in *Feria d'agosto.*

The dialectical tension at the heart of almost all of Pavese's works is evident here also. It is no longer embodied in the facile juxtaposition of Fascist and Communist offered in *Il compagno.* The antimony here springs from within its protagonist's consciousness and is reflected in the juxtaposition of the hill and the city; childhood and adulthood; the world of being and the world of doing and becoming. The ideas expressed theoretically in *Feria d'agosto* have a richer, more poetic development here, especially the theme of the yearning for return to the state of instinctive life. Although the reexamination of childhood memories as a reservoir of personal myth is proposed by Pavese as a desirable epistemological process, the attempt to re-create that reality through a surrender to the raw energies of nature is implicitly condemned as a moral taboo.

The motif of the *selvaggio* recurs insistently throughout the novel. In the opening chapter Corrado alludes to its mysterious presence in the hills: "Behind the tilled fields and the roads, the human dwellings, under my feet, the age-old, indifferent heart of the earth brooded in darkness, lived in hollows and among roots, lurked in hidden things, in the fears of childhood" (*PG,* 99). It is in contemplating the sky that Corrado habitually glimpses this "age-old indifference" of the powers of nature. In a short scene with distinct Joycean echoes, he steps away from an animated discussion on the war in order to savor the emptiness of the night sky: "I was lost for a moment in contemplating the stars and the void above. The same stars of my boyhood. The same stars that were shining on the city and on the trenches, on the dead and on the living" (*PG,* 172).

The sight of the sky also serves as a trigger for the juxtaposition of historical events with the timeless realm of nature in an early scene, rich with thematic allusions:

> I arrived at the spring in the hollow grown over with muddy, lush grass. Patches of sky and airy slopes appeared in the gaps between the trees. There was a frothy, almost brackish smell in the cool air. What did the war matter, I thought. What did blood matter with this sky and these trees? You could run around here, throw yourself in the grass, play at hunting and ambushes. This is the way that snakes, hares, and boys lived. . . . Only in the woods nothing changed, and where a body fell new roots flourished. (*PG,* 126–27)

The images in this episode are of central importance. The setting itself is a typical theater of the *selvaggio*, with its humid, overgrown seclusion reminiscent of "Nudismo" in *Feria d'agosto.* Here, in the wildness of the woods, the body of a war victim would gradually merge with the earth, providing nourishment for new roots. This is the setting that provokes in Corrado the temptation to surrender to the forces of nature, to return to the instinctive state of childhood, undistinguishable from animal existence. In his flight toward the hills of his childhood, Corrado later lives "the way that snakes, hares, and boys live." The image of the hare recurs repeatedly from this point forward.

Corrado's desire to escape from the war, from history and from the world of adult existence, is always connected with the desire to fuse with nature, to merge with animal life, or to become a child again. After the first account of his personal terror, Corrado observes: "I would like to have been a root or a worm to go deep underground" (*PG,* 146).

Later, another variation emerges: "I would like to have disappeared into hiding like a rat. Animals, I realized, did not know what was going to happen. I envied them" (*PG,* 163). But it is the image of the boy, closely linked with the emanations of the *selvaggio,* that dominates in Corrado's final moment of self-awareness at the novel's conclusion. And here too, the regression to childhood identity is connected with the sight of the sky, symbol of the abyss: "I realize now . . . that I lived only in a state of prolonged isolation, a useless vacation. I was like a boy who, in the middle of a game of hide-and-seek, finds a comfortable spot among the thicket and starts to watch the sky through the leaves, forgetting to come out again" (*PG,* 215).

In these passages the themes of *Feria d'agosto* reappear: the link between a vocation for solitude and the desire to surrender to the abyss of prerational life, always associated with childhood and the untamed wildness of the landscape. This yearning for fusion with nature and for a symbolic return to the womb of the Earth Mother is at the heart of the Corrado's quest. Its corollary is his social and political detachment, isolation, misogyny, and this refusal to enter into adult relationships of responsibility or affection. He is eventually able to recognize the futility of his quest, not through the rational accusations of Cate or through his own corrosive sense of remorse, but through the purgatorial journey to the heart of his own myths.

As Corrado approaches the Langhe hills at the end of his difficult journey back to his origins, he gradually realizes, witnessing the devastation all around him, that the place he was attempting to rediscover—the timeless, immutable domain of his earliest experience—no longer exists. Although he knows implicitly that he must now surrender his illusion, the old yearning endures, which Pavese suggests with the uterine symbol of the closed room: "For me it was strange and unacceptable that fire, politics, and death should overturn this past which was mine. I would have liked to find everything as it was before, as in a locked room" (*PG,* 203).

In the light of Pavese's earlier statement on the necessity of discovering personal myths in order to destroy them, the novel's conclusion takes on a specific moral meaning. Corrado's attempt to return to his origins and to reimmerse himself in the experience of childhood leads instead to the awareness of his unclarified internal myths and of the realities of his contingent history. It forces him in the process to acknowledge the futility and self-deception of all his previous existence. Yet his final meditations yield no facile resolutions and are shot through with a sense of nihilism and self-alienation. This is suggested by the image of the split self, reminiscent of the split self in the novel's opening chapter:

When the encounters and events of this past year begin to haunt me, I bring myself to ask: "What have I in common with that man who fled from the bombs, the Germans, his own remorse and sorrow?" It is not that I don't feel a twinge when I think of the dead, when I think of the nightmarish sights fleeing on the roads like dogs, I even tell myself that there hasn't been enough yet, and in order to get the horror over with, we the survivors should thrust ourselves into it, creating even more bloodshed. But it happens that I . . . already feel like someone else. I feel detached, as if everything that I did, said, or suffered had happened already, that it was in fact someone else's business, was already past history. (*PG*, 215)

Though the novel concludes with Corrado's heightened awareness of historical events, his compassion for the victims of the war, and the surrender of his illusions, it does not attempt to negate the importance of the archaic forces of the mythic and the unconscious in human experience. On the contrary, the intimations of a realm beyond the immediate world of events remains an enduring part of Corrado's journey toward self-discovery.

On two occasions Corrado comes across the confirmation of mythic time, of a cyclic calendar based on repetition and return. The first revelation of this kind occurs in the cloister in Chieri where he takes refuge from the war, exchanging "the woods for the sacristy." While exploring the contents of the priests' breviary, he discovers in the age-old liturgy of the Holy Office a vision of historical horror subsumed into ritual and myth. This mythic remembrance is a daily part of the collective life of the priests:

In [the breviary] I read about feast days and saints: every day had its own saint. I deciphered terrible stories of suffering and martyrdom. There was the story of the forty Christians thrown naked to die in an icy pool, whose legs were broken first by the executioner. There was another one about women flogged and burned alive, of tongues cut out, intestines removed. It was surprising to think that the yellowing pages of that ancient Latin text . . . could contain so much convulsive life . . . and so much bloodshed, cruel, yet up to date. (*PG*, 191–92)

Father Felice, the priest who befriends Corrado, seems to have gained, through this continual contact with the world of myth, a sense of practical detachment from the events of the war: "'It's a lot of nonsense,' he would say. 'It's manure this land needs, not bombs'" (*PG,* 186). The priest's explanation of the necessary monotony of the liturgical readings is also revealing: "Life is summed up in the cycle of the year. . . . The Catholic liturgy accompanies the year and echoes the work of the fields" (*PG,* 192). Yet he has an acceptance of violence as an inevitable part of human experience that seems astonishing to Corrado: "I envied him because I realized that he did not differentiate between this mortal peril and an earthquake or any other catastrophe" (*PG,* 186–87). By denying the importance of linear time, ritual experience heightens the awareness of a metaphysical reality.

In a second, much briefer episode, Corrado finds another manifestation of mythic time. Coming across a Carnival scene in war-torn Turin, he is amazed that "there were still people who were willing to travel about, to whiten their faces and parade themselves like that" (*PG,* 178). The Carnival is a symbol and celebration of the eternal cycles of nature between death and rebirth, suggesting a cyclical calendar that ignores the vicissitudes of historical events. Its key emblem, the mask or painted face, is linked with primitive rituals of exorcism and magical protection. Thus in the ruins of the city, this strange festive sight moves Corrado to contemplate the imminent renewal of spring: "Up on the hill under the sodden leaves, surely the first flowers were about to appear. I promised myself to look for them" (*PG,* 178).

The complex relationship between Corrado and Dino is linked with the novel's mythic substructure, with its emphasis on the theme of yearning for instinctual, prerational life. Corrado looks to Dino as a symbol and substitute for his own childhood self. In the novel's opening pages, before his first encounter with Dino, Corrado converses with this other self, describing it as a "little son." It is in relation to this lost self that the roots of his difficult struggle with others, with women, with political commitment, and with the Absolute are found. The symbolism of his return to his native hills is only another form of the journey back to that younger, primal self, a journey whose paradoxes become explicit only in the concluding chapter.

In *Feria d'agosto* Pavese had condemned the quest to re-create the instinctive world of childhood in order to achieve the annihilation of consciousness, rather than the clarification of myth. Though Corrado, almost from the beginning, implicitly identifies Dino as his son, he succeeds through a series of deliberate obfuscations and hesitations in refusing to accept that certainty. His self-deception is so effectively evoked through the narrating consciousness as to confuse many of

Pavese's critics. Corrado does not want to be a father. His entire inner direction—up to the end of his journey to the Langhe—is not toward the responsibilities of adulthood, but toward the rediscovery of the childhood self. Ironically, it is the child Dino who manifests the responsibility and protectiveness associated with the paternal role. It is Dino who protects Corrado's identity during their stay at the monastery and who later leaves for the hills to fight in the Resistance. This incident has no "realistic" or documentary function. In a child of seven or eight, Dino's sense of commitment seems utterly implausible. His actions are the symbolic projection of what the adult Corrado, trapped in his intimate quest for the past, is unable and unwilling to carry out.

Corrado discovers in the course of his journey that there is no possible refuge into prerational timelessness in the face of human events. Finally disabused of the intimate illusion that motivated his existence, he is consumed with remorse for his lack of solidarity and participation. He can find no lasting peace: "I conclude that to be alive by chance is not to live at all. And I ask myself whether I have really escaped" (*PG,* 182). Yet it is clear that Corrado does not believe that his participation in the war could have changed anything. Through his journey of self-discovery he has come to realize that the perennial world of nature and the time-bound reality of history are not as distinct as he had imagined. The bloodshed lurking within the domain of nature, the hillside, the *selvaggio,* is the inevitable legacy of men as well, and it is doomed to repeat itself, over and over, in human history. It is a part of human destiny. This pessimistic Nietzschean insight is also at the heart of *Dialoghi con Leucò,* in its vision of the overwhelming, irrational forces of the world bent on an eternal cycle of destruction and recreation.

With this novel Pavese attains mastery of his distinctive use of symbolic realism. Through the recurrence and accumulation of apparently realistic detail, Pavese weaves a rich web of embedded symbols. This can be observed, for example, in the delineation of Corrado's relationship with Elvira, which though sketched in with the utmost economy, has a vivid resonance and power. There is almost no description of the house where Elvira lives with her mother and where Corrado takes refuge from the bombings, apart from a recurring allusion to the "fresh white curtains" on the windows. In this image a whole world is evoked, a world of genteel hypocrisy and sterile conventionality. As a counterpoint to the curtains, another image comes into play: the scarlet flowers that Elvira grows in her garden. To Corrado the flowers have an obscene quality and he is unable to give them a name, despite his training in biology. They function in the narrative to suggest Elvira's suppressed eroticism: an eruption of the *selvaggio* within a closed, middle-class world.

The use of dialogue within *La casa in collina* provides, with its psychological incisiveness, a realistic counterpoint to the more allusive language of the main narrative. Through the conversations between Cate and Corrado, Pavese is able to convey some of the complex tensions unacknowledged in Corrado's consciousness as narrator. He also uses dialogues in a more conventionally documentary way, to bring alive the various responses to the war among the people in Corrado's setting.

With the experience of *La casa in collina,* where autobiographical tensions are exorcised and subsumed into mythic patterns, Pavese reached a degree of artistic integrity he had never achieved before. At the completion of this novel, he realized that his experimental stage was over and that he had at last found his own authentic narrative voice.

Chapter Seven

The Search for Destiny in the Final Novels

Il diavolo sulle colline

Pavese wrote *Il diavolo sulle colline* (*The Devil in the Hills*) between June and October of 1948. He was simultaneously engaged in setting up a new series of ethnological and anthropological publications at Einaudi, a project that had grown directly out of his personal interest in myth. Mythic themes have an essential importance in this novel and are interwoven, as always, with Pavese's deepest existential preoccupations. He explores here the already familiar issues of human freedom and limitation, the difficulties of innocence and the possibilities of salvation and survival, against a broad canvas of characters and social situations, so that the result is more eclectic and diversified than any of his preceding work.

The action of the *Il diavolo sulle colline* focuses on the discoveries of three male students during a crucial summer vacation as they pass from the innocence of youth into the knowledge and experience of adulthood. All three protagonists incorporate some autobiographical elements, though they are superficially distinguished from each other by virtue of temperament and social background. Pieretto, a skeptic and an iconoclast, is a city-dweller through and through. Oreste, the most ingenuous and socially inexperienced of the three, belongs to a farming family and lives in a rented room in Turin while studying medicine at the university. The anonymous narrator is also of rural stock. Though born and raised in the city, he cherishes some early memories of vacations in the countryside.

The story opens as the three friends embark on the pursuit of diversion in Turin and its suburbs at the start of summer. During a late-night ramble in the hills they encounter by chance a dazed young man, obviously under the influence of drugs, whom Oreste recognizes as Poli, the son of an upper-class family with a large estate not far from his own home in the country. The students are drawn to the mysterious youth, whom they discover to be a cocaine addict, and they accompany him to some of his customary haunts in the city. Poli introduces the three to Rosalba, his clinging, pathetic mistress, who soon afterward shoots and injures her lover and eventually kills herself with an overdose.

After Poli's hospitalization, the three friends are separated for a short period as Oreste returns to his village, and the narrator spends his days boating on the Po, first with Pieretto and later, less happily, with a woman. Apart from obvious themes focused around the central personality of Poli, Pavese introduces many themes in this expository section that take on greater significance later in the novel: the contrasting polarities of work and leisure, the importance of landscape, nudity, and misogyny. In the boating sequences the narrator establishes his delight in sunbathing. With a few brief comments, he reflects on a theme that gradually emerges as a crucial concern in the narrative: "Sitting in that boat I developed a taste for the open air and came to realize that the pleasure we get from water and earth is something that comes from the far side of infancy, from the far side of a garden or an orchard. On those mornings I began to think that all life is like a game beneath the sun" (*BE,* 113). The perception that "all life is like a game beneath the sun" foreshadows the three protagonists' subsequent fascination with the instinctive and the unconscious, and their temptation to explore the limits of human behavior. "The far side of infancy" and "the far side of an orchard" correspond to the primal stage of human existence as well as the primitive, untamed forces of being. It is the rational Pieretto who recognizes the danger implicit in the surrender to the pleasures of water, earth, and sun: "If you lived this sort of life every day . . . you'd become an animal" (*BE,* 114). And it is also Pieretto who indicates the link between the summer landscape and the decay of mortality: "There is nothing that smells like death more than the summer sun . . . the brightness of the light, the exuberance of nature. . . . Nature is death" (*BE,* 114).

The middle section of the novel shifts to the hilly landscape of Oreste's youth, where Pieretto and the narrator come to stay at their friend's home. The world of Oreste's family is modest and hardworking, in harmony with the needs of the land and the cycle of the seasons. Rather than attempting to help with the tasks of the farm, the three friends escape every day to a secluded hollow among the hills where they bask naked in the sun. This sunbathing ritual, which becomes a kind of pantheistic communion with nature, rapidly takes on an obsessive importance and is implicitly juxtaposed with the practical world view and untiring labor of Oreste's immediate family. The most significant episode of this central section is the visit of the three friends to the isolated farm of Oreste's cousins, Davide and Cinto, an environment even more rugged and genuine than Oreste's village.

After this brief, idyllic encounter with peasant life, the three young men learn that Poli has returned to his villa on the Greppo hill. It is here, on Poli's neglected, overgrown estate, that the rest of the novel unfolds, as Oreste, Pieretto, and the narrator come to stay with their wealthy friend and discover the seductions of a decadent environment. Almost immediately after their arrival, Oreste embarks on a flirtation with Poli's alluring wife, Gabriella, and a sense of unspoken tension begins to build. Yet the languid life at the villa progresses as usual with drinking sessions, outings, and long discussions of a pseudophilosophical sort. A near-accident occurs during a shooting party, echoing hidden hostilities, but no one is injured. Finally, after an all-night orgy, initiated by a group of visitors from Milan, Poli begins to spit up blood. Gabriella, who until now seemed to despise her husband, rushes faithfully to his side, brushing off Oreste and the others. Liberated from the spell of the Greppo and its occupants, the three friends return to the sanity and tranquillity of Oreste's village.

Though the final section of the novel has recognizable echoes of F. Scott Fitzgerald, whose work Pavese admired, the basic preoccupations of *Il diavolo sulle colline* are more closely related to *Feria d'agosto* and *Dialoghi con Leucò* than to the influence of the American novelist. The image of the hill appears in this novel in four different configurations: the hill overlooking Turin where Oreste rediscovers his childhood playmate, Poli, now a cocaine addict; Oreste's own native hill with its carefully cultivated fields and vineyards, testifying to generations of hard work; the Mombello hill where Cinto and Davide lead an apparently Edenic existence; and finally the Greppo hill, the demonic landscape of Poli's family estate where nature has been allowed to annihilate the toil of past generations, and whose dominion is death.

The thematic polarities characteristic of Pavese's work are expressed in new variations here. The contrast between work as a redemptive rational activity and unrestrained leisure as a death-inducing surrender to instinctuality receives its strongest statement in this novel. But the usual attributes of country and city are reversed. Here the cultivated countryside represents civilization and rationality and is envisioned as the repository of positive values. Conversely, the city—identified here and in the next novel with the idle upper classes—represents the negative pole, a descent into the hell of the *selvaggio.*

Unlike the image of the rural life in *Paesi tuoi,* where the peasants have been brutalized by their closeness to nature and their instinctive devotion to the needs of the land, this novel offers instead an idealized view of the conquest of nature by the hardworking discipline of farming people. Pavese's evocation of the rural world is at its most lyrical in the middle section of this novel. His idealization of peasant life is carried to an extreme, however, in the episode of the visit to Oreste's farming cousins, Cinto and Davide. The encounter with these two rugged peasants provides an important counterpoint to the subsequent scenes on the Greppo hill:

> [We did] the rounds of the house and the vineyards, and ate some *polenta* for lunch, catching a glimpse of women and children in the shadows. The room had a low ceiling and was as rustic as a stable. As we stepped outside we saw a cloud of starlings swoop up over the oak-dotted fields. Beside the stable there was a well, and Davide pulled up a bucket of water, plunged a bunch of grapes into it, and told us to eat. Pieretto was sitting on a log and laughing like a child. He kept on talking with his mouth full. (*BE,* 144)

The characterization of Pieretto in this short scene contrasts sharply with the argumentative skeptic who appears elsewhere in the novel. He has been momentarily transformed by the pastoral atmosphere of the Mombello farm. This is unmistakably Pavese's personal vision of paradise. The work of the farm has been done, the land is fertile, and the wine is good. Women serve in the background, never emerging to assert demands of their own, while the men eat, drink, and laugh together in an Arcadian landscape with the carefree innocence of children. Introducing a contrapuntal note, Oreste tells his cousins about Poli's shooting by Rosalba, while the narrator immediately observes the incongruity of this topic within the pastoral setting: "I realized as I listened that the story . . . seemed improbable and out of place. What could it have in common with that wine, that land, those two men?" (*BE,* 144).[1]

A different physical and moral environment presents itself on the Greppo estate, whose occupants seem committed to the pursuit of the irrational through the rituals of orgiastic festivity. Here, in the absence of rational human effort, the landscape has been abandoned to the wildness of nature. Though the state is overwhelmed with weeds, brambles, and climbing vines, its exoticism has a sinister allure. This atmosphere of decay is heightened by climatic circumstances, creating an impression of overwhelming obscenity, which prompts Pieretto's comment: "'The countryside in August is indecent. What's the meaning of all these seed pods? There's a smell of sex and death. And what about the flowers, the animals in heat, the ripe heaviness of pulp?'" (*BE,* 166–67).

Even before their arrival at Poli's villa, the three young men had already been searching for the atmosphere of permissive abandon embodied in the lush, overgrown landscape. Their eventual seduction by the mysterious powers of the Greppo is foreshadowed in the description of their sunbathing ritual in the hills near Oreste's farm:

> In the humid heat of the hollow I saw the glare of the sky and felt the earth tremble and hum. I thought of that notion of Pieretto's that the scorching countryside beneath the August sun makes you think of death. He wasn't mistaken. . . . That thrill we got from being naked there and being conscious of it, from hiding away from the gaze of others, from sunbathing till we were black as tree trunks, has something sinister about it, more bestial than human. In the high wall of the fissure I saw roots sprouting and filaments like black tentacles: the inner, secret life of the earth. (*BE,* 130)

This attempt to fuse with "the inner secret life of the earth" through exposing the body to the sun was previously explored by Pavese in "Nudismo" and "Mal di mestiere" and suggests a Nietzschean reunion with the Earth Mother. In these earlier meditations in *Feria d'agosto,* the self-destructive, death-invoking aspect of this temptation is implicitly condemned. Sunbathing is likewise presented in *Il diavolo sulle colline* as a drug—like Poli's use of cocaine—whose function is to explore the limit, to push behavior beyond the boundaries of convention, to risk breaking taboos in order to discover the deepest, primal self. This theme of transgression is a dominant element in the spiritual journey undertaken by the three protagonists.

It is Poli who explicitly articulates the yearning to transgress all limits and to reach the bottom. His self-destruction is presented almost as a religious quest, and is linked with the concept of *il fondo* ("the bottom"): "When everything is lost you find yourself. . . . There is an innocence . . . a clarity that comes from the bottom. . . . This innocence is what I am looking for. The more I know it, the more I am convinced that to be weak is to be human" (*BE,* 108). Poli seeks innocence through degradation, the divine through the diabolical. Here, as elsewhere in Pavese, there is a confusion between the search for the Absolute and the pursuit of the limits of human behavior. The lure of the depths is irresistible and is equated with the power of the primeval Earth Mother. For Poli, this path is sought through cocaine and the annihilation of rational consciousness. The pursuit of the lowermost depths is, however, fraught implicitly with danger. It is a journey from which one risks not being able to return, hence Rosalba commits suicide—in the wake of her obsessive attachment to Poli—and Poli surrenders eventually to tuberculosis.

It is significant that during the initial drug-influenced posturing of Poli in the hills above Turin, the young man claims to feel like a god. Pavese incorporates in this fantasy an age-old vision of human pride attempting to transgress mortal limits by laying claim to divine powers. *Il diavolo sulle colline* contains other similar religious references as well as several allusions to the concepts of sin, damnation, and salvation. Poli's function as Tempter on the hill overlooking the city has obvious scriptural echoes,[2] which in turn hark back to an earlier Hebrew tradition where the image of the "high place" is associated with the orgiastic excesses of Canaanite worship. The final orgy with which the sojourn on the Greppo ends is presented as a kind of black Mass and includes the mock worship of an image of Poli, a substitute for the devil. *Il diavolo sulle colline* has been described as an inverted parody of Dante's journey through the various phases of Limbo, Purgatory, and the Earthly Paradise (Turin, Oreste's village, and the Edenic vision of Mombello), culminating with the infernal sojourn on the Greppo estate.[3] Yet despite echoes of popular and literary eschatology, the real devil in Pavese's novel is not a conventional diabolical incarnation but the pull of the *selvaggio*: the eternal, irrational legacy of primal instincts. *Il diavolo sulle colline* evokes a spiritual struggle that ultimately owes more to Nietzsche and D'Annunzio than to Dante or the Christian tradition.[4]

The dominant themes in the novel thus reveal a marked affinity with the preoccupations of the decadent tradition. Pavese attempted to offset this focus, however, by inserting an explicit note of social consciousness. This results in a certain stylistic unevenness. The didacticism of the narrator's comments on Poli's neglected estate springs directly from Pavese's need to superimpose on the novel a contemporary note of class criticism: "The desolation, that isolation on the

Greppo hill was a symbol of [their] mistaken way of life. They did nothing for their hill and the hill did nothing for them. Their savage waste of so much land and so much life could not bear any fruit other than anxiety and futility. I thought back to the vines at Mombello and the rugged face of Oreste's father. To love a piece of land you had to work it, to sweat over it" (*BE,* 168).

The moralistic tone of this passage and the subsequent descriptions of bourgeois decadence led several reviewers and critics to treat this novel primarily as an attack on the moral degeneracy of the upper classes.[5] Pavese was aware of this interpretive trend from the time of the earliest reviews and did not discourage a discussion of the novel in these terms. Perhaps attempting to win the approval of friends on the Left, he insisted that *Il diavolo sulle colline* was conceived as the story of a conversion to social consciousness. His claims, however, are unconvincing, as can be seen in his defensive response to the harsh appraisal of the novel by his former teacher, Augusto Monti. Pavese wrote to Monti: "*Il diavolo sulle colline* is a youthful hymn to the discovery of nature and society, where three youths see everything as wonderful and only gradually come to realize the squalor of that futile world: a certain bourgeois world that achieves nothing and that believes in nothing" (*L,* 686).

It is difficult to identify in *Il diavolo sulle colline* the theme of redemptive revelation to which this letter alludes. Pavese's three protagonists finally depart from the degenerate environment of the Greppo estate not out of a sense of moral indignation but because of the intervention of Poli's tubercular attack. The tensions accompanying their seduction by the world of Gabriella and Poli prevail right to the end. The ambivalent sense of attraction and repulsion that consistently characterizes their response to the wealthy class may, in fact, reflect Pavese's own ambivalent feelings toward that class, a difficulty he did not openly acknowledge.[6] It is significant that the bourgeois Gabriella, who functions in the novel as a kind of Circe, casting a spell on the three youths and encouraging their moral degeneracy, remains one of the most charmingly drawn female figures in the entire Pavesian repertoire.

Despite Pavese's own retrospective claims, the moral vision that pervades *Il diavolo sulle colline* is not simplistically laid out along class lines. At moments in the novel the image of the bourgeois world appears as a convenient metaphor for corruption and decay, but the patterns of culpability and retribution have more to do with the familiar mythic tensions between work and indolence, between rationality and bestial abandon, than with the contrast between different social worlds. In this way the novel reflects the same morality articulated some years earlier in *Dialoghi con Leucò.* The economy of justice within *Il diavolo sulle colline* dooms Poli to death not simply because of his social class, but also because of his immaturity in surrendering to the domain of the irrational. According to a comment made by Oreste's father, the choice of responsible commitment to work and cultivation had been made by Poli's grandfather, during whose time the Greppo hill was fertile and flourishing.

Pieretto, Oreste, and the narrator are not innocent victims of diabolical power exerted by the wealthy Poli. Their moral world was not significantly different from that of their wealthy friend to begin with. In an early scene in the novel this similarity is made explicit: "Pieretto went on to explain that Poli did nothing worse than what we were already doing. Uprooted and middle class as we were, we spent our nights on park benches making conversation, had sex with whores, and drank wine. He had other means. He had drugs, freedom, and classy women" (*BE,* 98–99).

Bàrberi Squarotti has offered a convincing critique of the lack of realism in Pavese's description of the bourgeoisie, which, in his view, "is merely a metaphor [which does not seek to establish] a precise truth about local or provincial life."[7] These observations opened up the critical response to *Il diavolo sulle colline,* which is now interpreted more as a symbolic projection of Pavese's intimate existential problems than as an allegory of social corruption.

It seems clear that Pavese was attempting in this novel to sublimate his own terror and conflict surrounding the issues of death, solitude, and sexuality. Yet he diluted the power of his deepest insights by interweaving the polemical note regarding class consciousness and by limiting psychological impact through the creation of three protagonists rather than one. Furthermore, his device of introducing major existential issues in the dialogues between the characters is not as effective as he thought it was (*MV,* 321). These "student discussions," which delighted the author, now seem dated and overblown. The observations made by Poli, Oreste, Pieretto, and the narrator—on subjects ranging from religion to suicide, from drugs to the forces of nature—sometimes seem to parody or trivialize passages in *Il mestiere di vivere* and *Dialoghi con Leucò.* Poli's self-dramatizing disquisitions on addiction and spirituality offer no original illuminations. In this novel, far from exorcising his internal ghosts, his terror of the common destiny of solitude and death, Pavese intellectualizes them in a heavy-handed manner, with the result of compounding the unresolved tensions and paradoxes at the heart of the novel's inspiration.

Tra donne sole

Tra donne sole (Among single women)[8] was written between March and June of 1949. It was published later that year in *La bella estate,* a volume that also included the 1940 novella *La bella estate* as well as *Il diavolo sulle colline,* and which won for Pavese the coveted Strega Prize. While still in the process of writing *Tra donne sole,* Pavese described it as "a great novel" that attempted to explore the "false, tragic world of the upper class" (*MV,* 334). Unlike *Il diavolo sulle colline,* it is set almost exclusively within the city. *Tra donne sole* constitutes the final dissolution of the city as a positive image in Pavese's work. With greater consistency than in *Il diavolo sulle colline,* Pavese explores civilized society in *Tra donne sole* as the repository of the brutal forces of instinctive life, of the *selvaggio.*

The novel opens with the return of Clelia, the thirty-four-year-old first-person narrator, to her native Turin after an absence of many years. She arrives at the height of the Carnival season with the task of setting up a Turinese branch of a Roman fashion house. Clelia, a self-made woman, has risen from humble origins in the back streets of Turin to a successful career as a couturière. She is a solitary, independent individual who checks into her hotel alone, deliberately ignoring the insistent ringing of the telephone and abruptly dismissing the chambermaid's attempt to engage in conversation. She eventually emerges from her room to investigate a noisy scene in the corridor outside her door, and witnesses a young woman being carried away on a stretcher. The girl, unconscious and still wearing a party dress, has attempted to kill herself with an overdose. The pathetic figure of this unknown woman introduces the theme of death in contrast with the surrounding festivity, a juxtaposition repeated throughout Clelia's account of her return to the city of her youth.

Clelia is soon introduced into the social circles of the Turinese upper classes, a world that has become accessible to her only by virtue of her professional success. It is in this milieu that Clelia meets Rosetta, the woman who had attempted suicide in the hotel. Rosetta belongs to a bourgeois family and enjoys all the benefits of a privileged existence.

Clelia also becomes acquainted with some of the other women in Rosetta's circle and most importantly with Momina, a hard-edged, cynical woman, with whom Rosetta had had a sexual relationship some years before and who now seems intent on pushing Rosetta beyond the limits of her endurance. Despite the demands of her work, Clelia accompanies Rosetta, Momina, and their friends on a frenzied hunt for amusement and pleasure. She also makes a brief attempt to establish contact with an old friend in the run-down neighborhood of her childhood, and discovers that communication with the people from her past is no longer possible. Yet life with the elegant Turinese social set does not intrigue or satisfy Clelia. She observes the shallowness and cruelty of her upper-class acquaintances and the meaningless eccentricity of the artists they patronize. As Rosetta gradually sinks into despair, neither Momina nor Clelia try to help her but seem to condone her suicidal temptation. Clelia drifts away from these friends as she is forced to become more involved in the problems presented by her work. Eventually, she enjoys a brief erotic adventure with Becuccio, the foreman in charge of renovating the interior of the fashion salon. By the time she reestablishes contact with Momina, Clelia discovers that Rosetta is dead.

The action of the novel thus spans a brief period of reprieve from the moment of Rosetta's first failed attempt to kill herself to the time of her actual death some weeks later. In its progression from attempted suicide to successful suicide, the narrative reflects the circular pattern characteristic of Pavese's fiction. This circularity is reinforced through the insistent repetition of related themes and motifs. From the opening paragraph, the image of festivity predominates—the garish, essentially ambivalent face of the Carnival season. The opening image of ritual celebration and diversion is echoed throughout the novel in several allusions to parties, receptions, and outings, including a theatrical presentation. Some of these images are suffused with intimations of death. Clelia's personal memories of the Carnival season include this ambivalent association, because of the loss of her father during childhood at the height of the pre-Lenten festivities. For her, the sight of the colorful Carnival booths inevitably brings to mind that important death many years before.

The climactic episode evoking the link between festivity and death is the grotesque party given by the artist, Loris, "to celebrate the death of his second period." The ritual is staged in mock solemnity with a coffin and lighted candles. Just as the party in *Il diavolo sulle colline* was followed by Poli's surrender to his fatal disease, this party is followed by Rosetta's final surrender to the temptation of suicide. Pavese's presentation of the theme of *festa* against the backdrop of high society is in sharp contrast with his vision in other works of the joyful festivities of the peasant world. Divorced from the rhythms of cultivation and harvest, from the notions of tribute and fertility, the social celebrations of the idle elite reveal only emptiness and morbidity.

The whole of life is conceived in this novel as a shallow performance. The motif of playing a part, of making existence itself an artifact, is inherent in many elements of the narrative. A sense of artificiality prevails. Interiors and clothing are presented in a manner that suggests their function as props and costumes. Clelia is aware that her cherished fur coat functions as a mask in the necessary game of social mobility. From the early scene at the party of the aging dowager, Donna Clementina, it is obvious that the society that grants Clelia social access will never accept her as an equal. Although she may wear the clothes of an upper-class woman and play that role for amusement, she knows that in the eyes of everyone she will always be a mere dressmaker.

The themes of work, artifice, and performance are inextricably interwoven here. Clelia is an achiever, a woman committed to the process of self-realization through work. It might seem that this is her most authentic attribute, but this too is a game. As a fashion designer, her function is to create the costumes that will affirm the privileged status of the rich. Her specific task in establishing a local branch of the Roman fashion house is to supervise the creation of an elegant interior, full of mirrors and ornamentation: a make-believe set designed to entice her clientele. Despite her surface image of self-sufficiency, Clelia is not as independent as she seems, being subject to the whims of her boss in Rome, the moods of her architect, Febo, and the eventual economic power of the clients. She is in fact trapped within that make-believe world that creates the promise of her freedom.

While still in the midst of the task of setting up the salon, Clelia articulates an amusing, if provocative fantasy to her newfound wealthy friends. According to Clelia, it is her upper-class friends who should go to work as clerks at the new fashion house. When asked who would then provide the clientele, Clelia slyly answers that their servants could play that part. This age-old device of exchanging roles between master and servant—achieved through a change of costume—is one of the central practices of the traditional Carnival. Here the concept functions as a deft link between the motif of Carnival and Clelia's deep realization that her social mobility is merely an illusion and a masquerade.

Another related motif is that of prostitution. Clelia claims that she would prefer to design clothes for prostitutes, since prostitutes work for a living. Instead, she is obliged to dress wealthy women who for diversion might attempt to masquerade as prostitutes. In a bizarre scene, Clelia's elegant women friends are led by their escorts to a bar facing a brothel in a lurid Turinese neighborhood. Here the men play a guessing game to determine which of their women friends could most easily pass for a whore. Meanwhile, as a backdrop to this odd ritual, a Carnival image briefly reappears: "Just before . . . we had seen a stand in the street with a little man in white selling *torrone* and chestnut candy" (*BE*, 324).

The recurrent motifs of diversion and performance reinforce the absence of authentic feeling in Clelia's world. A sense of incurable solitude pervades all her relationships, including the two erotic interludes described in the course of the novel. In the first of these episodes, the architect Febo sexually assaults Momina and Clelia in a hotel room and meets with only minimal resistance. The scene is evoked in a few rapid strokes, bringing into focus above all the irritated indifference of the two women, and concluding with Clelia's sarcastic comment to Febo: "Now will you let us sleep?" Clelia's adventure with Becuccio, though not without tenderness, has a similar hollow ring. It seems above all a game. Clelia and Becuccio put aside their hierarchical roles as manager and foreman for one unrestrained encounter, and then immediately revert to their previous positions in an almost perverse performance of detachment and indifference. Becuccio, though a Marxist, knows the rules of the game. He observes the conventions of middle-class decorum by returning to the formal manner of address. Later, when Clelia invites him to a party with her friends, he declines with the excuse that he does not circulate in elevated social circles. Thus even Becuccio, the only positive character in the novel apart from Clelia, plays out a role—involving a strange blend of middle-class manners and proletarian politics—right to the end.

Rosetta is the only one of Clelia's Turinese friends who expresses the need to reject the games imposed by her milieu. Like Poli in the previous novel, she appears to have a yearning for the Absolute. Yet, unlike Poli, Rosetta will not attempt to reach the depths of self-degradation in order to affirm an ambivalent purity.[9] Her death is at one level a protest against the unauthentic, make-believe world she sees around her. In spite of this, even her suicide seems contaminated by the conventions of that world. There is something theatrical about the manner in which she choreographs her death, renting an empty artist's studio with a window conveniently facing the Superga hill, the emblem of her unresolved yearning for peace and spiritual detachment. Before Rosetta's suicide Loris, her artist friend, had staged a death scene, complete with coffin and candles. In her posture seated alone in the empty studio, facing the hill and the sky, she is simply offering a more refined, aesthetic version of the macabre tableau already created by Loris. This is one of the most Pirandellian moments in Pavese's work, where life appears to imitate art.[10] Not long before Rosetta's death, Loris had made explicit allusion to this intermingling of life and art: "I like that fantasy of reality in which the situations seen in art spill over into life. Where the personal element begins doesn't interest me" (*BE,* 241).

Though Clelia is at a distance from Rosetta's drama, it provides an important element in the experience of her return to her native city, and it is mainly through her contact with the younger woman that she embarks on the "discovery of herself and of the emptiness of her world" (*MV,* 334). Rosetta, in her unspoken quest for the Absolute, her intolerance for the savage pettiness of supposedly civilized life, and her unresolved feelings for Momina, leaves no exit open other than self-destruction. Though she claims that she was unaware of the motives for her first suicide attempt in the hotel, it is clear that her friends regard self-destruction as Rosetta's ineluctable destiny. Their irritated reaction to her first failed attempt also reveals a certain pragmatic acceptance that Rosetta was about to accomplish a necessary act. In Loris's studio, these friends complain that they feel inhibited in staging a theatrical performance about death with Rosetta present, and observe: "If Rosetta had really died, [the play] could be done. . . . that stupid one should have got on with it, it would have been better" (*BE,* 240). Appalled by this callous perception of Rosetta's destiny, Clelia reiterates the theme of make-believe: "I'm used to hearing scandals and petty stories of Roman society in our store, but this talk among friends that a third friend hadn't managed to kill herself got to me. I almost thought that the performance had already begun and that everything happening was invention as in the theater" (*BE,* 241). The black humor of Loris's circle regarding Rosetta's compulsive vocation for suicide is finally echoed in Momina's ultimate announcement to Clelia of the young woman's eventual death: "That stupid girl has gone and killed herself again" (*BE,* 328).

Though Clelia does not share the callous attitudes of Rosetta's friends, the despair that she witnesses in Rosetta is ultimately beyond her comprehension. Clelia's experience of solitude and her understanding of destiny are different. She has attempted to solve the problem of alienation through the quest for worldly success and has learned to tolerate compromise and renunciation. She has come to accept the necessity of a self-protective isolation: "I told myself that if I wanted to do something or get something out of my life, I should not tie myself to anyone or depend on anyone" (*BE,* 216). Her return to the neighborhood of her youth is not motivated by the desire to break that isolation through human contact, but simply to measure how far she had come. For Clelia, "the greatest thing about the tenement courtyard was to compare it with [what she had achieved] now" (*BE,* 244). She had nevertheless cherished a secret fantasy of receiving admiration and recognition from the people of her past: "I had told myself so often during that time that the goal of my life was in fact to succeed, to become someone, to return one day to those alleys where I had been a child and to enjoy the warmth, the wonder, the admiration of those familiar faces, of those little people" (*BE,* 253). She discovers, instead, that "the faces of those little people had disappeared," and she receives no welcome. Nevertheless, Clelia's encounter with her childhood playmate Gisella is the source of important revelation, and enables her to contemplate the distinction between ambition and destiny.

In watching Gisella—now a gray, faded presence—Clelia realizes that change cannot be willed and that she herself is as powerless over her destiny, her ultimate identity, as the nervous, embarrassed woman before her. Here Pavese's familiar note of determinism emerges as Clelia confronts the immutability of fate: one is what one was, and one is obliged to repeat the models learned in the beginning of life. Clelia observes in Gisella's gestures and expressions the mirror image of the old woman who had taken her in as a girl: "I saw Gisella behaving like the old woman. . . . The old woman had made Gisella in her own image" (*BE,* 253). At this moment Clelia begins to suspect the superficiality of her own apparent autonomy and success, and wonders if she too has become the mirror image of her mother. She asks herself if even her own most characteristic attributes ("my ambition, my mania for doing things on my own, for managing without others") were simply the unconscious replication of her mother's example (*BE,* 254).

The immutability of destiny thus provides the thematic counterpoint in this novel to the evasive games, the shifting masquerades of social convention. Clelia finally confronts the futility of all ambition, realizing that "you often obtain things at a point when they are no longer of any use" (*BE,* 253) and that "you achieve things when you can get along without them" (*BE,* 301). Ultimately, Clelia has returned to Turin not to enjoy the reassurance of her worldly success but to reconfirm her destiny of solitude and to confront her limits. Clelia lives without myths. She had substituted for myth the fantasy of worldly success only to come face-to-face with the limitations of that self-deception. Of all of Pavese's works this is the most resigned. In Clelia, Pavese created the figure of a survivor, of an individual who can propel herself forward by means of discipline and determination. Her story is essentially one of renunciation, since her life will never be more than mere survival, and the luxuries that she has won—the furs, the outings, the pleasure of summoning and dismissing men as she needs them—are hollow consolations.

All three of the main female characters—Clelia, Rosetta, and Momina—are to some degree autobiographical. Unlike the three protagonists of *Il diavolo sulle colline,* however, they represent dramatically contrasting aspects of their author's personality. Clelia's odyssey from the shabby neighborhood of her youth to the fashionable establishment she is setting up in the heart of the city is an obvious parallel to Pavese's own progress from humble beginnings to the height of literary success. As with Pavese, there is a melancholy element to Clelia's sense of achievement, manifest in her occasional doubts that getting there was worth the effort. Her ambivalent attitude toward the upper class—vacillating between contempt and stifled envy—is also typical of Pavese, as Calvino pointed out in his comments regarding this novel and *Il diavolo sulle colline.* But, most of all, Clelia resembles the author in her ability to propel herself forward, to work, to achieve, to maintain a practical, disciplined rhythm, regardless of her doubts and disillusions. Rosetta, on the other hand, in her disgust with life and her longing for peace that only death can offer, expresses a different aspect of the author's psyche. It is Rosetta, not Clelia, who is an avid reader of books and who has studied at university. Yet these cultural and intellectual resources are of no value to her (or ultimately to Pavese) in the ongoing struggle with existential despair. Even Momina, one of the harshest characters in all of Pavese's works, is reminiscent of the author. Her dislike of people, her rejection of sex, the relentless cruelty she manifests toward Rosetta, all echo the tone of self-hating abuse that emerges from time to time in Pavese's diary. The interaction between these three characters provides a powerful psychological tension in the novel. It is Momina's destructive negativity that dominates, however, and that eventually contaminates Clelia. As a parable of Pavese's inner drama, as a reflection of his deeply divided self, *Tra donne sole* has no equal among his other works of fiction.

The most remarkable quality of the style in this novel is its cold clarity and economy. The emotional impact of the events is carefully measured and controlled. This restraint gives the narrative a remarkable tension and power. The conversations have a lighter, more vital rhythm here than in the previous novel, and falter only when Pavese tries too hard to illustrate through them the themes of social corruption among the privileged classes of postwar Turin. Here, as in the previous novels, Pavese succeeds in bringing dialogue to life through the use of hesitation, elipsis, and silence.

Pavese's female narrator is credible within the totally artificial world that the novel constructs. Nevertheless, his attempts to draw attention to her femininity seem self-conscious and forced.[11] In the process of finishing the novel Pavese himself began to doubt the strength and credibility of his characters and wondered, in a diary note, whether he had "been playing with clay figures or miniatures" (*MV,* 336). Yet he also knew that the peculiar genius of his narrative was not in the conventional practice of creating forceful characters. He observed in the radio interview given two years later, speaking of himself in the third person: "Pavese is not concerned with the creation of characters. Characters are for him a means, not an end. They are useful to him only in the construction of intellectual fables whose theme is the rhythm of events" (*SL,* 266).

Tra donne sole owes its compelling rhythm neither to the psychological impact of its narrator, nor even to the gripping existential dilemma of Rosetta, but to Pavese's familiar technique of recurrent images and symbols—his "poem-story" technique. Thus, as the result of the narrator's repeated references, Clelia's fur coat acquires emblematic weight of its own, including the suggestion—indicated by Calvino—of a hairy male body. Rosetta's extravagant blue evening dress, on the other hand, finally reveals itself as a shroud. Beccuccio's leather armband, through rhythmically repeated allusions, builds up the suggestion of a modest, authentic existence. Likewise, the figure of a cat, which appears at several moments throughout the narrative, acquires a vital role in the end, as the messenger of Rosetta's death. These recurrent images weave the narrative from scene to scene, unobtrusively at first, yet finally revealing a mythic rhythm.

La luna e i falò

La luna e i falò, Pavese's final novel, is his most complex work of fiction and is considered by the majority of critics to be his greatest. While his ideas for this work were still in gestation in the summer of 1949, Pavese wrote to his friends, Adolfo and Eugenia Ruata, announcing with undisguised elation that he was about to begin "the construction of a modest *Divine Comedy*" (*L,* 659). Several visits to Santo Stefano Belbo that year helped him to rediscover his affinity for the landscape of the Langhe and to sharpen and define the vision that was to emerge in *La luna e i falò.* Pavese wrote the novel in a surge of energy that autumn, perhaps already sensing that it was his last. Some months later, on the title page of the copy of the first edition that he presented with a note of dedication to his old friend Pinolo Scaglione, he wrote: "This is probably the last book I shall ever write."[12]

Anguilla, the protagonist and narrator of this final novel, is sharply reminiscent of the heroic cousin in the early poem "I mari del Sud"—a middle-aged man who has returned to the landscape of his childhood after years of wandering throughout the world. The account of Anguilla's return to the hills of the Langhe after a prolonged absence provides the framework of *La luna e i falò.* The events of this visit are interlaced with discoveries, memories, and meditations on the past, thus weaving a rich tapestry of scenes from different moments in time that are assembled in a subjective, nonchronological sequence.[13]

La luna e i falò resembles *Tra donne sole* only in that both novels are the story of a return to the places of childhood and a discovery through that return of the sources of identity, illusion, and destiny. Whereas *Tra donne sole* is set almost exclusively within the city, the countryside dominates in *La luna e i falò.* A spatial counterpoint to the rugged hills of the Langhe is provided, however, in Anguilla's memories of the vast, inhuman landscape of America. Like *La casa in collina,* this novel is set within precisely defined historical perimeters. The framework of the story, recounting Anguilla's return to the Langhe, unfolds in the summer of 1948. From this temporal vantage point, Anguilla evokes scenes from his childhood, adolescence, and early adulthood and some episodes from his American experiences. He also learns of the events that had occurred in the Langhe during the wartime struggle for the liberation of northern Italy through the account of Nuto, his only surviving childhood friend. This revelation of violence finds echo in the present, since in the course of Anguilla's short stay in the village, tragedy erupts again, revealing the cyclic pattern of irrational forces that transcend human understanding.

Despite the vividness with which Pavese evokes a precise period in recent history and the distinctive features of a rural community in Piedmont, the novel has a timeless, legendary atmosphere at odds with this documentary dimension. Through the nonlinear presentation of scenes from different moments in the past, related to each other by virtue of internal echoes, similarities, and repetitions, an evocative cadence is set up. The thematic importance of Anguilla's return is echoed on the structural level through the repetitive circularity of the narrative. The various progressions back and forth in time suggest the ineluctable repetitiveness of natural events.

Anguilla's journey back to the Langhe is motivated by a quest for identity and roots. His attachment to the countryside of his youth is an ambiguous one, since he was abandoned at birth and was raised as a ward of the state by an impoverished peasant family in a village some distance from where he was found. Though unaware of the precise location of his birth, he feels the necessity of claiming that landscape as his own: "I came back to this village and not Canelli, Barabesco, or Alba, because I had a reason to. . . . I've traveled enough around the world to know that all flesh is equal and worth the same, but you get tired of traveling, and that's why you try to sink your roots in the ground to make land and a country for yourself, so that your flesh will mean something and last a little longer than the simple round of the seasons" (*LF,* 7). Connected with Anguilla's quest for roots is the explicit desire to "last a little longer than the round of the seasons," a hope that betrays his preoccupation with mortality and the passage of time. This longing for permanence will be constantly challenged by his experience as he rediscovers the landscape of his youth.

The two poles of Anguilla's memories of early life are the crudely built cottage on the Gaminella hill, where he was raised, and La Mora, a prosperous farm on the edge of the village, where he went to work as an adolescent and secretly fell in love with the proprietor's daughters. Anguilla's foster family as well as the former owners of La Mora have by now disappeared, leaving both houses in the hands of different occupants. Of all his childhood friends and acquaintances only one still survives. Nuto, who as a youth functioned as Anguilla's guide and confidant, has become a carpenter in the village. The two men resume their friendship, and Nuto becomes Anguilla's guide again, accompanying him to some of the cherished places of the past.

Anguilla contemplates the sad end of each one of his adoptive relatives. Padrino, his foster father, had died an outcast after the early death of his two daughters, one of a tumor, the other struck by lightning. He also contemplates the fate of the former occupants of La Mora, the two beautiful sisters whom Anguilla had silently worshipped, as well as their younger half-sister. Irene, the eldest girl, a tall, blond beauty, had fallen ill and almost died of typhus, before marrying and moving away with a husband who was known to beat her brutally. Silvia, dark-haired and passionate, had bled to death at home after a crudely performed abortion. From Nuto, he finally learns that Santina, who was still a child when Anguilla left the village, had grown up to be the most beautiful of all the sisters, with eyes as dark "as the heart of a poppy." She had been courted at length by a powerful Fascist official. Later, during the armed Resistance, she had taken to the hills to fight with the Partisans. When it was finally discovered that she was a double agent, she was shot to death by her comrades—in Nuto's presence—and her body was burned in a great bonfire. It is with the image of the scar left on the earth by Santina's funeral pyre that *La luna e i falò* comes to a close.

Anguilla's desire for permanence is shattered at the first sight of the Gaminella farmhouse upon his return. To his amazement, the hazel trees surrounding the old house have vanished, causing him a sense of panic: "I never expected to find that the hazel trees were not still there. This meant that everything was over. The change shocked me so much that I didn't call out; I didn't go into the yard" (*LF,* 8). Like Clelia in *Tra donne sole,* Anguilla had hoped to find the welcoming, familiar faces of the past, and discovers instead a terrible emptiness and absence: "I'd come back, I'd gone out on the road, I'd made money, . . . but the faces, the voices, and the hands that should have touched me and recognized me were gone. . . . What was left was like a town square on the day after the fair, a vineyard after the harvest, or coming back alone to a restaurant after a woman has walked out on you" (*LF,* 57).

Yet even while mourning the transformations wrought on the places of his memory, Anguilla realizes that the essence of the landscape itself had not changed: "It was strange how everything had changed and was yet the same. Not even one of the old vines remained, not even an animal. . . . And yet, looking around, the huge flank of Gaminella, the paths on the distant Salto hills, the farmyards, the wells, the voices, the hoes, everything was the same, everything had that smell, that taste, that color of those days long ago" (*LF,* 27). He also discovers that the past has a way of repeating itself. In Cinto, the son of the new owner of the Gaminella cottage, he perceives a reflection of his childhood self. Cinto has many of the gestures, reactions, and interests that Anguilla had as a boy. Unlike Anguilla, he is not illegitimate; but he is lame, a mark that singles him out from other children as Anguilla's illegitimacy had isolated him. Cinto lives in the most abject poverty, and yet—like Anguilla years earlier—he seems capable of transcending the misery of his circumstances through his lively interest in the world around him and through his friendship with an older boy, Piola, who fulfills the same role for him as Nuto had for Anguilla. Anguilla befriends Cinto, rediscovering through his conversations with him some of the experiences of his own youth. This is a friendship that must be pursued with discretion, for fear of the wrath of Cinto's father, Valino, a destitute tenant farmer who savagely beats the boy at the slightest pretext. Like Anguilla, Cinto eventually emerges as the sole surviving member of his family at the Gaminella farm, and it is Anguilla who inadvertently ensures his survival by providing the pocketknife with which the lame boy defends himself against the demented violence of his father.

This act of violence is central to the novel's structure, prompting Nuto's ultimate disclosure of Santina's terrible end and reinforcing the mystery of human destiny, always at the mercy of the power of the *selvaggio.* It is Cinto who brings Anguilla the news of Valino's final act of madness. The boy's father, after beating to death the two women who lived with him, had set fire to the farm and the animals. Then, unsuccessful in his attempt to capture Cinto, he had hanged himself from a tree in the vineyard. Hand in hand with Cinto, Anguilla returns to the burning cottage and the scorched, disfigured hillside of his youth to contemplate the changes wrought by time and destiny on the privileged places of memory.

From Nuto, Anguilla learns that Valino's frantic act of destruction followed in the wake of the unjust demands of the landowner, who had asked for a greater share of Valino's meager crops than he could afford to concede. His death is interpreted by Nuto as the outcome of social injustice. Valino was a sharecropper and subject to the harsh injustices of an age-old system which the supposedly enlightened climate of postwar Italy had as yet failed to supplant. Nuto's outrage against the circumstances that had led to Valino's impoverishment and ultimate self-destruction introduces a polemical note into the narrative. This theme will be repeated in other episodes that reveal the disappointing social and political realities of postwar Italy, particularly in the episode describing the burial of the two unknown Fascists, which is accompanied by the reactionary rhetoric of the local priest and schoolteacher.

The incident of the burning farm relates not only to the novel's sociohistorical setting, but also to its mythical subtext. Fires abound in Pavese's fiction, beginning with Berto's act of arson in *Paesi tuoi* and continuing through the festive bonfires in the short stories, "Il mare" and "L'eremita," as well as the human bonfire that concludes "Le feste." The bonfires, which are also the subject of "I fuochi" in *Dialoghi con Leucò,* reflect Pavese's continuing fascination with ethnological accounts of ritual practice and belief. Both Valino's act of setting fire to the farmhouse and its occupants, and the Partisans' preparation of Santina's funeral bonfire, transcend the historical and sociological situations in which these episodes are framed. They suggest a mythic rite, linked with the forces of nature and the cycles of fertility.[14]

It is Nuto, steeped in rural lore, who tells Anguilla that bonfires awaken the earth and prepare it for an abundant harvest. Cinto, too, knows the magic of bonfires, and tells Anguilla of their power to make the land fertile. Pavese intimates, however, that bonfires have a propitiatory as well as a festive function. They seem called into being by the obscure powers of nature as a necessary ritual tribute. Valino's demented act of self-immolation fits into this scheme, suggesting a symbolic rite of restitution.[15]

One of the Anguilla's guiding intuitions in returning to the hills of his youth is the mythic power of that landscape, a power he had previously rejected. Years earlier, Anguilla, who presents himself as a skeptic, had turned his back on the timeless world of the Langhe to travel on a quest for adventure, movement, and progress. He had sought a new life in America precisely because he perceived that country as a nation of bastards, of people lacking roots and identity like himself. Yet despite his initial conviction that America was indeed his true home, he came to realize with the passage of time that the very elements that had drawn him there had become the source of overwhelming loneliness and uneasiness.

Pavese's depiction of the American Southwest has an odd visual starkness that some critics attribute to his familiarity with Hollywood films of the 1930s and 1940s. Yet his vision of America is shot through with a nightmarish atmosphere that is absent in the Westerns of that period.[16] Despite some jarring dialogues rendered in stilted English, Anguilla's "American" memories are rendered with an extraordinary assurance and power. The chief characteristics attributed to America in this novel are movement, uprootedness, and sterility. These qualities are reflected not only in the landscape, but also in the people. Anguilla's encounter with the heart and spirit of Americans is evoked through memories of his relationship with two women, Nora and Roseanne, both of whom are alienated from their families, from the places of their birth, and from the earth itself. Anguilla, in an attempt to make sense of his presence in the alien Californian landscape, asks Nora to make love on the ground. Not only is she incapable of understanding his request, but she also insists on getting drunk before she will allow him to touch her. Roseanne, on the other hand, refuses to drink any form of alcohol for fear of spoiling her good looks. Propelled by the desire to achieve fame as a model or an actress, she has taken up with Anguilla only because of the possibility of financial support, and is prepared to exploit his generosity right to the end. In these sequences, shot through with characteristic misogyny, there is the suggestion of a culture dominated by narcissism, greed, and repressed emotion.

For Anguilla, the most alienating aspect of American life is the absence of a bond between the people and the landscape. Deprived of cultural traditions that acknowledge this bond, like the festivals and bonfires of rural Piedmont, Americans seem lost in a perpetual movement and vacuity, a vacuity that reflects and intensifies the terrifying emptiness of the desert.

The account of Anguilla's American sojourn culminates with his memory of a night spent stranded in the desert of the Southwest. Here he finds himself completely alone near a railroad track, miles from the nearest town. The only sounds are the howling of a coyote in the distance and the incomprehensible hum of the telegraph wires that flank the length of the tracks. When a train finally passes, it roars by like an apocalyptic vision, a violent intrusion on the lonely silence of the desert. Above the scene the moon presides. This is not the benevolent moon invoked by Nuto, who knows its power over the cycles of fertility and implicitly accepts the use of festive bonfires to encourage its influence over the harvest. The American moon looms over a barren landscape—where the power of bonfires is unrecognized—with a sinister promise of violence and terror: "There was a reddish light. . . . From the low clouds a slice of moon had appeared like a knife wound and filled the plain with blood. I watched it for a while, and was truly terrified" (*LF,* 48).

This crucial scene helps to illuminate Anguilla's decision to return to the Langhe and to confirm a sense of identity there. No longer able to tolerate a world of constant movement and uprootedness—a world that seems out of harmony with the rhythms of the earth—he finally acknowledges the need to seek his identity in the landscape of his youth, where custom and tradition offer meaning to the relationship between people and the earth they inhabit.

Anguilla's quest for meaning in his place of origin is mixed with a yearning for permanence. He is convinced of the timeless nature of life in the Langhe hills: "I knew that all in all only the seasons count, and that it is the seasons that make your bones, it is the seasons that you eat up as a boy. . . . In the hills time does not pass" (*LF,* 44).[17] Through his return to those hills, he seems to be attempting to abolish the knowledge of his own ineluctable end, mistakenly equating mythic timelessness with immortality. The motives for his return, based on this illusion, are gradually clarified and purged through his encounter with the realities of human transience and with the revelation of a dimension of life transcending linear time, a dimension based on concentric cycles of return rather than progress or permanence.

Pavese suggests that the outcome of Anguilla's journey to the heart of his own myths is the achievement of maturity through the acceptance of destiny. In this novel, unlike many of the earlier works, maturity is to be found in the countryside, in the source of childhood memory, rather than the city. Yet Pavese is not attempting here a facile idealization of the countryside in relation to the city. The rural world is not presented in the same glowing light in this novel as in *Il diavolo sulle colline.* On the contrary, Valino's life of unstinting toil leads only to misery, madness, and self-immolation. Nevertheless, there is an understanding generated within the atmosphere of the countryside and reinforced in peasant rituals, that human events are of no great importance, that individual identity is a paltry thing in relation to the majesty and terror of the moon, the procession of the seasons, and the cycles of fertility. The vast tableau of death and violence that Anguilla contemplates upon his return to the Langhe teaches him only the uselessness of human grandiosity. Ultimately a human life has the same value to the earth as the life of an animal, a fruit, or a flower. Things come into being, ripen, and decay in an endless cyclic progression. The essence of maturity lies in the acceptance of mortality as part of that immutable timelessness. This idea is encapsulated in the quotation from *King Lear* that Pavese placed at the beginning of the novel: "Ripeness is all."[18]

The retelling of the destiny of the three beautiful sisters serves to reinforce Anguilla's ultimate acknowledgment of the cyclical timelessness of nature and the ephemeral character of human existence. Irene, Silvia, and Santina, transfixed in the eternity of memory, now emerge in a legendary light. Each of their stories has parallels in that of the others. All three sisters are fated to disappear after a brief season of passion and hope. The cyclic, repetitive form of their stories is intended to reflect the immobility of myth. In Anguilla's memories, the sisters are frequently associated with flowers and fruit, the exquisite harvest of a passing season, and they embody for him the beauty, delicacy, and transience of life itself. Their fate is emblematic of human fate, the common destiny of death.

The account of Santina's involvement in the events of the war reflects Pavese's deepest historical pessimism and cosmic fatalism. Santina's shift from the Fascist to the Partisan camp and back again does not seem motivated by any ideology or purpose. She is driven along her predestined path in a way that is mysterious to everyone, even to herself, although she already has the intuition, expressed in a passing comment to Nuto, that she is going to be burned. In the evocation of her death Pavese suggests the image of a sacrificial victim. She is referred to here not by the childlike diminutive Santina, but by her true name, Santa—the holy one. Just before she is shot by her comrades, as though anticipating the ritual act, she changes into a white dress.[19] Thus she is sanctified and transfigured in the mythic holocaust of her funeral fire.

Anguilla's visit to the Langhe is framed between the initial discovery of the bodies of two unidentified Fascists, killed three years earlier, and Nuto's final admission of Santina's end. Between these moments, there unfolds a litany of brutality, murder, suicide, and other violent deaths. Calvino observed in an article on this novel: "Everything that Pavese says converges in one direction only, images and analogies gravitate toward a single obsessive preoccupation—human sacrifices."[20] Implicit in *La luna e i falò* is the suggestion that murderous violence is an inevitable, immutable component of the human condition. There is also the notion that this violence is prompted by cruel, transcendent powers beyond human understanding. Yet the novel is not completely consistent in this theme. The fatalistic implications of Pavese's mythic presentation of violence are counterbalanced in the historical values expressed by Nuto.

It is Nuto's particular wisdom to incorporate mythic and historical concerns. While accepting the ancient lore of peasant civilization, the cult of the earth, and the power of the moon, Nuto, a Marxist, is also committed to the idea of social justice and progress. Nuto believes in the usefulness of solidarity and action, and implies that real change can be accomplished through human effort and the rejection of violence. He offers a rational, sociological interpretation of events to Anguilla, in a tone that occasionally borders on the rhetorical. Despite the didactic tone of some of Nuto's observations, however, he remains one of the most complex and richly drawn characters in all of Pavese's work. Nuto attempts to provide the voice of reason in a deranged world. Calvino has aptly compared him to Virgil, the sagacious spirit who accompanies the pilgrim Dante in his journey through the Inferno.[21]

Although Pavese's reference to this novel as a modest *Divine Comedy* was certainly inflated, there are some significant connections with Dante's epic. The most obvious is the theme of going back or going down, the *katabasis,* a spiritual journey through a landscape of horror and violence that leads to a process of self-knowledge. Like the protagonist of Dante's *Comedy,* Anguilla is a man of middle age whose personal journey toward awareness involves the contemplation of the violent upheavals of recent history, especially the tragedy of civil strife. Like the pilgrim Dante, Anguilla comes to acknowledge the dominion of transcendent powers and the surrender of individual life to cosmic destiny. Anguilla's surrender, however, is existential and not religious. It is made without faith or hope. The mythic powers of Pavese's universe are unknowable and unpredictable. Their mystery yields only death.

Another parallel with Dante's epic can be observed in the variations in narrative style found in this final novel, a quality for which Pavese has been severely criticized. In the most memorable passages of *La luna e i falò,* an elegiac tone predominates. This is true especially in the evocation of Anguilla's bittersweet memories of Irene and Silvia, culminating with the account of the Feast of Our Lady of Good Counsel. The girls, described metonymically rather than realistically, become fleeting oneiric presences. This effect is heightened in the peculiar use of temporal references which are both precise and deliberately vague. For example, some chapters begin with allusions to "those times," "that winter," or "September." Though seemingly specific, these temporal indications are in fact difficult to place chronologically because of the nonlinear progression of the narrative. The elegiac dimension of the novel is also intensified in Proustian moments of recaptured time: "For many years all I needed was to catch the smell of the linden trees in the wind at evening, and I would feel different. I would feel truly myself and I wasn't even sure why" (*LF,* 102). Similarly, the taste of the ripe figs on the Gaminella hill triggers long-forgotten sensations.

The passages that describe the Anguilla's memories of La Mora diverge sharply from the passages describing his experiences in America as well as his return to the village. The American passages reveal a level of stylization that verges on the Gothic.[22] The sometimes sordid realities of contemporary Piedmont are rendered, on the other hand, in a variety of different tones. Pavese has been criticized for introducing into this dimension of the novel a language that betrays a note of propaganda, supposedly with the hope of ingratiating himself with his critics on the Left. Tibor Wlassics points out that Pavese's evocation of the social and political realities of the village sometimes echoes the didactic rhetoric widespread in party politics during the postwar period.[23] Yet it might be observed that Pavese's very invocation of the literary precedent of the *Divine Comedy* (styling his own work a "modest" version of Dante's great poem) implied a model in which a varied range of rhetorical styles were invoked, sometimes with didactic, "nonpoetic" results.

La luna e i falò encapsulates and develops almost all the thematic and stylistic elements of Pavese's previous work. Its protagonist's real name is never revealed, but the mythic connotations of his nickname, Anguilla (meaning "eel"), are clear. The eel is known for its migrating patterns, its ability to traverse huge distances and find its way back to its destiny.[24] Like Anguilla, Pavese visited the Langhe in 1949, not with the intention of staying there, but with the hope of clarifying his own myths, of reducing them to *logos.* The novel that took shape from that experience was his crowning achievement, and he dedicated it upon publication to his new love, the American actress Constance Dowling, whom he had recently encountered. It was she who also inspired the small collection of poems he wrote in the spring of 1950, later published as *Verrà la morte e avrà i tuoi occhi* (Death will come and will have your eyes). These poems have received attention mainly because of their intimations of death, foreshadowing Pavese's suicide some months later. Like the tragic vision of *La luna e i falò,* they evoke a rhythmic association of woman, earth, and death. In these brief, hypnotic cadences the poet seems to contemplate the final seduction of a journey back to the Great Mother:

> Come
> erba viva nell'aria
> rabbrividisci e ridi,
> ma tu, tu sei terra.
> Sei radice feroce.
> Sei la terra che aspetta.
> (*P,* 181)

> Like live grass
> you shiver and laugh in the air,
> but you, you are earth.
> You are the fierce root.
> You are the waiting earth.

Chapter Eight

Conclusion: Pavese's Critics and His Legacy

Despite the explicit plea for discretion made in his suicide note, Pavese's life and death have been the object of unrelenting speculation and discussion. More has been written about him than about any other Italian author of the twentieth century. Pavese's suicide, eventually interpreted as the gesture of an entire generation,[1] was, in fact, simply a private act. It was the direct result of his fragile mental health, characterized by recurrent bouts of extreme depression and exacerbated by the external pressures that converged at a single moment in time. Public fascination with this troubled, perplexing personality and his dramatic last act has often eclipsed or distorted the critical perspective on his remarkable artistic and intellectual achievements.

The scope of Pavese's contribution became evident only after his death. His novels enjoyed enormous popularity not only in Italy but throughout the world, and they were soon translated into many languages. Though no systematic critical assessment was available for some time, two diverging views of Pavese gained currency. On the popular level, he came to be regarded along with Vittorini as the major exponent of the neo-realist novel,[2] with all the implications of social consciousness that that category brought with it. In the meantime, however, critics on the Left brought into focus his lack of ideological consistency and his regressive, decadent inspiration.

An essay written by Carlo Muscetta shortly after the publication of *Il mestiere di vivere* in 1953 exemplified the opinion of the Left. Observing in Pavese's spiritual stoicism the reflection of a decadent sensibility, Muscetta gave an essentially negative evaluation of the writer's art.[3] In 1954, in a short article inspired by a similar perspective, Alberto Moravia dismissed the literary qualities of Pavese's poetry and fiction, claiming that the cultural importance of Pavese's work was greater than its artistic value.[4] A year later, Carlo Salinari also emphasized the decadent sensibility at the heart of Pavese's inspiration. While analyzing the critical importance of his development of "symbolic realism," Salinari presented Pavese as the end point of the entire decadent tradition in Europe. On the positive side, he also claimed that Pavese was the first *letterato* of truly European stature to emerge in Italy for many years.[5]

Much of the criticism of Pavese offered during the 1950s and 1960s proceeded from biased generalizations and, with some exceptions, studies attempting a methodical critical assessment of his works were very few. The publication of Lajolo's biography *Il vizio assurdo* in 1960 served to further confuse the issues and to perpetuate the notion that an evaluation of Pavese's poetry and fiction should be linked with the details of his day-to-day existence. Lajolo attempted to illustrate the events of Pavese's life with references to his poetry and fiction, thus subordinating the importance of the writer's art to the account of his psychological and social problems. Though the limits of such an approach were noted almost immediately by Pavese's more astute readers,[6] *Il vizio assurdo* enjoyed widespread popularity and acclaim. A play written by Diego Fabbri in collaboration with Lajolo—on whose book it was based—was eventually produced on Italian national television in 1978. This served to circulate and reinforce on a mass level the distorted image first generated by Lajolo's earlier work, that of Pavese as a hysterically flawed and pathetic individual.

The extensive Freudian analysis of Pavese's life and works undertaken by Dominique Fernandez in 1967 has become one of the most widely quoted sources in the secondary literature.[7] Nevertheless, Fernandez places excessive emphasis on the details of Pavese's life and particularly on his emotional difficulties, as a tool for understanding his poetry and fiction. There are also briefer, less detailed attempts at psychoanalytical criticism in the secondary literature, notably the biographical chapter offered by Armanda Guiducci[8]—influenced by the theories of Melanie Klein—and the monograph by Philippe Renard,[9] which builds an interpretation based on the principles of Jacques Lacan. All of these studies are regrettably reductive and flawed. More useful, though also limited, is Armanda Guiducci's lengthy monograph, *Il mito Pavese*; while not purporting to be a study of Pavese's work, it offers a speculative analysis of the broad cultural influences that converged in the composition of those works.[10]

In 1964 the publication of an issue of *Sigma* devoted to the analysis of various aspects of Pavese's works became a significant milestone in the development of a rigorous critical trend. The twelve scholarly articles printed in this issue not only provided stimulus for future inquiry, but also set the example for a systematic, disciplined evaluation of Pavese's output. The articles on the significance of Pavese's use of language were especially influential, as were those on Pavese's elaboration of the notion of myth. Since 1964, many monographs on the author have been published, some taking their lead from the focused studies collected in the *Sigma* special issue, and others harking back to the attempts at psychobiography offered by Lajolo or in the more skilled but ultimately limited study by Fernandez. The most recent milestone in the literature on Pavese is the 1985 monograph by Tibor Wlassics, which, in its probing analysis of the incrustations that have accumulated in the secondary works, has raised the standard of Pavese studies to a new level.

The importance of Pavese's role in the perennial struggle to re-create the Italian literary language—the so-called *questione della lingua*—is now a matter of general consensus. His theories on myth and his formulation of a personal mythic symbolism remain more controversial. His preoccupation with myth is clearly linked with his decadent heritage, an influence for which he has been repeatedly criticized. Pavese was undoubtedly marked by his exposure to the tradition of European decadence. In his early years he carried on a conscious battle to transcend the limits of that sensibility, invoking the example of American writers and eventually attempting to create a radically new form of poetry. Despite his early and thorough attempt to become a modern, rational, progressive writer, he could never fully abandon his fascination with aestheticism and the myths of the late romantic sensibility.

His struggle to balance life with art was never resolved successfully. As a result of his emotional difficulties, Pavese's artistic and intellectual pursuits became not a mere temporary repository for existential tensions, but threatened to become a substitute for life itself. It has been on this point that his critics have been most severe. It should be observed, however, that for Pavese art could not completely substitute for life. In an ironic way, his deeply felt anxieties and alienation led him to desire to identify with the alienated. This existential yearning in part explains his membership in the Italian Communist party after the war; but his artistic integrity accounted for his ultimate rejection of the Party principle that culture must be subordinated to ideology.

Pavese was not only a poet and novelist but a cultural leader and innovator. His substantial contributions as editor, translator, and essayist broke new ground. In his work Pavese was decisive, disciplined, and strong. Despite the tone of self-abasement that surfaces from time to time in his letters and diary regarding his personal life, his attitude toward his work was marked by a contrasting self-confidence. His only fear was that his artistic inspiration might one day run dry. Life without the option of self-creation through writing would be impossible.

In 1939 Pavese quoted in his diary the French writer Lavelle: "La seule chose qui compte, c'est d'être, non point d'agir" ("The only thing that matters is to be, not to act") (*MV,* 146). Yet Pavese's whole life was dedicated to the process of doing, constructing, and working. This ceaseless activity, prompted by the need to prove himself worthy of being in the world, came from his deepest existential anxieties, transformed into rational endeavor. Too much attention has been paid to Pavese's final act of suicide and not enough to his unrelenting discipline and to his ongoing effort to transcend personal anxieties through the construction of an enduring artistic legacy.

Notes and References

Chapter One

1. Davide Lajolo, *Il vizio assurdo* (Milan: Il Saggiatore, 1960); rev. ed., *Pavese: Il vizio assurdo* (Milan: Rizzoli, 1980).

2. Tibor Wlassics, *Pavese falso e vero: vita, poetica, narrativa* (Turin: Centro Studi Piemontesi, 1985).

3. Wlassics (ibid., 27–42) identifies and discusses eight areas that are problematical in biographical accounts of Pavese due to inaccuracies perpetuated by Lajolo and others. These areas include the issue of Pavese's unhappy childhood; the evaluation of his contribution as a translator and scholar of American literature; the details of his anti-Fascist activities and detention; the discussion of his sexual and emotional problems; the nature and intensity of the religious crisis he experienced toward the end of the war; the issue of his political commitment in the postwar period; and the significance of his suicide.

4. Ibid. See also Wlassics, "Pavese Forgeries," in *Selected Proceedings, 32nd Mountain Interstate Foreign Language Conference* (Winston–Salem, 1984), 393–404, and Luciana Giovannetti, "Un Pavese 'nuovo' dall'America," forthcoming in *Pavese oggi, Atti del convegno* (Santo Stefano Belbo: Centro Studi Cesare Pavese, 1987). When *Il vizio assurdo* was being translated into English in 1983, Lajolo himself granted permission to the translators, Mario and Mark Pietralunga, to make substantial cuts in the text. The Pietralungas made the decision to omit from their translation letters attributed by Lajolo to Pavese, since none of this correspondence could be authenticated in manuscript. Mario Pietralunga nevertheless rejects the forgery theory put forward by Wlassics.

5. For the details of Pavese's early environment see Bona Alterocca, *Cesare Pavese* (Aosta: Musumeci, 1985), a source described by Pavese's niece, Cesarina Sini, as the most reliable biography available to date.

6. Cesarina Sini, in a personal interview, has confirmed the commonly accepted image of Pavese's mother as a stern and demanding woman. As Elio Gioanola suggests, however, such traits were not unusual in this cultural context: "Which one of us, born in Piedmont, of rural or lower middle-class origins did not have a puritanical mother?" (*La poetica dell'essere* [Milan: Marzorati, 1972], 17).

7. *Poesie edite e inedite,* ed. Italo Calvino (Turin: Einaudi, 1962), 83.

8. *Lettere 1924–1944,* ed. Lorenzo Mondo (Turin: Einaudi, 1966), 3.

9. Ibid., 11.

10. Ibid., 26.

11. All quotations from Pavese's letters are to *Opere,* vol. 14, *Lettere 1926–1950,* ed. Lorenzo Mondo and Italo Calvino (Turin: Einaudi, 1968).

12. Writing about *Il mestiere di vivere,* Susan Sontag suggests that Pavese exemplifies a uniquely modern, post-Christian phenomenon: "[We] are interested in the soul of the writer . . . because of the insatiable modern preoccupation with psychology, the latest and most powerful legacy of the Christian tradition of introspection, opened up by Paul and Augustine, which equates the discovery of the self with the discovery of the suffering self" (*Against Interpretation* [New York: Delta, 1965], 42).

13. Vittorini was to become, along with Pavese, one of the leading novelists and literary figures of his generation. For an account of his important contribution to the cultural resistance to Fascism, see Joy Hambeuchen Potter, *Elio Vittorini* (Boston: Twayne, 1979).

14. Tina Pizzardo, *Il Messaggero,* 23 and 24 August 1980.

15. These letters are reproduced in Giuseppe Neri, *Cesare Pavese e le sue opere* (Reggio Calabria: Parallelo 38, 1977), 41–44.

16. Lajolo offers a lengthy, highly embellished account of Pavese's relationship with Pizzardo. He states erroneously that Pavese learned upon return from the *confino* that Pizzardo had already married another man. This version has been repeated in many subsequent biographical accounts of Pavese.

17. Although Pavese wrote *Il carcere* before *Paesi tuoi,* the former was not published until 1948.

18. The Italian Social Republic came into existence at Salò on Lake Garda after the official fall of Mussolini in 1943 as an ally of Germany. Its armed forces were referred to as "i Repubblichini," a perjorative version of "repubblicani" ("republicans").

19. Paolo Spriano, official historian of the PCI, offered a different interpretation of this passage in a speech at an international convention on Pavese in September 1987, claiming that Pavese's despair came from a sense of remorse for his inability to commit himself fully to the Communist party. On the contrary, the journal entry clearly reflects Pavese's recognition of his lack of aptitude for political involvement and his regret at being caught up again in matters essentially alien to his character: "I contemplate my impotence, I feel it in my bones, and (yet) I have committed myself to political responsibility, which is crushing me. There is only one answer: suicide" (*MV,* 359). Pavese's final depression and his complex sense of powerlessness have been oversimplified by his critics, who have mistakenly attributed his suicide entirely to a sense of romantic loss or to a sense of political failure.

Chapter Two

1. *Lavorare stanca* has been translated by William Arrowsmith as *Hard Labor* (Baltimore: Johns Hopkins University Press, 1979).

2. Pavese's earlier experiments were influenced by D'Annunzio, as well as by the Crepuscular poets, particularly Gozzano. Traces of Gozzano are not

entirely absent from the poems of the *Lavorare stanca* period. See Lorenzo Mondo, "Fra Gozzano e Whitman: le origini di Pavese," *Sigma* 1, nos. 3–4 (1964):3–21.

3. For an analysis of the evolution of Pavese's metrical choices in *Lavorare stanca,* see Marziano Guglielminetti, "Racconto e canto nella metrica di Pavese," *Sigma* 1, nos. 3–4 (1964):22–33.

4. In the 1943 Einaudi edition, this poem, which is dedicated to Augusto Monti, is dated 1931. Nevertheless, the manuscript of "*I mari del Sud*" is dated 7–14 September 1930. Pavese's deliberate reconstruction of the period of composition is an attempt to set "*I mari del Sud*" apart from other less original (and still unpublished) early poems. It is also an indication of the diligence with which he sought to control and construct his public image as a poet.

5. Franco Riva offers an analysis of dialect elements in Pavese's early poetry in "Note sulla lingua della poesia di Pavese," *Lingua nostra* 17 (1956):47–56.

6. Pavese placed "*Fumatori di carta*" and all his other poems with a political theme in the "Legna verde" (Green wood) section of the Einaudi edition of *Lavorare stanca*.

7. See Annamaria Andreoli, "La voce di Jahier," in *Il mestiere della letteratura* (Pisa: Pacini, 1977), 51–53.

8. This poem echoes a theme that provided the central inspiration of *Dialoghi con Leucò,* and implies a mythical parallel between the state of childhood and the age of the Titans. The power of this era of pure instinctuality, closely linked with the forces of nature, is eclipsed by the onset of rational life, symbolized in myth by the advent of the Olympian deities.

9. Published in *Poesie edite e inedite,* and in *Opere,* vol. 11 (Turin: Einaudi, 1973).

10. Mila, preface to *Poesie* (Turin: Einaudi, 1961), vii–xi.

11. See Marco Forti, "Sulla poesia di Pavese," *Sigma* 1, nos. 3–4 (1964):34–48.

Chapter Three

1. *Ciau Masino* first appeared in print in *Opere.* See *Racconti,* 9–133. The collection has never been translated into English. Its title means both "Hi Masino!" and "Bye Masino!" in Piedmontese dialect.

2. Through a detailed, sociolinguistic analysis of the language of this story, Gaetano Berruto demonstrates the complexity of Pavese's narrative experimentation at this early stage of his career. See Berruto, "*La Langa* di Cesare Pavese: Una lettera 'sociolinguistica,'" *Lingua nostra* 37 (1976):96–106.

3. Anco Marzio Mutterle, "*Ciau Masino*: Dal Plurilinguismo al Monologo Interiore," *Belfagor* 5 (1970):559–91.

4. In *Feria d'agosto* (Turin: Einaudi, 1946).

5. Ibid., 43–62.

6. The title of the English translation, *The Political Prisoner* (London: Peter Owen, 1957), lacks the symbolic nuances of Pavese's title and falsely suggests a political theme.

7. Anco Marzio Mutterle, *L'imagine arguta: lingua, stile, retorica di Pavese* (Turin: Einaudi, 1977), 5–39 and passim.

8. See Wlassics, *Pavese falso e vero,* 99; Wlassics's discussion of *Il carcere* is found in ibid., 91–101.

Chapter Four

1. The title, which alludes to the proverb "Moglie e buoi dai paesi tuoi" ("Pick your wife and your cattle from your own neck of the woods"), translates literally as "Your villages," or colloquially as "Your neck of the woods" or "Your part of the country." It was published in English as *The Harvesters* (London: Peter Owen, 1961).

2. Vittorini's letter to Pavese, dated 3 June 1941, is quoted in a footnote in Pavese's collected letters (*Lettere 1924–1944* [Turin: Einaudi, 1966], 593).

3. In 1946 Pavese observed in the essay "L'influsso degli eventi" (The influence of events): "The American who most influenced me—because of his tempo, his narrative rhythm—was James Cain, though no one was able to discern that when *Paesi tuoi* came out" (*SL,* 223). See Wlassics, *Pavese falso e vero,* 103–7.

4. For a thoughtful discussion of Pavese's understanding and development of a style based on the rhythmic recurrence of images, see Wlassics, *Pavese falso e vero,* 65–75.

5. Emilio Cecchi suggests, in fact, that this novel is simply a reformulation of Verga's effort. See Cecchi, "Cesare Pavese," *Paragone,* August 1950, 19.

6. A diary entry for 10 December 1939 confirms this: "A symbol . . . is an imaginary link that weaves its web through the narrative. It is a question of recurrent instances, which indicate a persistent imaginary sense and a hidden reality that comes to the forefront. An example of this is the 'breast' in *Paesi tuoi,* a true epithet that expresses the sexual reality of that landscape" (*MV,* 152).

7. Giorgio Bàrberi Squarotti, "Pavese o la fuga nella metafora," *Sigma* 1, nos. 3–4 (1964):165–88.

8. Many of Pavese's diary notes during the period of the novel's composition show a preoccupation with the concept of narrative realism. See, in particular, the entry for 9 March 1940 (*MV,* 166).

9. The triptych *La bella estate* was republished as volume 8 of *Opere.* In

a brief note accompanying this triptych Pavese alludes to some important elements common to the three novels: "It is a matter of moral climate, a mix of themes, a recurring mood in the free flow of the imagination. . . . A theme that recurs in each of the plots is that of temptation. . . . Another is the frantic search for vice, the daring need to break the rules, to reach the limits. Another is the way that a natural sanction falls upon the weakest and the guiltiest, on the 'youngest'"(*BE*, 333).

10. This dichotomy is central to the short story, "*Il campo di grano*" (*R*, 330).

11. Wlassics, *Pavese falso e vero,* 113.

12. I disagree with Doug Thompson's claim that the narrator of this novel is an anonymous friend of Ginia's. See Thompson, *Cesare Pavese* (Cambridge: Cambridge University Press, 1982), 80.

13. Gioanola, *La poetica dell'essere,* 219.

14. For a stylistic analysis of this novel, see ibid., 225. See also Corrado Grassi, "Osservazioni su lingua e dialetto in Pavese", *Sigma* 1, nos. 3–4 (1964):58–71.

15. The following is typical of this construction: "Ginia obeyed and ran home and told Severino that she was having dinner with Amelia; she fixed her hat and went out as it was raining" (*BE,* 48).

16. When approached by Giambattista Vicari with the request of submitting work to *Lettere d'oggi*—of which Viccari was editor—Pavese agreed with apparent reluctance to having the novel published in serial form. The following year it was printed in book form.

17. Armanda Guiducci, *Invito alla lettura di Cesare Pavese* (Milan: Mursia, 1972), 79.

18. For an analysis of the symbolic function of the olive tree, see Wlassics, *Pavese falso e vero,* 123–24.

Chapter Five

1. Furio Jesi, "Cesare Pavese, il mito e la scienza del mito," *Sigma* 1, nos. 3–4 (1964):95–120.

2. See Johannes Hösle, "*I miti dell'infanzia,*" *Sigma* 1, nos. 3–4 (1964):203.

3. Introduction to *La letteratura americana,* xxxi.

4. On 28 December 1938 Pavese wrote: "The very suspicion that the subconscious is God, or that God lives and speaks in our subconscious has exalted you. If, with this idea of God you review all the thoughts scattered throughout this diary on the subconscious, now your past takes on a different aspect. Above all your laborious quest for the symbol is enlightened by its intimate significance" (*MV,* 269).

5. Wlassics addresses this problem in *Pavese falso e vero,* 127–34.

6. Eugenio Corsini, "Orfeo senza Euridice, I *Dialoghi con Leucò* e il classicismo di Pavese," *Sigma* 1, nos. 3–4 (1964):121–46.

7. Maria Luisa Premuda, "I *Dialoghi con Leucò* e il realismo simbolico di Pavese," *Annali della Scuola Normale di Pisa* 26 (1957):221–49.

8. This classification was first suggested in Corsini, "Orfeo senza Euridice."

9. Lorenzo Mondo, *Cesare Pavese* (Milan: Mursia, 1961), 77.

10. Mutterle, *Immagine arguta,* 84.

Chapter Six

1. The poems first appeared in *Le tre Venezie* 21, nos. 4–6 (1947) and were published posthumously in *Verrà la morte e avrà i tuoi occhi* (Turin: Einaudi, 1951).

2. See Alberto Asor Rosa, *Scrittori e popolo* (Rome: Samona e Savelli, 1965), 198–99, 210–16.

3. Sergio Pautasso, *Guida a Pavese* (Milan: Rizzoli, 1980), 106.

4. See Gian Paolo Biasin, *The Smile of the Gods* (Ithaca: Cornell University Press, 1968), 172.

5. Gianni Venturi, *Pavese* (Florence: La Nuova Italia, 1969), 92.

6. Bassani's original review of *Il compagno* is reprinted in Giorgio Bassani, *Le parole preparate* (Turin: Einaudi, 1966), 138–39.

7. Bàrberi Squarotti, "La fuga," 175.

8. Thompson, *Cesare Pavese,* 160; see Wlassics, *Pavese falso e vero,* 137–42.

9. See Bàrberi Squarotti, "La fuga," 177.

10. Philippe Renard, *Pavese, prison de l'imaginaire, lieu de l'écriture* (Paris: Larousse, 1972), 158.

11. The biblical text to which *Prima che il gallo canti* refers is the story in the Passion narrative in which Jesus foretells his imminent betrayal by Peter with the words: "Before the cock crows twice you will deny me three times" (Mark 14:30; see also Luke 22:34; Matthew 26:34; and John 18:27).

12. See chap. 1, n. 18.

13. Venturi, *Pavese,* 106.

14. This comment by a reviewer on the Left was quoted by Giansiro Ferrata in his review of *Prima che il gallo canti* in *L'Unità,* 9 February 1949, and by Gioanola, *La poetica dell'essere,* 308.

15. Pavese summed up his response to leftist criticism of the novel in his letter of 20 March 1950 to Rino del Sasso, a Communist critic: "I wanted to depict a solitary, hesitant type, who in spite of—or perhaps because of—his cowardice, discovers or at least glimpses some new values (the sense of death, humility, the understanding of others). If you say that I didn't measure up to that attempt, you may be right, in fact, you are certainly right; if you say that these themes should not be dealt with, then I shrug my shoulders.

The world is big and there is room for everyone. . . . Art should discover new human truths, not new institutions" (*L,* 710–11, citing Lajolo, *Vizio,* 348–48, because original is unavailable).

16. Mutterle, *L'immagine arguta,* 112.

17. Gioanola, *La poetica dell'essere,* 315.

Chapter Seven

1. An analysis of the pastoral elements of the Mombello episode is offered by Antonio Musumeci in *L'impossibile ritorno* (Ravenna: Longo, 1980), 115.

2. Matthew 4:1–11 and Luke 4:1–13.

3. Renard, *Pavese, prison de l'imaginaire,* 183–87.

4. The forces of the *selvaggio* are heralded in *Il diavolo sulle colline* by a ritual roar in the night (*BE,* 91), a motif that previously appeared in *La spiaggia.* Wlassics suggests that this characteristic motif has its basis in D'Annunzio. Wlassics, *Pavese, falso e vero,* 167.

5. See, for example, Franco Mollia, *Cesare Pavese* (Padua: Rebellato, 1960), 124, and Giuliano Manacorda, "Pavese poeta saggista e narratore," *Società* 2 (1952):233.

6. In a letter written to Pavese shortly after this novel and *Tra donne sole* were published, Calvino observed that he disliked Pavese's depiction of the privileged class. He added: "It doesn't matter if you love it or hate it, but you have to know what your position is. You haven't made up your mind, and this is obvious in the way you keep returning to the subject." Calvino's remarks appear in a footnote to Pavese's collected letters (*L,* 665).

7. Bàrberi Squarotti, "La fuga," 183.

8. Both the English and American translators of this novel have taken the same liberty in rendering the title as "Among Women Only," changing Pavese's emphasis. In the original title "*sole*" is an adjective rather than an adverb; it may be read as "Among Single Women," or even "Among Lonely Women."

9. Renard, *Pavese, Prison de l'imaginaire,* 200–201.

10. Critics and commentators have not hesitated to point out the premonitory parallels with Pavese's own suicide two years after this work was written.

11. Calvino offered Pavese some harsh but insightful comments on the characterization of Clelia: "The thing that I find most disorienting here is this hairy horse-woman who speaks in the first person with a deep voice and the smell of tobacco on her breath. . . . It is obvious that it's you who is there with a wig and false breasts, declaring: 'There you are. This is what a real woman should be like'" (*L,* 665).

12. Pinolo Scaglione, Pavese's childhood companion from the Langhe

countryside, had settled permanently in Santo Stefano Belbo where he had developed a thriving carpentry business. It was Scaglione who provided the model for Nuto in Pavese's final novel.

13. See Louis Kibler, "Patterns of Time in Pavese's *La Luna e i falò*," *Forum Italicum* 12 (1978):339–50.

14. For an interesting interpretation of Pavese's bonfires, see John Freccero, "Mythos and Logos: The Moon and the Bonfires," *Italian Quarterly* 4 (1961):16.

15. See Renard, *Pavese, prison de l'imaginaire,* 217.

16. See Peter M. Norton, "Cesare Pavese and the American Nightmare," *Modern Language Notes* 77 (1962):24–36.

17. According to Musumeci: "Anguilla's return is an attempt to conquer time through space. Space, especially the space where childhood is spent, defines the identity of the individual, and is presented as a sign of permanence against the erosion of time. . . . The mythic quest consists, in essence, of the attempt to obliterate time through space" (*L'impossibile ritorno,* 132).

18. In his 1949 essay, "L'arte di maturare," Pavese uses the full quotation: "Man must endure / his going hence e'en as his coming hither. / Ripeness is all" (*SL,* 330).

19. For Pavese as for biblical apocalyptic, the color white is often associated with violence or terrifying revelation.

20. Italo Calvino, "Pavese e i sacrifici umani," *Avanti!,* 12 June 1966, 3.

21. Ibid.

22. Norton, "American Nightmare."

23. Wlassics, *Pavese falso e vero,* 188.

24. The symbolism of the eel is explored in Eugenio Montale's poem, "L'anguilla," and later "translated" by Robert Lowell in his poem "Intimations."

Chapter Eight

1. Leslie Fiedler, "Introducing Pavese," *Kenyon Review* 16 (1954):544–45.

2. This view of Pavese as a neo-realist novelist has now been totally superseded.

3. Carlo Muscetta, "Per una storia di Pavese e dei suoi racconti," *Società* 8 (1952):614–41.

4. Alberto Moravia, "Pavese decadente," in *L'uomo come fine* (Milan: Bompiani, 1964), 187–91.

5. Carlo Salinari, "La poetica di Pavese," in *Il Contemporaneo,* 1 October 1955; reprinted in *Preludio e fine del realismo in Italia* (Naples: Morano, 1967), 87–97.

6. Claudio Varese, "Cesare Pavese VII," in *Occasioni e valori della letteratura contemporanea* (Bologna: Cappelli, 1967), 194–99.
7. Dominique Fernandez, *L'échec de Pavese* (Paris: Grasset, 1967).
8. Armanda Guiducci, *Invito alla lettura di Cesare Pavese* (Milan: Mursia, 1971).
9. Renard, *Pavese: Prison de l'imaginaire.*
10. Guiducci, Armanda, *Il mito Pavese* (Florence: Vallecchi, 1967).

Selected Bibliography

PRIMARY SOURCES

Pavese's works are listed here in chronological order according to genre and date of composition. Unless otherwise noted, the publication information refers to the first edition. Most of Pavese's works have been translated into English. Where an English translation exists, I have indicated this with the siglum ET.

1. Fiction

Ciau Masino. In *Racconti,* 9–133. Turin: Einaudi, 1968. Stories, 1931–32.

Notte di festa. Turin: Einaudi, 1953. ET: A. E. Murch, *Festival Night.* London: Peter Owen, 1964. Stories, 1936–38.

Il carcere. In *Prima che il gallo canti.* Turin: Einaudi, 1948. ET: W. J. Strachan, *The Political Prisoner.* London: Peter Owen, 1959. Short novel, 1938–39.

Paesi tuoi. Turin: Einaudi, 1941. ET: A. E. Murch, *The Harvesters.* London: Peter Owen, 1961. Novel, 1939.

La bella estate. Turin: Einaudi, 1949. ET: W. J. Strachan, in *The Political Prisoner.* London: Peter Owen, 1959. Short novel, 1940.

La spiaggia. Rome: Lettere d'oggi, 1942. ET: W. J. Strachan, *The Beach.* London: Peter Owen, 1963. Short novel, 1940–41.

Feria d'agosto. Turin: Einaudi, 1946. ET: A. E. Murch, *Summer Storm.* London: Peter Owen, 1966. Stories and prose, 1941–44.

Racconti. Turin: Einaudi, 1960. Short stories, 1936–44.

Fuoco grande. Turin: Einaudi, 1959. ET: W. J. Strachan, in *The Beach.* London: Peter Owen, 1963. Unfinished novel, with Bianca Garufi.

Il compagno. Turin: Einaudi, 1947. ET: W. J. Strachan, *The Comrade.* London: Peter Owen, 1959. Novel, 1946.

La casa in collina. In *Prima che il gallo canti.* Turin: Einaudi, 1949. ET: W. J. Strachan, *The House on the Hill.* New York: Walker, 1959. Novel, 1947–48.

Il diavolo sulle colline. In *La bella estate.* Turin: Einaudi, 1949. ET: D. D. Paige, *The Devil in the Hills.* New York: Noonday Press, 1959. Novel, 1948.

Tra donne sole. In *La bella estate.* Turin: Einaudi, 1949. ET: D. D. Paige, *Among Women Only.* London: Peter Owen, 1953. Novel, 1949.

La luna e i falò. Turin: Einaudi, 1950. ET: Marianne Ceconi, *The Moon and the Bonfires.* New York: Farrar, Straus and Young, 1953. Novel, 1949.

2. Poetry

Lavorare stanca. Florence: Solaria, 1936. 2d ed. Turin: Einaudi, 1943. ET: Margaret Crosland, *A Mania for Solitude: Selected Poems, 1930–1950.* London: Peter Owen, 1969; William Arrowsmith, *Hard Labor.* Baltimore: Johns Hopkins University Press, 1979.

La terra e la morte. In *Le tre Venezie* (Padua: 1947). Posthumous edition in *Verrà la morte e avrà i tuoi occhi.* Turin: Einaudi, 1951. ET: Margaret Crosland, *A Mania for Solitude: Selected Poems, 1930–1950.* London: Peter Owen, 1969. Poems, 1945.

Verrà la morte e avrà i tuoi occhi. Turin: Einaudi, 1951. Poems, 1950.

Poesi edite e inedite. Edited by Italo Calvino. Turin: Einaudi, 1962. Poems 1930–50.

3. Letters, diary, essays, and mythic meditations.

Lettere 1924–1944. Turin: Einaudi, 1966.

Lettere 1945–1950. Turin: Einaudi, 1966.

Lettere 1926–1950. 2 vols. Turin: Einaudi, 1968.

La letteratura americana e altri saggi. Turin: Einaudi, 1951. ET: Edwin Fussell, *American Literature: Essays and Opinions.* Berkeley: University of California Press, 1970. Essays, 1930–50.

Il mestiere di vivere. Turin: Einaudi, 1952. ET: A. E. Murch, *This Business of Living.* London: Peter Owen, 1962. Diary, 1935–50.

Dialoghi con Leucò. Turin: Einaudi, 1947. ET: William Arrowsmith and D. S. Carne-Ross, *Dialogues with Leucò.* Ann Arbor: University of Michigan Press, 1966. Mythical dialogues, 1945–46.

4. Works translated by Pavese from English to Italian

Anderson, Sherwood, *Dark Laughter—Riso nero.* Turin: Frassinelli, 1932.

Defoe, Daniel. *Moll Flanders.* Turin: Einaudi, 1939.

Dickens, Charles. *David Copperfield.* Turin: Einaudi, 1939.

Dos Passos, John. *Big Money—Un mucchio di quattrini.* Milan: Mondadori, 1937.

———. *Forty-Second Parallel—Il 42o parallelo.* Milan: Mondadori, 1935.

Faulkner, William. *The Hamlet—Il borgo.* Milan: Mondadori, 1942.

Henriques, Robert. *Captain Smith—Capitano Smith.* Turin: Einaudi, 1947.

Joyce, James. *A Portrait of the Artist as a Young Man—Dedalus.* Turin: Frassinelli, 1934.

Lewis, Sinclair. *Our Mr. Wrenn—Il nostro signor Wrenn.* Florence: Bemporad, 1931.

Melville, Herman. *Benito Cereno.* Turin: Einaudi, 1940.

———. *Moby–Dick.* Turin: Frassinelli, 1932.

Morley, Christopher. *The Trojan Horse—Il cavallo di Troia.* Milan: Bompiani, 1941.

Stein, Gertrude. *The Autobiography of Alice B. Toklas—Autobiografia di Alice Toklas.* Turin: Einaudi, 1938.
———. *Three Lives—Tre esistenze.* Turin: Einaudi, 1940.
Steinbeck, John. *Of Mice and Men—Uomini e topi.* Milan: Bompiani, 1938.
Toynbee, Arnold. *Civilization and History—La civiltà nella storia,* with Charles De Bosis. Turin: Einaudi, 1950.
Trevelyan, G. Macaulay. *The English Revolution of 1688–1689—La rivoluzione inglese del 1688–89.* Turin: Einaudi, 1941.

SECONDARY SOURCES

1. Books

Alterocca, Bona. *Cesare Pavese.* Aosta: Musumeci, 1983. Practical, unassuming account of Pavese's life by a former journalist friend.
Biasin, Gianpaolo. *The Smile of the Gods.* Ithaca: Cornell University Press, 1968. Careful, scholarly analysis of Pavese's major themes.
Catalano, Ettore. *Cesare Pavese, fra politica e ideologia.* Bari: De Donato, 1976. Ideological critique of Pavese's contradictions.
Fernandez, Dominique. *L'échec de Pavese.* Paris: Grasset, 1967. Outdated psychoanalytical study of Pavese's life and major themes.
Giaonola, Elio. *La poetica dell'essere.* Milan: Marzorati, 1971. Still valid as a discussion of Pavese's existential themes and poetics.
Guglielminetti, Marziano, and Zaccaria, Giuseppe. *Cesare Pavese.* Florence: Le Monnier, 1977. Basic but useful survey of Pavese.
Guiducci, Armanda. *Il mito Pavese.* Florence: Vallecchi, 1967. Discussion of Pavese's cultural and artistic influences.
Lajolo, Davide. *Il vizio assurdo.* Milan: Il Saggiatore, 1960. ET: Mario and Mark Pietralunga, *An Absurd Vice.* New York: New Directions, 1983. First full-length biography of Pavese, the value of which is now in dispute.
Mondo, Lorenzo. *Cesare Pavese.* Milan: Mursia, 1961. Careful and sensitive account of Pavese's life and work.
Musumeci, Antonio. *L'impossibile ritorno.* Ravenna: Longo, 1980. Analysis of thematic recurrence of the myth of return.
Mutterle, Anco Marzio. *L'immagine arguta: Lingua, stile, retorica di Cesare Pavese.* Turin: Einaudi, 1977. Linguistic study of Pavese's fiction.
Paloni, Piermassimo. *Il giornalismo di Pavese.* Legnano: Landoni, 1977. Study of Pavese's essays in newspapers and magazines.
Pappalardo La Rosa, Franco. *Cesare Pavese e il mito dell'adolescenza.* Milan: Laboratorio delle Arti, 1977. Analysis of the myth of adolescence in Pavese.

Ponzi, Mauro. *La critica e Pavese.* Bologna: Cappelli, 1977. Anthology of criticism, with bibliography.

Renard, Philippe. *Pavese: Prison de l'imaginaire, lieu de l'écriture.* Paris: Larousse, 1972. Analysis of Pavese's major works in a Lacanian key.

Thompson, Doug. *Cesare Pavese.* Cambridge: Cambridge University Press, 1980. Study of Pavese's life and works that attempts to clarify his cultural background for the English-speaking reader.

Tondo, Michele. *Invito alla lettura di Cesare Pavese.* Milan: Mursia, 1983. Balanced introduction to Pavese's works.

Wlassics, Tibor. *Pavese, falso e vero. Vita, poetica, narrativa.* Turin: Centro di Studi Piemontesi, 1985. Fresh, scholarly study of Pavese's major fiction, and a rigorous, systematic effort to break through the clichés that have accumulated in the critical and biographical literature. Includes excellent critical bibliography by Luciana Giovannetti.

2. Chapters of Books and Articles

Bàrberi Squarotti, Giorgio. "Lettura di *Lavorare stanca.*" In *Cesare Pavese trent'anni dopo.* Santo Stefano: Centro Studi Cesare Pavese, 1980, 37–62. Analysis of the early poems.

———. "Pavese e la fuga nella metafora." *Sigma* 1, nos. 3–4 (1964):165–88. Seminal study of Pavese's symbolic narrative.

Barnett, Louise K. "Notes on Pavese's Critical View of American Literature." *Forum Italicum* 8 (1974):381–89.

Beccaria, Gian Luigi. "Il lessico, ovvero la 'questione della lingua' in Cesare Pavese." *Sigma* 1, nos. 3–4 (1964):87–94. On the use of dialect elements in Pavese's language.

Calvino, Italo. "Pavese e i sacrifici umani." *Avanti!,* 12 June 1966, 3. Short essay on Pavese's final novel.

Corsini, Eugenio. "Orfeo senza Euridice: i *Dialoghi con Leucò* e il classicismo di Pavese." *Sigma* 1, nos. 3–4 (1964):121–46. Analysis of Pavese's use of classical sources in *Dialoghi con Leucò.*

Fiedler, Leslie. "Introducing Cesare Pavese." *Kenyon Review* 16 (1954):536–53. First essay on Pavese in English; remains a classic.

Foster, D. W. "The Poetic Vision of *le colline*: An Introduction to Pavese's *Lavorare stanca.*" *Italica* 42 (1965):379–89.

Forti, Marco. "Sulla poesia di Pavese." *Sigma* 1, nos. 3–4 (1964):34–48. Balanced overview of Pavese's poetic development, based on Calvino's critical edition.

Freccero, John. "Mythos and Logos: *The Moon and the Bonfires.*" *Italian Quarterly* 4, no. 16 (1961):3–16.

Ghezzi, Aurelia, "Life, destiny, and death in Cesare Pavese's *Dialoghi con Leucò,*" in *South Atlantic Bulletin* 45 (1980):31–39. Discussion of the themes of *Dialoghi con Leucò.*

Ginzburg, Natalia. "Ritratto di un amico." In *Le piccole virtù.* Turin: Einaudi, 1962. ET: "Portrait of a Friend: in Memoriam Cesare Pavese." *London Magazine* 7, no. 2 (1968):21–27. Sensitive account of the writer's personality by a close friend and colleague.

Grana, Gianni. "Cesare Pavese." In *Orienatmenti culturali: La letteratura italiana: I contemporanei.* Milano: Marzorati, 1962, 2:133–67.

Grassi, Corrado. "Osservazioni su lingua e dialetto nell'opera di Pavese." *Sigma* 1, nos. 3–4 (1964):49–71. On dialect influence in Pavese.

Guglielminetti, Marziano. "Racconto e canto nella metrica di Pavese." *Sigma* 1, nos. 3–4 (1964):22–33. Analysis of Pavese's metrical innovations.

Heiney, Donald. "*The Moon and the Bonfires.*" In *America in Modern Italian Literature.* New Brunswick: Rutgers University Press, 1964, 171–86.

———. *Three Italian Novelists: Moravia, Pavese, Vittorini.* Ann Arbor: University of Michigan Press, 1968.

Hösle, Johannes. "I miti dell'infanzia." *Sigma* 1, nos. 3–4 (1964):202–16. A study of Pavese's "myth of childhood."

Jesi, Furio. "Cesare pavese, il mito e la scienza del mito." *Sigma* 1, nos. 3–4 (1964):95–120. A useful essay on the residual influence of the late romantic worldview in Pavese's ethnological sources.

Kibler, Louis. "Patterns of Time in Pavese's *La luna e i falò.*" *Forum Italicum* 12 (1978):339–50.

Manacorda, Giuliano. "Pavese, poeta, saggista e narratore." *Società* 8 (1952):221–37.

Merry, Bruce. "Artifice and Structure in *La luna e i falò.*" *Forum Italicum* 5 (1970):351–58. Study of time structures in Pavese's last novel in the light of Propp's *Morphology of the Folktale.*

Mondo, Lorenzo. "Fra Gozzano e Whitman: le origini di Pavese." *Sigma* 1, nos. 3–4 (1964):3–21. Describes early influences on Pavese's poetry.

Moravia, Alberto. "Pavese decadente." In *L'uomo come fine.* Milan: Bompiani, 1963, 149–53. Dismissal of Pavese's artistic talent and indictment of his decadent influences by a major contemporary writer.

Mutterle, Anco Marzio. "*Ciau Masino*: dal plurilinguismo al monologo interiore." *Belfagor* 25 (1970):559–91. Seminal study of the language of *Ciau Masino.*

Norton, Peter M. "Cesare Pavese and the American Nightmare." *Modern Language Notes* 77 (1962):24–36.

Premuda, Maria Luisa. "I *Dialoghi con Leucò* e il realismo simbolico di Pavese." *Annali della Scuola Normale di Pisa* 26, nos. 3–4 (1957):221–49. Seminal study of Pavese's mythic dialogues.

Salinari, Carlo. "La poetica di Pavese." In *Preludio e fine del realismo in Italia.* Naples: Morano, 1967, 87–97. Interpretation of Pavese as the last great decadent writer.

Schneider, Franz K. "Quest, Romance and Myth in Pavese's *The Devil in the Hills.*" *Italica* 49 (1972):393–425.

Sontag, Susan. "The Artist as Exemplary Sufferer." in *Against Interpretation.* New York: Delta, 1965, 39–48. On Pavese's diary.

Varese, Claudio. "Cesare Pavese VII." In *Occasioni e valori della letteratura contemporanea.* Bologna: Cappelli, 1967, 194–99.

Index